THE GARDENS OF DESIRE

Marcel Proust and the Fugitive Sublime

Stephen Gilbert Brown

STATE UNIVERSITY OF NEW YORK PRESS

Published by

STATE UNIVERSITY OF NEW YORK PRESS, ALBANY

© 2004 State University of New York

All rights reserved

Printed in the United States of America

No part of this book may be used or reproduced in any manner whatsoever without written permission. No part of this book may be stored in a retrieval system or transmitted in any form or by any means including electronic, electrostatic, magnetic tape, mechanical, photocopying, recording, or otherwise without the prior permission in writing of the publisher.

For information, address
State University of New York Press,
90 State Street, Suite 700, Albany, NY 12207

Production, Laurie Searl
Marketing, Michael Campochiaro

Library of Congress Cataloging-in-Publication Data

Brown, Stephen Gilbert, 1949–
 The gardens of desire : Marcel Proust and the fugitive sublime / by Stephen Gilbert Brown.
   p. cm.
 Includes bibliographical references and index.
 ISBN 0-7914-6113-0 (alk. paper)
  1. Proust, Marcel, 1871–1922—Criticism and interpretation. 2. Desire in literature. I. Title.

PQ2631.R63Z545417 2004
843'.912—dc22

2004045293

10 9 8 7 6 5 4 3 2 1

The Gardens of Desire

This book could not have been created without the assistance and inspiration of two men: my father, Harry N. Brown, who worked to provide for my education at the University of California, Santa Barbara; and Prof. Douwe Sturman, whose existential humanist readings opened the way to the inimitable gardens of Proust's genius. It is to their inspiring example that I therefore dedicate this book.

Contents

Acknowledgments		ix
Introduction: Entering the Garden		1
chapter 1	The Kiss of Death: Desire in the Garden of Good and Evil	21
chapter 2	The Art of Sapphic Desire: The Curse of the Little Phrase	51
chapter 3	The Hymenoptera of Self and Other: The Making and (Un)Making of Knowledge	93
chapter 4	Three Moments of Desire: The Ideal, the Real, and the Remembered	143
chapter 5	*Recherche* and the Rankian Gaze	175
Conclusion: The Art of Madness		217
References		237
Index		241

Acknowledgments

Though this book's cover and title page bear my name, its creation owes much to the inspiration and assistance of a select group of colleagues I would here like to acknowledge. At the University of South Florida, I wish to thank Prof. J. P. W. (Pat Rogers) for giving me the opportunity to pursue graduate studies in Proust in his seminar, to refine the focus of this book, and to get his valuable feedback on several key chapters. I would also like to thank Professors Sara Deats and Phil Sipiora for allowing me to model Rankian readings of literary works in their graduate seminars on Shakespeare and The Ex-Patriots. At the University of Tampa, I wish to thank Dean Jeff Klepfer (Psychology) for approving the $5000 Delo grant that enabled me to commence the research on this book, for allowing me to develop and teach the Honors English course that enabled me to refine a Rankian reading of A la Recherché, and for giving me the opportunity to model Rankian readings of literary works as a guest speaker in his Honors Psychology course. I also want to extend a heartfelt thanks to the students in those Honors courses, whose lively and informed participation provided the immediate impetus to begin writing this book. At the University of Nevada, Las Vegas I wish to thank my colleagues in the English department, and particularly Prof. John Irsfeld and Prof. Darlene Unrue, for the steadfast support they have given to this project in the tenure review process, in research grants, in merit considerations, and in their appreciative comments. I owe a special word of thanks to Priscilla Finley, Research Librarian at UNLV, for her apt and enthusiastic assistance. I also want to express my gratitude to Prof. Kostas Myrsiades, Editor of *College Literature*, for publishing two articles related to this project. I owe a heartfelt thanks to Alexa Dvorsen, who during our years in Yosemite introduced me to the diaries of Anais Nin, in whose Paris volumes I first encountered the psychological theories of Otto Rank. A very special thanks goes to James Peltz, Editor-in-Chief at SUNY Press for his interest, support, and guidance on this project from the outset. I am also indebted to Priscilla Ross and Laurie Searl at SUNY Press for the faith and guidance they have respectively shown. A word of heartfelt gratitude goes to friends and colleagues Norm Albert and

Nancy Buonocoursi, Sid Dobrin and Christian Weisser for their steadfast support over the years. A special thought, as well, goes to Connie Sutton Fox for being there through the thick and thin of it all. I wish, also, to thank my dear colleague, Prof. David M. Marcus, for the wise counsel and warm friendship he has always kept. Finally, I want to express by deep appreciation to Bobbi Nicole Wilson whose loyalty, love, and friendship have been a heart-beacon through the vicissitudes of the last twenty years.

introduction

Entering the Garden

Proust remains as light and inviting as a feather bed, a nearly infinite mass of prose gently sighing up and down, like a calm sea glinting with myriad coins of moonlight. . . . Scott Moncrieff's ornate and sinuous English prose, based upon the first, highly faulty French texts, was the gate that opened into Proust's incomparable gardens, and one resists any alternation to sites of enchantment. . . . Scott Moncrieff's was a labor of love, and Proust has attracted other such labors in the form of precious small books of devotion.

—John Updike

A PROUSTIAN IDYLL: THE ORIGINS OF A "READING"

This too is a book of devotion.

I share Updike's sentiments for Moncrieff's flawed translation: if some of the accuracy of the original text may have been sacrificed in translation, little of its charm has been—which seemed more important to me at the time I began writing this book, and still does. Added to this was the knowledge that Moncrieff's translation had met with Proust's approval—as if the author was speaking through this particular translator. In a letter to Moncrieff shortly before his death, Proust writes that he is "very flattered and touched by the pains you have taken over the translation of *Swann* . . . of all my translators in different languages, you are the only one to whom I have written. Perhaps it was seeing the fine gifts you have brought to this translation . . . kindly give your publishers my compliments on a most noteworthy translation of Swann." The objections Proust raises regarding Moncrieff's translations of his title for the work and for its first volume are "tempered with much praise" (*Selected Letters* 1918–1922, 448–449). Proust's own success as a translator of Ruskin lends further credence to his assessment of Moncrieff's translation of *A la Recherhce*. In subsequent years, and through numerous readings, Moncrieff's two-volume edition became invested with additional charms, which had nothing to do with the text itself: with the charm of my own experience, seemingly coded onto its pages and covers. When I gaze at the two-volume Moncrieff translation today, some thirty years after having first opened it, it is indeed like re-opening lost chapters of my own experience, fragments of which have been preserved within this book: in the sweat-stained binding, in a tar-stained thumb-print upon a page, in the grains of sand that trickle from between the bindings as if from a leather hourglass. As do the marginalia, scribbled in various inks, with varying degrees of legibility, which enable me to "date" a particular entry: the more readable "texts" signifying an older period of experience—each the "signature" of a different reading, from a different period of my life.

The oldest readings evoke Santa Barbara, resurrecting undergraduate experiences—and particularly the voice, gestures, and existential wisdom of a particular professor: Douwe Sturman (Rhodes Scholar, friend and colleague of Aldous Huxley, but first and foremost, a Proustian) in whose Modern European Novel class I was first introduced to *A la Recherche*. The culmination of that undergraduate experience was a year-long seminar in Proust, during which the class met in Sturman's den for our weekly sessions of idolatrous explication.

A defining moment, insofar as it sewed the seed of a profession: one that united the pleasures of an avocation (reading Proust) with the practical appeal of a vocation (teaching literature). As enchanting as the prose currents of Proust's narrative were the existential riffs of Sturman's interpretations, which made the experience of "reading" Proust akin to reading two authors—and which modeled at an early period the synergy between art and interpretation in general, and between literature and criticism in particular. I'm not sure which I enjoyed, or profited from, the most: Proust's "text" or Sturman's existential humanist "reading" of it. *A la Recherche* is among other things a multiple metonymy of the self.

These threads are inextricably bound within this "text," altering and compounding it, in the way Proust's "accordion-like" addendums altered his original narrative. It is much more than a mere text that fascinates and illuminates in its own right. Its own "heat" is layered with the heat it absorbed from the sands of Devereaux Beach, from the glare off the Pacific, and from Professor Sturman's interpretations, slipped between its pages like existential bookmarks, offered from a podium or a rocking chair, accompanied by a gaze over the rim of his reading glasses that expressed an intellectual kinship with his students, as if we were all card-carrying members of a secret cult whose only qualification for membership was an idolatrous appreciation of Proust.

I was wont in those days to read *Recherche* while floating in my homemade sea kayak, content to ship oars with a volume cradled in my lap and drift on the currents of its prose—until the day a shark fin broke the surface in the vicinity of my dangling foot.

The end of an idyll.

Or so I thought at the time. Years later, while rereading the work I chanced upon a fingerprint preserved in tar in the margins: a memento from the '67 oil spill whose gooey globules gave a flypaper quality to the tawny tide-line then, as they do now. Yet something of the particular quality of that hour, of that silky sea rusted with kelp, had also been preserved, as if in fictional formaldehyde—until unsealed in this moment far removed in time and space, when I happened to come upon this particular page again. While I was absorbing the contents of *Recherche,* it was secretly absorbing the contents of my self—and my surroundings. The mere act of bringing its words and my eyes into contact was enough to trigger an exchange of old essences, forever preserved between its pages, like the lupines and columbines Cherie used to "press" between its pages on picnics into the alpine meadows of the Colorado Rockies. In the process of surrendering it secrets, it acquired mine.

We are possessed by the books we possess.

This two-volume edition ranked among my dearest possessions—along with the N. C. Wyeth illustrated edition of *The Yearling,* from which my father used to read me to sleep as a boy. Both were "accidentally" lost one summer when an electrician who was rewiring my university office left all my books in the hall overnight, where a janitor unwittingly mistook them for trash. The shock of this loss was exceeded only by the loss of a manuscript in Mexico to which I had devoted a year of my life. Once it subsided, however, I was consoled by a happy realization: now I had a perfect excuse to launch my own "search" for lost essences, by frequenting antiquarian book fairs and musty used book shops. In a dim and dusty back room of an antiquarian book dealer in Micanopy, Florida, I chanced upon a pristine edition of Moncrieff's two-volume set. A ladder quickly brought me within arm's reach of its position on a crowded shelf, where it seemed to float as if suspended in a solution of dust, darkness, and sunlight.

I removed a hardbound volume from its box and opened it to the first page, at once fearful of the price I would find penciled in the top corner and resolved to pay it nonetheless. I giddily paid the $15 to the old book lover at the cash register, recalling the $75 I had paid for the same two-volume set as an undergrad at U.C.S.B.—a small fortune that seriously impacted my beer and pizza budget. Now I was the beneficiary of a pleasant realization: the more valuable the book became to me, the less it cost. Micanopy seemed to incarnate an hour from turn-of-the-century Florridy—as if it belonged between the pages of *The Yearling* with Wyeth's illustrations. Moreover, it was the gateway to the "big scrub" where Marjorie Kinnan Rawlings had set her barefoot bildungsroman. This little Spanish moss crossroads is now associated with these cherished editions of *The Yearling* and *Recherche:* like their pages, the lichen-draped streets of Micanopy encapsulate a musty whiff of time.

Now I have a fresh set of margins to fill, which are already crowded, not with the notes of Sturman's humanist existential interpretation, but with the almost illegible "signs" of my own Rankian reading. The words that found their way onto these pages began their journey in those crowded margins—an illegible scrawl embroidering page after page of Proust's text.

This book has enabled me to conjoin the two greatest intellectual influences of my life: Marcel Proust and Otto Rank. Two intellectual currents which for years flowed apart, for want of something in common, have finally merged. I now find these two texts have something to say to one another, find that their contents deeply inform one another—even as the "two ways" communicate to each other at the end of *Recherche*. I had for years cherished Rank's *Art and Artist* because of the light it shed on the mysterious and manifold origins of the creative impulse, more insightfully and comprehensively in my view than the theories of Freud—or of any other writer for that matter. For years I had ruminated on the relationship between genius and madness, creativity and neurosis, as if upon a riddle that had no solution. Then one year in my mid-twenties my friend Alexa "turned me on" to Anais Nin. I was living in Yosemite at the time, working as a cook at the Yosemite Lodge. Intrigued by Alexa's appreciation of Nin's diaries, I asked if I might borrow a volume. A few days later we met in the Ahwahnee Hotel, to mooch the coffee that was wheeled into the Baronial hall every afternoon at 4:00 P.M. on a draped bus tray and to rap about writing in front of the fireplace—itself seemingly designed by and for a race of giants. The Parisian volume of Nin's diary passed from Alexa's hand to mine. And it was there I first encountered the name of Otto Rank. The appreciative comments of Nin and Henry Miller about Rank's theories on the neurotic origins of the creative impulse prompted me some months later to seek out the primary source, *Art and Artist: Creative Urge and Personality Development* (1932), which I found deep in the aisles of the library at the University of Hawaii-Hilo, where I was working toward a fifth-year teaching credential in English and History.

I bored through Rank's dense revelations with the greedy excitement of one who finally has his hands on that for which he has long searched. I knew with each stunning sentence that the search was over, and a keen sense of happiness and relief began to mount within. What I held between my hands, bound between the red covers of *Art and Artist*, was a portion of my self which another had delivered to me, had freed from within me. In a language I had never read, Rank had captured a little lightning of the self. I spent the rest of that year of graduate study (and the quarter century since) trying to digest the particular wisdom of those pages. Like *Recherche*, its complex density invited and rewarded multiple readings. How one mind had fathomed so much was a riddle I could not comprehend. I was freed from a problem that had fixated my mind for years—and of all the effects this work produced, perhaps the keenest was this sense of deliverance. It was a deliverance into my self and from my self.

Meanwhile, the two-volume *Recherche* followed me everywhere—continued to accrue amongst its pages layers of my own experiences. An invisible sediment that accumulated on the bedrock of this prose sea. I read and reread these two masterworks (one a work of art, the other an analysis of the origins and effects of art) as if they had nothing in common, even as they satisfied the same need to find my self objectified in the words of an other.

The years went by.

I again found myself in graduate school, this time at the University of South Florida, having left secondary education to pursue a Ph.D. in English. I knew that, among other things, I wanted to model Rankian readings of literary works in my graduate classes. I began with a Rankian reading of Joyce's *Portrait* in Professor Sipiora's class on The Ex-Patriots of Paris. This was followed by Rankian readings of *Titus Andronicus* and *Hamlet* in Professor Deats's course on the Elizabethan Revenge Tragedy. Then I caught wind of an exciting rumor that Professor J. P. W. (Pat) Rogers, the eminent literary historian, was offering a graduate seminar on Proust. This rumor proved true. Faced with the necessity of producing two papers on *Recherche*, impelled by the desire to please and impress Professor Rogers, anxious to break new critical ground, and unable to resist the temptation to combine my two greatest intellectual passions, I found myself for the first time theorizing the associations of these two epic works. The more I considered them in light of each other, the more associations I began to discover—to the point where I had to start writing them down, lest they disappear for good. When I considered *Recherche* in light of *Art and Artist*, I began to see it anew—especially those portions of The Search where the narrator is writing about writing. The conviction began to grow that *A la Recherche*, as a bildungsroman of the artist, could be usefully "read" from a Rankian psycho-critical perspective—that the career of Proust's narrator could be interpreted as a "case study" illustrating the theories elaborated in *Art and Artist,* particularly as they inform the origins and effects of the creative impulse.

Professor Rogers's seminar afforded me the opportunity to model a Rankian reading in a critical setting, to "try out" my interpretation in discussions with colleagues, in two papers to Professor Rogers, and in a conference presentation at the International Association of the Fantastic in the Arts (IAFA), where I read one of my papers, "A Talking Tour of the Proustian Dreamscape: Amphibious Lovers and Monstrous Creatures." I am consequently indebted to Pat Rogers not only for the opportunity to develop this "reading" in a critical setting, but for the guidance and feedback that helped focus it in key places, particularly in chapter 4, "Three Moments of Desire: The Ideal, The Real, and the Remembered."

When I open the book, it still releases the whiff of a Yosemite waterfall, conjures the red-cellophane mirror of the Cook Inlet at slack tide. The spectrum of its own truths expands into a deeper spectrum of the self. In reading it, we gaze into the self—and gaze again upon the selves we were when reading it: at Santa Barbara, Yosemite, Hawaii, Alaska, and Florida—as if gazing through a telescope at galaxies that are "red shifting" away from us. The words upon the page are windows into the Other and into the self. By virtue of their ability to acquire what we are, they acquire as well the ability to reveal what we are.

Recherche is not only a book, but a yearbook.

A dog-eared page is now host to a phantom offshore wind that used to riffle the pages, losing my spot for me, making them flap like a sail in a sloughing breeze. The shiny white pages still enshrine the August sunshine, even as a coffee stain rebuilds a Yosemite cabin and the drifted snows whose chilled tedium the book helped me endure. The book enacts one of its most memorable and much-interpreted passages: the garden reading scene of Marcel. As we read this book, it is "reading" us—and our surroundings. Proust's observation is definitive: "Some name we read in a book in bygone years, for example, contains among its syllables the strong breeze and brilliant sunshine of the day when we came across it" (PR 1005).

I have therefore chosen to use Moncrieff's monumental, if flawed, translation not only because of its arbitrarily poetic effects, or because it met with Proust's approval, but because of my deep personal connection to this edition. All volume and page references are therefore to the C. K. Scott Moncrieff and Frederick A. Blossom translation of *Remembrance of Things Past (A la Recherche du temps perdu)*, 2 vols. (New York: Random House, 1927–1934). However, when referring to the work itself, I prefer Proust's original title, or abbreviations of it *(Recherche/ A la Recherche)* in contradistinction to Moncrieff's bastardization of it. I have also used the following abbreviations for its seven volumes, which I list in chronological order: SW *(Swann's Way)*, WBG *(Within a Budding Grove)*, GW *(Guermantes Way)*, CP *(Cities of the Plain)*, LP *(La Prisonnière)*, LF *(La Fugitive)*, PR *(Past Recaptured)*. Because they are more faithful to Proust's original titles, I use the abbreviations LP *(La Prisonnière)* and LF *(La Fugitive)* when referring to these volumes. Another distinction I adhere to is that between the author (Proust) and the narrator (Marcel). The "I" of the narration I refer to as "Marcel," or as "the narrator." This is not an absolute prejudice, however, insofar as there are places in the text where referring to Proust is appropriate, if not unavoidable. For the most part, however, I endorse the postmodern tendency, as does Paul Bové, of recognizing and respecting a difference between "the biographical Proust who pens the novel [and] the textual creature, the 'posited author,' whose existence is a function of the difference between the narrator and the biographical 'Proust' toward whom the text seems to be gesturing" (Afterword 149). While it may be safe to assume that Marcel is speaking in place of Proust, it is risky (at best) to presume that he is speaking for the author.

THE PROUSTIAN CONVERSATION: TWO CRITICAL TRADITIONS

> With the passage of time, critical methods too have been changing and Proust's book has proved rich and complex enough to support many diverse approaches.
>
> —Germaine Brée

A recent body of postmodern scholarship is radically transforming our understanding of *Recherche*, as well as altering the manner in which we "read" this inimitable, if problematic masterpiece. For the last quarter-century the scholarly conversation in Proust has been dominated by the theories of Lacan and Derrida, has been driven by the psycho-critical/grammatological discourse arising from the fusion of Lacanian psychoanalysis and Derridean linguistic theory, producing a psycho-critical/linguistic discourse that challenges received notions of Proustian textual analysis, that calls into question some of the most fundamental assumptions regarding *Recherche*, and that theorizes the work from a perspective that breaks with the earlier (New) critical tradition. Reading against the grain of an earlier modern tradition, this provocative postmodern critical tradition has broken new ground in Proustian analysis. This postmodern turn in Proustian scholarship was but one result of the contra-Marxist intellectual uprising that occurred in France in 1968—the year in which Proustian criticism fractures into two traditions: an earlier, modern tradition dominated by New Criticism and itself comprising a first "golden age" of Proustian interpretation: Beckett (1931), Brée (1955), Moss (1962), Bell (1962), Shattuck (1963), Bersani (1965), Cattui (1967), Jephcott (1972), Stambolian (1972), Appignanesi (1973), and Brady (1977), to name just a few. This modern critical tradition continued into the 1970s despite its residual influence after 1968 upon an emerging postmodern psycho-critical/grammatological discourse that brought the most fundamental assumptions of this earlier tradition under radical attack. Inspired by the post-'68 turn from Marx and his tradition toward "linguistically synchronic models" (Bové 153), this second tradition commenced with the works of Deleuze (1972) and Doubrovsky (1974), was sustained by the analysis of de Man (1979), Kasell (1980), Humphries (1983), and others, and continues to shape the direction of Proustian discourse, as evidenced by the work of Gray (1992) and Kristeva (1993, 1996).

Inspired by Doubrovsky's radical break from the critical tradition, the postmodern gaze "has freed the critic/reader into the possibility of producing (endlessly) new readings that recount the circulation of a text's signs around and through the system of its guiding fantasies" (154). Further, these two distinct critical traditions have been bridged by a Freudian psycho-critical tradition whose pre-1968 works reinscribed the orthodoxy of Freudian theory (Miller and Bell), even as the post-'68 works, drawing on Lacan's radical reinvention of Freudian theory, broke with this earlier tradition of psycho-criticism (Deleuze, Doubrovsky, Gray, and Kristeva). Indeed, tensions emerge within this postmodern tradition between the readings of Deleuze and Doubrovsky over the issue of textual unity.

The interrogation of the early modern tradition by postmodern criticism has focused on a series of critical moments in the career of Proust's narrator, the multiple interpretations of which have sparked a lively and continuing debate, fueling the conversation as it moves into a new century and millennium. These critical cruxes foreground the following "moments" of The Search: the "privileged moments" of the madeleine, the good night kiss, the *Francois le champi* reading scene, the garden reading scene, the steeples at Martinville, the trees of Hudimesnil, the sado-Sapphic performance at Montjouvain, the Albertine-asleep vignette, Albertine's discourse on the "ices," Charlus's brothel scene, the climactic proliferation of involuntary memories at the reception of the Princess de Guermantes, and Marcel's relationship to writing at the novel's end. These narratological topoi comprise a selective set of the sites upon which postmodern criticism has focused its interrogation of *Recherche*, generating a body of work through two generations of postmodern scholars, those of the 1990s revisiting the sites so usefully informed by their predecessors—like archeologists of knowledge working a series of particularly productive "digs," excavating fragments that elaborate the mosaic of postmodern "readings," even as they expose tensions between them.

These readings contradict many of the assumptions and assessments of earlier scholars, and deconstruct the text's authority in particular. The narrator's search is in turn searched by the postmodern gaze for those moments when it seemingly unwrites itself—when it is unwritten and rewritten by the very "subconscious" it purportedly writes onto the page, the victim of its own repression—which returns through the postmodern gaze to call into question the most fundamental assumptions about *Recherche*. At times, these counterassertions seem scandalous, as Paul Bové argues, to those readers "raised in the decorous tradition of Trilling, Levin, Booth, and Shattuck" (Afterword 149). Drawing on Lacanian and Derridean theory, these provocative, controversial rereadings of *Recherche* problematize the assessments of an earlier critical tradition regarding the text's unity, narrative mastery, and position in the bildungsroman tradition. Yet, like many an emergent discourse, the psycho-critical/grammatological critique of *Recherche* has grown into its own orthodoxy: an orthodoxy that invites critical challenge and radical departures. This book, in its challenge to the received notions of the postmodern Proustian tradition is itself inspired by the resistant spirit that inspired that tradition in its departure from an earlier modern orthodoxy. Further, by assimilating both traditions, I hope to reconcile, without altogether effacing, some of the tensions between them—for these tensions are protean.

As the critical record evidences, *Recherche* warrants and rewards analysis from a Freudian/Lacanian psycho-critical perspective. Indeed, of all the interpretive perspectives brought to bear on Proust's text (New Critical, Marxist, Feminist, Freudian, Lacanian, Derridean, Queer Studies, Cultural Studies et al.), none has exerted a greater influence than the Freudian psycho-critical tradition. *Recherche*, by virtue of its thematic material, comprises perhaps the definitive text for Freudian interpretation. Its pervasive oedipal themes invite Freudian analysis—indeed, insist upon it. And make no mistake about this: Freudian interpretation has helped decode the Proustian sign. Yet, in the final analysis, Freudian/Lacanian psycho-criticism yields an understanding of the origins (to say nothing of the effects) of the creative impulse that is selective and reductive. As Doubrovsky asserts, this postmodern interrogation "poses a major challenge to various culturally conservative adaptations of Freud's theory of sublimation" (Bové 153). Indeed, it may even be asserted that Freudian psycho-criticism of *Recherche* may say more about its own prejudices and desires than the text it purportedly analyzes, as if Proust's "translated aestheticized fantasies 'colonize' the unconscious of the critics and critical discourses that rise up to feed upon them," in an effort to appease their own desires. But the attempt of these feedings, of these ingestions, is, in Doubrovsky's terms, "either great effort for little reward or endless and anomic spewing of desire in unstable and deceitful critical echoings" (153)—as if baited by a text whose desires return to arouse their own.

It is time to remove the viewfinders that privilege the influence on the creative urge of sublimated sexual impulses—to the exclusion of other factors: of the will to form, of an educative ideology, of neurosis, of an ideology of sacrifice, of a desire to eternalize the soul, and of the artist's own struggle with art. The search for the origins of the creative impulse lead beyond Freudian theory, which is more useful as a starting point than as a definitive interpretation not only of the origins but of the effects of the creative urge. Something more is wanted by way of interpretation—and it is my contention that the theories of Otto Rank as enunciated in *Art and Artist* provide this something more: not the last word, nor the definitive word, but a word that leads to a deeper engagement with the origins and effects of the creative impulse in general, and as they are informed by disorders of the self in particular.

Yet no scholar of Proust, to my knowledge, has attempted to "read" *Recherche* from a Rankian perspective, despite the shared interest of Proust and Rank in the psychology of invention, and in the origin and effects of "separation anxiety" as embodied in their major works: *Recherche, Trauma of Birth,* and *Art and Artist.* Indeed, Rank's focus on "separation anxiety" in *Trauma* was seized upon by his Freudian critics as its greatest limitation. As Heinz Kohut observes *in The Restoration of the Self* (1977), Rank commits the same error in *Trauma* for which he criticized his Freudian colleagues, replacing an obsession with the "conditions of early life" with a fixation on the "separation anxieties" produced by birth. This "shift in outlook"

> impoverishes the analyst's perception of the varieties of significant human experiences and brings about a narrowing of the focus of his attention upon a single thread in the complex weave of the patient's psychopathology. This error was, for example, committed by Rank whose theory of the "trauma of birth" led him, according to Freud (1937, pp. 216–217), to a single-minded therapeutic preoccupation with the problems of separation anxiety. (101)

However, given Freud's overreliance on childhood trauma, this seems like a case of the "kettle calling the pot black." Further, it is just this emphasis on "separation anxiety" that warrants a Rankian reading of *Recherche*, which is nothing if not a representation of the effects of "separation anxiety," the most significant of which is the "search" that arises from it. As I will argue in this work, that search constitutes an attempt to overcome the effects of separation from the maternal sublime.

Concern with the "separation anxieties" associated with birth constitute the first great intellectual focus of Rank's career, to be followed by a second focus on the psychology of the artist. In *The Jewish Origins of the Psychoanalytic Movement* (1981), Dennis Klein observes the radical significance of Rank's early focus on "separation anxiety," as theorized in *Trauma*:

> In this work, he argued that the basis of neurosis was not oedipal, but preoedipal, the separation of the hold from the mother.... Rank thus described neurosis as the ambivalence occurring between the desire to return to the prenatal existence and the fear of repeating the separation trauma. (107)

This statement has important implications for the "merger-hungry" personality of Marcel which exerts a deterministic influence on the self-Other dyad throughout *Recherche* (Kohut 380). These heretical "ideas on the preoedipal relationship with the mother, the separation crisis or primal anxiety," which resulted in Rank's banishment from the Vienna circle, are now considered to be one of his major contributions to the field. As Klein observes, "Rank's significance for psychoanalysis has been the introduction of these ideas into the mainstream of the field" (107). In *The Search for the Self* (1978), Kohut similarly underscores Rank's early preoccupation with "separation anxiety," observing that Rank approached "psychoanalytic therapy as an experience in mastering separation anxiety" (411):

> Thus, if we see the task of psychoanalysis in the Rankian mode as a working-through and ultimate mastery of separation anxiety, then the intrinsic criteria for termination [of the therapy] will relate to the achievement of the capacity for psychosocial independence. (415)

The origins and effects of "separation anxiety" not only comprised a central theme of Rank's writing, but the alleviation of those effects constituted the primary aim of his therapy—even as the causes and effects of "separation anxiety" comprise the central theme of *Recherche*, the writing of which was the primary means of alleviating those traumatizing effects. Thus, Rank's theories on "separation anxiety" can usefully inform the career of Marcel, whose origins are firmly rooted in this particular anxiety and whose driving force is the desire for "psychosocial independence" from the mother: a traumatizing anxiety that not only manifests itself in incestuous, homoerotic, matricidal, and suicidal impulses, but more significantly for this study, in the creative impulse. Hence, that which is viewed in some quarters of the field as a limitation (Rank's emphasis on "separation anxiety'), is for the purposes of this study an asset: one that invites and rewards the critical juxtaposition of these two works. However, a mutual interest in the origins and effects of separation anxiety is not the only criterion that warrants the association of Proust and Rank—though this alone would justify it.

Rank's interest in (and theories about) the theme of redemption also justifies a Rankian reading of *Recherche*, which similarly foregrounds the theme of original sin and eternal salvation, of damnation and redemption. Like Marcel, Rank "turned to art to express his longing for renewal" (116), reflecting in this turn the deep influence of Nietzsche on his thought. Rank's writings, both fictional and nonfictional, foreground the liberatory struggle of a "redemptive figure" (Klein 117), reinscribing the career of Marcel, whose quest is nothing if not an attempt to liberate from within himself a redemptive creative self. For Rank, as for Proust, this "redemptive figure" is the genius. *Art and Artist*, like *Recherche*, is a monument to the redemptive and antiheroic figure of the genius, and to the cult of genius it inscribes. Rank, consequently, shared Proust's idolatry of Wagner, whose music similarly embodied this "redemptive vision" (Klein 118). Consequently, *Art and Artist* and *Recherche* may both be usefully viewed as "expressions of artistic self-affirmation, as well as of the Promethean struggle for universal regeneration" (118). Rank's therapeutic method was indeed founded on a profound faith "in the eternal regenerative possibilities of man's nature" (124). His hopes for the future of the human race were a direct effect of his faith in "the power of psychoanalytic interpretation to affirm man's longing for creativity" (128). His view of the work of art is Proustian insofar as it envisions art "as the satisfaction of the will that was yearning for liberation" (128). He saw art as the cure for neurosis, and to the extent that the psychoanalyst participates in this cure, he or she is at the forefront of "artistic regeneration" (129).

A mutual preoccupation with "separation anxiety" and "artistic redemption" is not the only thing that justifies the critical association of Proust and Rank. Their respective emphasis on redemption may owe something to their Jewish heritage, to being one of "God's Chosen People" (145). This influence deeply informs the themes of redemption, of artistic regeneration, as figured in *Recherche*, in which the salvation of the individual genius is figured amidst the Sodom and Gomorrah–like damnation of society.

In addition to Rank's study of the psychology of the artist, his familiarity with countless works of art provides further justification for a Rankian reading of *Recherche*. He was not only co-editor of *Imago*, the psychoanalytic journal of the arts (Klein 105), but by all accounts "possessed unusual analytic abilities for the interpretation of legends and myths, as well as of individual artists or their masterpieces," as evidenced by his dissertation: a psychoanalytic interpretation of Wagner's *Lohengrin* (1911). For these reasons, I believe Rank's theories on the psychology of the artist can usefully, if selectively, inform the careers of Marcel Proust and "Marcel."

In an effort to enrich and broaden the psycho-critical Proustian tradition, I want to theorize *Recherche* from a Rankian perspective. It is not my intent to supplant Freudian interpretations of *Recherche*, but to move beyond them while acknowledging the pioneering contribution they have made (and continue to make) to our understanding of the text. I believe a Rankian reading not only informs many of the aforementioned critical cruxes fomenting scholarly debate today, but evidences the usefulness of Rankian psycho-criticism to literary criticism in general: a psycho-criticism that has largely been under erasure since Rank's own rebellious departure from the orthodoxy of Freudian theory in 1924, the year that saw the publication of *Trauma of Birth*. Yet, as Klein observes, "the paucity of scholarship" on Rank does not "reflect the importance of the contribution he made to the psychoanalytic movement" (104).

FREUDIAN VERSUS RANKIAN PSYCHO-CRITICISM

> In criticism there is something for everyone—as long as you see that whatever the metalanguage used, there is no ultimate decoding of the metaphorical language of the work into a rigorously metonymic language that would "lay out" its meaning.
> —Doubrovsky

Recherche is perhaps the definitive psychological novel in the modernist canon. As such, it particularly lends itself to critical interpretation from a psychoanalytic perspective. Freudian interpretation of *Recherche* has proven particularly useful in unpacking the oedipal overtones of the mother-son dyad, as well as in analyzing the ubiquitous contents of the narrator's unconscious mind: as manifested in dreams, involuntary memories, and in a host of repressed desires (matricidal, homoerotic, sado-masochistic, and incestuous impulses). Where Freudian analysis in general, and of *Recherche* in particular, is found wanting, however, is in its reductive analysis of the origins of the creative impulse, with its traditional emphasis on sublimation.

Rank's rift with Freud, and with the Vienna circle (Jones, Adler, Sachs, Eitingon, Abraham, and later, Jung) commenced with his publication of *Trauma*, and continued to widen with each successive publication. Freud told him, "You are the dreaded David who with his *Trauma of Birth* succeeds in deprecating my work" (Taft 79). Rank's friends in the group refused to speak to him; he was branded a heretic, a neurotic, was accused of sabotaging the psychoanalytic movement; even as his writing was criticized as "too unsystematic, too free, too universalized, too one-sided" (77).

Rank's response to the persecution and banishment of his peers was to join the expatriate community in Paris, which he does in 1929, and where his books *Der Kunstler* (The Artist) and *Trauma* attract the attention of Henry Miller and Anais Nin respectively, facilitating the formation of their own Parisian literary circle. Rank devotes much of the remainder of his writing career to refining his ideas on the psychology of the hero, the neurotic, and the artist, which achieve full maturity in the work for which he is best known, *Art and Artist: Creative Urge and Personality Development* (1932). He elaborates his differences with Freudian psychology in a paper delivered at Yale titled "The Psychological Approach to Personal Problems" (Feb. 28, 1929):

> [N]either Freud, nor Jung, nor Adler sufficiently considers the creative part of the personality, namely that which is not purely biological as Freud sees it, nor purely racial as Jung conceives it, nor purely social as Adler thinks, but which is purely individual. . . . I tried to explain the creative type by using Freud's psychology and his terminology, but I found that I could not do it without going beyond Freud. (qtd. in Taft 138)

And go beyond Freud he does—at least with respect to the psychology of the artist. *Art and Artist* embodies a far more nuanced and comprehensive analysis of the origins and effects of the creative impulse than the purely biological hermeneutic applied by Freud. Whereas Freud posits one source of the creative impulse (a sublimated sexual/reproductive urge), Rank proffers multiple origins: neurotic conflict, a desire to eternalize the soul, to replace what has been lost, the will-to-form, etc. In going beyond Freud's interpretation of the creative urge, Rank not only asserts that its origins are nonsexual, but that it has "something positively antisexual in its yearning for independence of organic conditions. Correspondingly, my conception of repression differed from Freud's; for him it is the result of outward frustration, while I trace it to an inward necessity" ("Preface" xxiii). Further, this process of sublimation is a collective process insofar as it is common to all. Freud's theory, however, fails to explain how or why this repressed material is transformed into art in one individual, but not in another.

To explain the origins of the creative impulse, Freudian psychology turned away from the artist's adult experience (which had been the focus of "pre-analytical" biography) to an analysis of "the decisive importance of infantile impressions" (Rank 62). The problem with Freud's oedipal theory of creativity is that while every child has these experiences, not every child becomes an artist. As Rank observes, "[T]his conception got no further, however, than the banal statement that even the artist was not immune from those typical experiences of childhood" (62). Freud and his school saw in those typical childhood experiences the causes both of neurosis and creativity, "though without being able to explain the difference between one outcome of them and another"—an omission that included "the whole problem of artistic creation" (*Art and Artist* 62–63):

> Beyond this statement analytical psychography has to this day not progressed.... And although the Oedipus complex, and the sexual problem of the child that is bound up with it, still forms the centre, this is rather the sign of a fatal stoppage than a proof of the superlative importance of this family problem. (63)

Because the "artiste manqué," a type of artist which Proust's narrator resembles, dwells in an individualized universe of suffering, the collective ideology of the Oedipus complex is insufficient for explaining the origins of the artistic impulse. For Rank, the individual's personalized universe is assigned greater importance than Freud's "collective psychology" (63). In contradistinction to the determinism of Freud's collective oedipal complex, Rank assigns greater agency to the individual's will, drawing on the ideas of Nietzsche and Schopenhauer to formulate his own "will psychology," citing the careers of artists as illustrative case studies.

From a Rankian perspective, the Oedipus conflict is but one of many types of neurotic conflicts that are creatively appropriated by the artist, through which he or she overcomes the trauma. Thus, the "inhibitive family ties... manifested as erotic desire (towards mother and sister)" are absorbed into the creative impulse, are externalized by it, and are thereby detached from the creative individual—a process embodied in the career of Proust's narrator, Marcel. The artist's reaction to the oedipal conflict constitutes a creative and "deliberate affirmation of the existence forced on us by fate" (65). Marcel can do nothing to alter the given circumstances of fate that have decreed his separation from the mother in life as in death, but he can detach himself from this traumatizing reality by transforming it into art. This "separation anxiety" is but one of many types of neurosis that lead to artistic production, even as neurosis is but one of several underlying sources of the creative impulse, of all "those creative tendencies which go beyond the mere function of propagation." Rank continues:

> In any case, we fail to see how the sexual urge, which is designed to primarily preserve the race, should produce even the most primitive ornamentation, still less a higher art form. The attempt made by psychoanalysis to find such a solution is today recognized to have been a failure. . . . (84)

The "collective" nature of Freud's theories fails to account for the more particularized origins of the creative impulse in the artist. Consequently, "Freud's therapy did not help at all for the psychological understanding of the creative process":

> The only tangible statement which Freud's theory could give us about the artistic process was that which asserted that the impulse to artistic productivity originated in the sex impulse. But it is easy to see that this explanation . . . takes us no further in reality, being a pure paraphrase of the individual meaning already obvious in the very concept of genius (gignere = to beget). But psychology could not explain how from the sex-impulse there was produced, not the sex act, but the art work, and all the ideas called in to bridge this infinite gulf—"compensation," "sublimation," etc.—were only psychological transcriptions for the fact that we had here something different, higher, and symbolical. (26)

Rank's recognition of the "symbolical" is significant insofar as it anticipates the postmodern emphasis on language, which is nothing if not a system of "signs" or symbols. Postmodern approaches to *Recherche* have attempted to surmount this limitation of Freudian theory by informing it with Derridean linguistic theory. Hence the proliferation of psycho-critical/grammatological, Lacanian/Derridean readings of Proust (Deleuze, Doubrovsky, Kristeva et al.). Nevertheless, the liberatory impetus of these postmodern Proustian projects has been mitigated by their inability to escape their "own inscription within the system of Oedipal fantasies" (Bové 155), by their own narcissistic obsession with the "fantasy controlled world of writing" (156).

This is not to suggest that everything in *Recherche* should be reductively interpreted through the lens of Rankian psychoanalytic theory. Much of the novel's contents does not lend itself to such an interpretative framework, and indeed can be usefully "read" from diverse critical perspectives. There are, however, critical portions of the work that can be usefully interpreted from a Rankian perspective: specifically, those metafictive passages where Proust/Marcel comments about art in general, and about writing in particular. These sites of The Search comprise the focus of this study insofar as they illustrate Rank's theories on the origins and effects of the creative impulse, even as Marcel's problematic "apprenticeship to signs" comprises a useful case study of Rank's developmental paradigm of the modern artiste manqué (Deleuze 4).

Every act of interpretation is an act of translation. We can never apprehend a text's "signs" in a pure, unmediated state. We can only offer extremely situated, metonymic decodings which superimpose the author's signature with our own. The interpreted literary sign is in fact a cosign. I freely acknowledge that this work is nothing more, nor less, than a collection of signs imposed upon a collection of fragments.

BEYOND THE "KITSCHIFICATION" OF PROUST

If the modern critical tradition focused on a close textual analysis of *Recherche*, then the postmodern critical tradition has focused on the "'violence and desire' of its appropriations" (Gray 152). Similarly, the emerging discourse of cultural studies centers its analysis on the "'violence and desire' of contemporary appropriations of Proust":

> for few canonical modernist writers have provoked such response in popular culture as Proust, whose proliferating presence in jokes, puns, cartoons, advertisements, magazine articles, and the newspaper columns of Russell Baker has made him something of a media cliché. If he is not yet quite what Baker, the self-proclaimed "man who took Marcel Proust out of the cobwebs in the literary stacks and made him a vital presence at the center of American consciousness" asserts, Proust is certainly encountered with intriguing regularity on the surfaces of contemporary culture. His current reader thus approaches the *Recherche* amidst a thick atmosphere of popular myth and cliché, violent and desiring appropriations that refigure the text as a sort of vernacular, popularized simulacrum. (152)

As Marcel's creative self obsessively appropriates the "essence" of the Other (be it a field of hawthorns, a Normandy coastline, an Oriental church at Balbec, a Titianesque Venice, a feudal aristocracy, a Sapphic Albertine, or the genius of Vinteuil, Bergotte, and Elstir), so he is appropriated by literary critics (including this one) and by pop culture: his individualized universe collectivized by his readers, interpreters, and consumers as a means of reproducing themselves. Thus, art becomes the vehicle for the collective's reproduction of itself, as evidenced not only by these aggressive interpretations, but also by the aggressive "kitschification," of Proust, which Gray likens to an homogenizing "viral contamination"(155):

> In an age that values speed, brevity, efficacy, performance, and appearance, Proust "signifies" slowness, length, labor, contemplation, resistance, transcendence.... Proust is the scandalous imperative ... to move backward in time rather than ever more frantically on. And contemporary culture has no time for time. (153–54)

Recherche is thus dismembered into consumable metonymic fragments not only by a signifying intellectual culture, but by a kitschifying pop culture. My intent therefore is to re-member some of the dismembered fragments of *Recherche*, to re-member a presence that is often lost amidst the absence of its kitschy appropriations and the glare of its own fragmented, pop-culture reflections. Gray's assessment is worth noting: "The obsessiveness of cultural attention to Proust suggests we need to look beyond the self-indulging pleasures of kitsch and idolatry. The very 'fetishizing' of Proust betrays a cultural dread" (170). We must eschew idolatry for analysis, even as Proust's idolatry of Ruskin was eventually subsumed by his own liberatory analysis of Ruskin's idolatry of faith: a critical epiphany which, from a Rankian perspective, finally and dramatically enabled the pupil to escape the shadow of the master and step into his own creative light. We are still bathed in the idolatrous light of that individual revolution. Yet to see the thing for what it is we must step out of the glare of our own idolatry, while acknowledging that all we can ever apprehend is not a work of art, but only the interpretative signs of the self.

This violent, appropriative desire of academe and pop culture may be the effect of a narrative that foregrounds the violence of desire, as well as those pleasurable, illicit gardens where desire is aggressively pursued: not only in the artificial gardens of Aunt Leonie and the Duchess de Guermantes, nor only in the wild gardens of the Combray countryside or the outdoor gardens of the Bois and the Allee des Acacias, but in the secret gardens of the imagination where Marcel desires to possess the secrets of the Sapphic sublime, of the homoerotic sublime, of the Normandy and Venetian sublime, and most ardently of all—of the artistic sublime. The garden is, as Germaine Brée correctly perceives, a central trope of *Recherche:* "From [its] nocturnal birth on the borderland of sleep, the Proustian world retains the unreal atmosphere, vaguely disquieting and menacing, of those magic gardens and palaces which in fairy tales spring up from the heart of darkness or from some strange forest" (3).

The effects of desire are violent and inescapable, deterministic and neurotic. The desire to possess is obsessive—is in reality a displaced desire to possess the self by objectifying it in words. The narrator's search is one vast "wrong turn" into an objective reality, inspired by the false assumption that it is there, in the material world, that he will find that for which he is searching: the spiritual and immortal fragment of an ideal self, crystallizing around the sign of "genius." The material signs of this self (the madeleine, the steeples of Matinville, etc.) merely enervate the liberatory struggles of this imprisoned self. Throughout the search, this self is the real fugitive: a fugitive not only from the material world, from the mother, and from love and society, but from itself—until finally found and freed in the word.

THE PROUSTIAN SUBLIME

Proust's conception of the sublime, so essential to the overall conception of *A la Recherche*, derives from Ruskin's treatment of the sublime, which it reinvents.

Ruskin's conception of the sublime, in turn, is derivative of its "eighteenth century originators" whose "theories of the sublime had become the dominant concern of aesthetic speculation" (185). As George P. Landow observes in *The Aesthetic and Critical Theories of John Ruskin*, theories of the sublime, which are rooted in "romantic criticism," are fundamental to a "study of Ruskin, not only because he discusses the sublime himself but because ideas derived from the sublime otherwise influence his views on art." Landow continues:

> The notion of reaction is at the center of theories of the sublime: the spectator, upon encountering sublimity in art or nature, reacts emotionally . . . theories of sublimity, which were frequently concerned with violent emotional reactions, made the intensity of the aesthetic experience a matter of concern. (70–71)

Beauty is consequently figured "not in terms of external qualities of the object but in terms of the psychological experiences of the beholder" (93). An object's beauty is not inherent, but associational, a function of its association with the self, a byproduct of the "accidental connection of ideas and memories with material things, owing to which those material things are regarded as agreeable. "(Ruskin, qtd. in Landow 104). Ruskin's theories of the sublime deeply inform Proust's treatment of the "privileged moments" in *A la Recherche*. Regarding the sublime, the object becomes a portal to the subject, by virtue of the associations and emotions it arouses, as part of "an aesthetic which is patently subjectivist and associationist" (240).

The sublime deeply informs Ruskin's (and therefore Proust's) perception of landscape, even as it is conscripted by Ruskin's orthodox faith: the sublime in nature, as in art, is evidence of that "faultless . . . inconceivable, inexhaustible loveliness which God has stamped upon all things" (*Modern Painters* 3.48). The origins of Proust's departure from Ruskin's aesthetic theory are rooted in the latter's treatment of the sublime in general, and of his tendency to configure it in terms of religion in particular (a point I will develop at greater length in chapter five). The second aspect of Ruskin's sublime that triggers Proust's aesthetic apostasy is Ruskin's tendency to privilege the object over the subject, is his deflation of the subjective as enunciated in his theory of "the pathetic fallacy"—the tendency of the emotions to distort perceptions of the objective: "it so distorts exterior reality that it represents truthful depictions of only an interior state" (384). Ruskin's desire to "avoid the dangers of a limiting subjectivity . . . leads him to prefer the epic and the dramatic—the more 'objective forms'" (386). Ruskin's theories of the sublime and the ideal artist comprise a renunciation of the excesses of the subjective: "the whole of his power depends on his losing sight and feeling of his own existence, and becoming a mere witness and mirror of truth . . ." (*Modern Painters* 5.125). Ruskin's aesthetic project endeavors to recuperate the object as a free-standing, transcendent signified: a status necessitated by his faith, and which he never relinquishes even in the depths of his apostasy from orthodox Christianity.

In Proust, the objective sublime is not seen as a manifestation of God, but of the ideal self: is intimately associated with the psychology of the self, and with the "ideal hunger," "mirror hunger," and "merger hunger" aspects of the personality in particular. Proust liberates Ruskin's concept of the "allegorical" or the "prophetic imagination" as a means to religious salvation, deploying it instead in the privileged moments of the sublime as a vehicle of personal salvation and "spiritual welfare." As configured by Ruskin, and conscripted by Proust, "the imagination allows us to escape the bounds of time and space for the sake of our spiritual welfare" (Landow 373). However, instead of being yoked to religion, in A la Recherche this "prophetic imagination" is yoked to a religion of genius. Thus, Ruskin and Proust part intellectual company over their respective views of the subject-object dyad, insofar as Proust figures the privileged object entirely in terms of the self, privileging a subjectivity that is characterized not by the distortions of a pathetic fallacy, but by the determinism of a pathetic sublime, which, alas, proves fugitive until "enclosed in the rings of a beautiful style." Hence, the origins of this book's title, *The Gardens of Desire: Marcel Proust and the Fugitive Sublime*.

chapter one

The Kiss of Death:
Desire in the Garden of Good and Evil

> I ought to have been happy; I was not. It struck me that my mother had just made a concession which must have been painful to her, that it was a first step down from the *ideal* that she had formed of me, and that for the first time she, with all her courage, had to confess herself beaten. It struck me that if I had just scored a victory it was over her; that I had succeeded, as sickness or sorrow or age might have succeeded, in relaxing her will, in altering her judgment; that this evening opened a new era, must remain a *black date in the calendar*.
>
> —SW 29, my emphasis

A BLACK DATE IN THE CALENDAR

IN *A LA RECHERCHE DU TEMPS PERDU* (1922–27) Proust provides two case studies that usefully illustrate the theories of Otto Rank regarding the neurotic origins of the creative impulse. The first involves Marcel's long apprenticeship to art; the second foregrounds the career of the "old music master of Combray," Vinteuil. This Rankian reading of *A la Recherche* is driven by (and therefore must commence with) a series of questions: does Marcel's suffering constitute a "neurosis"? If neurosis is rooted in pathological fear, what is the fear from which Marcel suffers? Is there evidence in the narrative of a cause/effect relationship between neurosis and creativity?

As the aforementioned passage evinces, the reader need search no further in The Search than its inciting "action," than this "black date in the calendar" to discover evidence of the protean symbiosis between neurotic conflict and the symbolic realm of invention—which either affords an escape from conflict, a means of objectifying it, or a means of escaping it by objectifying it.

The final six words of the aforementioned passage inform the origin of Marcel's conflict, even as they generate shock waves of meaning that resonate throughout *A la Recherche*. On the level of imagery, "date" and "calendar" metonymically reinforce the master trope of time, while "black" tropes on the darkness that lies at the very heart of Combray, and of the novel itself—concretized in the blackened bedroom, spiritualized in Marcel's neurotic fears. Further, "black" resonates with connotations of death: in this case, the death of innocence and joy, the death of the "ideal" self ("a first step down from the ideal she had formed of me"). This death of the ideal self in the "drame coucher" (good night kiss crisis) enervates the need to recuperate this self, prompting a search for its material counterparts in art, nature, nobility, love, and friendship. This outward search is, moreover, a surrogate for the real search: a quest for the means to liberate from within the self an ideal self, concretized under the sign of the "artist." The Search is nothing if not a struggle to recover an ideal self lost in this originary "black date in the calendar." This passage is not only an obituary for the death of Marcel's ideal self, but masks matricidal impulses that prefigure the death of the mother ("beaten," "a victory over her," "sickness or sorrow or age").

If "black date in the calendar" is an emblem of death, it is also signifies the darkness of birth. If on the one hand it conjures the tomb (and the tomb of the ideal), then on the other it evokes the womb: that mysterious neurotic darkness in which art is born. This "black date" connotes not only the death of an ideal self, but its rebirth through art as a direct consequence of the torment it spawns. It is altogether fitting, therefore, that a work that is nothing if not a bildungsroman of the artist commence with that "black date" on which the narrator's creative impulse is born, amidst the separation anxieties associated with the "good night kiss," which is for Marcel a "kiss of death," as well as a kiss of eternal life insofar as it signifies the death of an ideal self to profane desire and its redemptive rebirth to art.

The kiss, conferred in the darkness of night, is an ambivalent emblem of Marcel's "separation anxiety" and "merger hungry" personality. Consequently, it is invested at once with the savor of the profane and the sacred, of original sin and eternal salvation, of damnation and redemption, of oblivion and immortality. This ambivalent conflation of the profane and the sacred in the drama of the "good night kiss" inaugurates the pattern that conjoins vice and genius in works of art: *Francois le champi* (an allegory of incest), the magic lantern (an allegory of adultery), Vinteuil's sonata and septet (musical allegories of same-sex desire), Elstir's portrait of Odette (a courtesan), and Swann's association of a Botticelli with Odette. Throughout *Recherche*, genius is inseparable from vice: it is vice that humanizes genius, and genius that redeems vice—in what comprises a dialectical exchange between higher and lower selves, in which the baseness of vice is superimposed with the redemptive virtue of genius, even as materiality is superimposed with spirituality throughout *Recherche*. An intent of this study is to identify and track these narrative patterns or progressions: in this case, the superimposition of vice with genius, of the material with the spiritual.

One cannot understand the fundamental meaning of *Recherche* without first understanding the manifold psychological implications of the "drame coucher." The entire search arises from this inciting trauma, is rooted in its ambivalent material, is an effect of this protean crisis. The profane desire to "merge" with the maternal sublime that is thwarted here enervates the "merger hunger" that is futilely displaced onto the opposite sex (Gilberte, Albertine), and then onto same-sex relationships (Saint Loup, Charlus). The a priori desire that governs the self of The Search is a desire to surmount its own sexual differentiation: a desire repeatedly thwarted in reality until fulfilled on the illusory plane in art. The narrator's deepest neurotic fears are associated with the "drame coucher": a fear grounded in Absence, an anxiety associated with separation from the beloved, and which establishes the pattern of separation anxiety for every love affair in the novel.

THE GARDEN OF ORIGINAL SIN:
THE GUEST WHO CAME TO DINNER

If the Guermantes way is associated with the suffering of Marcel's separation anxiety (insofar as it keeps him afield too late to be kissed good night), then the Méséglise way is similarly a topos of sorrow by virtue of its association with Swann, whose presence at the dinner table compounds Marcel's separation anxiety. As Gilles Deleuze observes in *Proust and Signs* (1972), "[I]t is [Swann] who, from the start, possesses the law of the series or the secret of the progression, and confides it to the hero in a 'prophetic admonition': the beloved as Captive":

> We may locate the origins of this series in the hero's love for his mother; but here too we encounter Swann, who by coming to Combray to dine deprives the child of the maternal presence. And the anguish the hero suffers over his mother is already the anguish Odette caused Swann himself. (69–70)

Marcel blames Swann for diminishing his pleasure by having to "snatch" his kiss in front of others (18). As Harold Moss observes in *The Magic Lantern of Marcel Proust* (1962), "Swann's ringing of the garden gate bell . . . carries the sound of doom to Marcel" (21).

Swann's penetration of this Edenic childhood garden resonates with multiple meanings. It prefigures a type of romantic suffering that pervades the entire work, establishing the primacy of the beloved's absence over her presence in arousing desire. As Moss avers, "[I]t is the enigmatic nature of woman, it is the torture of her absence rather than the pleasure of her presence, that constitutes the clue to passion" (52). Whereas other writers spill volumes of ink upon the beloved's presence, it is his or her absence (and the psychological effects of it) that concerns Proust. The most deterministic of these effects is the enervation of desire. No absence, no desire. Absence is the deterministic, if ironic, precondition for the presence of desire. Indeed, the beloved's habitual presence is an impediment to desire insofar as it inhibits the imagination's production of fear and jealousy, upon which desire feeds.

Proustian desire is neurotic in nature insofar as it foregrounds the sorrows of separation anxiety. More significantly, this neurotic anguish stimulates the creative impulse indirectly by enervating the jealous imagination, whose hyperactivity stimulates the growth of the creative imagination. Further, the need to cope with the romantic wounds of the material world prompts Marcel's turn away from the material to the immaterial, as a means of satisfying his idealizing desire. This leads directly to the first works of his idealizing imagination: a Norman gothic Balbec church, a Turneresque Normandy coastline, Berma's reinscription of the classic Greek ideal in *Phedre*, Ruskin's Venice, or the feudal sublime embodied in the names of Geneviève de Brabant and Guermantes. The real is supplanted by the ideal, which in turn seeks to superimpose itself upon the real—in vain, until the ideal and the real are reunited in the end through involuntary memory, their merger eternalized in a work of art whose principal aim and most salutary effect is to gratify the "merger hunger" of a disordered self. Pain in the material world induces Marcel to search for pleasure in the realm of the symbolic, prompts the inward turn into the self, which evolves into an epic struggle to liberate from within itself that creative self which alone can eternalize the mother, can justify the sacrifice of the mother to art, can unite both mother and son in an immortal embrace that gratifies forever the "merger hunger" of the soul. All prisoners in *Recherche* are surrogates for the ideal self imprisoned within itself: Genevieve imprisoned in her tower, the female imprisoned within Charlus, the lost selves of Marcel imprisoned in the petites madeleines, the steeples of Martinville, and the trees of Hudimesnil, etc.

Every date in the calendar of The Search reinscribes this first "black date in the calendar" of Marcel's soul—bears the dark imprint, the neurotic fingerprint of this original sin. The "drame coucher" casts a spiritual shadow over the narrative landscape of *Recherche*, which not even the luminosity of St. Hilaire's stained glass windows or the pastoral brilliance of the hawthorns can entirely efface. That distinction is reserved for the final transfiguration, into whose redemptive light this spiritual darkness is finally absorbed.

The "drame coucher" initiates another narrative progression. The primacy of the absent mother prefigures Swann's fixation with an absent Odette and Marcel's own obsession with an absent Albertine—as well as his fixations with an absent Balbec and an absent Venice. His preoccupation with the absent is both an effect and a cause of Marcel's diseased imagination, of the "disease of the ideal" (Moss 49). Doubrovsky underscores the deterministic influence of the mother's "presence/absence [which] gives rhythm to the fullness/emptiness of the vital flux, determines the sequence of ecstasy/anguish, repletion/depression pinpointed in Combray I and infinitely repeated in the narrator's life. There is no mode of existence other than this legacy of early childhood" (19). The absent/present binary produces the bind and inflicts the wound that incites The Search, which culminates seven volumes later in The Word. Again, Doubrovsky's comments are instructive: "By a rigorous law, if the Other's continual presence determines absence to yourself, presence to yourself demands the Other's eternal absence—without whom, however, it is impossible to be yourself" (23). The solution to this double bind is to "become your own mother" by mothering a child in the form of art: "[W]hat is not possible in the real is executed in the imaginary, through art" (30). The anguish of a maternal absence agitates the imagination, which converts the absence into a presence on the plane of illusion. The neurotic effect of separation anxiety is the true mother of Marcel's invention.

The "merger hunger" that is thwarted by the mother is not only displaced onto heterosexual loves and same-sex friendships, but onto people, places, and things as well. This is evidenced by Marcel's need to merge the ideal and the real in Berma and the Guermantes, in Balbec church and in an erotic-artistic Venice. As Moss observes, this ideal self is "half a metaphor constantly searching for its relevant image" (54). The desire to have the ideal self mirrored in the mother, when thwarted, engenders a search for Others that mirror the ideal self (Saint Loup, Bergotte, Vinteuil) or for objects that personify this self (the petite madeleines, the Martinville steeples, the Hudimesnil trees). The desire for these privileged Others betrays yet another aspect of Marcel's diseased self: the "mirror-hungry personality" (Kohut 378). In *The Search for the Self*, Kohut defines this manifestation of the disordered self as follows: "[T]he mirror-hungry personalities thirst for selfobjects whose confirming and admiring responses will nourish their famished self" (378). Marcel's personality bears resemblance to yet another type of the disordered self: the "ideal-hungry personality" which "is forever in search of others whom [it] can admire for their prestige, power, beauty, intelligence, or moral stature"(378). As Marcel's career evidences, his disordered self seems to be a compendium of three disparate, yet overlapping personality types: the "merger-hungry," the "mirror-hungry," and the "ideal-hungry," which are in play throughout The Search, but which are particularly asserted during the "privileged moments."

Swann's penetration of Aunt Leonie's garden is the worm of sorrow that penetrates the apple of innocence, the serpent that corrupts the lovers in the Edenic garden with the promise of knowledge, in which Swann's rhetorical seduction of the mother through art replicates the serpent's seduction of Eve.

Aunt Leonie's garden is not merely a trope for the Edenic childhood garden of "perpetual springtime" (Moss 20); it is as well an emblem for the Edenic garden of "original sin": of the eternal corruption of love and happiness by the penetration of sin and sorrow. Leonie's garden is a topos of corrupted innocence, of exile into damnation and mortality.

The dining room is the first topos of forbidden desire and the possessive jealousy it breeds. It is a precursor of Montjouvain, the bathhouses of Sapphic love, and the sensuous streets of Venice: all as "desirable and hostile as the dining room that prevented the narrator's mother from kissing her son in Combray. There are sons who love their mothers (and mothers who love their sons) like the Gormorrheans" (Kristeva 76). It is alas that "garden from which a child is expelled" (Moss 21) that is invested with the melancholy enchantment of a paradise lost, for which the exiled sinner vainly seeks surrogates in the real world and which he finally repossesses through art.

Marcel's obsessive surveillance of the beloved, as well as the nature of the suffering he endures, foreshadows the sorrows of Swann during his love for Odette—establishing a correspondence between Marcel and his older double, here given an ironic twist by Swann's sorrow-inducing presence in the garden of the maternal sublime. As Moss writes,

> [H]e becomes a spy, the watcher whose beloved object is kept under surveillance until what he must irrationally possess becomes his . . . here we have all the precipitating emotions that will determine Marcel's emotional life. Since there is no security in a possession based on anxiety, the act must be repeated over and over again. Love is not a choice but a desperate reassurance, and the greatest power such a love has is the cessation of anxiety. The repetition of this ritual is the psychological key to the character of Marcel, in which suffering and love are inextricably bound. (22)

Swann's sorrow over Odette is a metonym for Marcel's agonies over the mother and Albertine, in what constitutes a tripartite development of the neurotic suffering associated with separation anxiety that spans seven volumes. Marcel's desire for the mother is replicated in his desire for the Other, which repeats the separation anxiety of the good night kiss tableau. As Moss avers, maternal "love itself is a disease psychic in origin . . . the pervasive maternal fog through which he sees all sexual relations" (48). The profane desire of the mother-son dyad, and the pathology of the self associated with it, produces acute symptoms, not the least of which is the "disease of the ideal" rooted in Marcel's imagination (49), which in turn incites his errant, Quixote-like quest for a paradise of the ideal to replace that from which he is exiled in childhood by his sense of maternal abandonment: the one fact of life he can neither alter nor accept.

Moss develops the implications of "the garden," observing that it is not only an image of paradise lost, but of paradise regained, not only of dispossession but of repossession, not only of exile but of salvation, not only of that which is fugitive but of that which is enduring. It is a trope for the garden of the maternal sublime, for the garden of youth and beauty, for the garden of profane desire, for the garden of a flowering intellect, for the garden of the aristocratic sublime, and finally for the Edenic garden of art that subsumes them all, and beside which the gardens of friendship, love, and society devolve into counterfeit gardens.

The garden of Aunt Leonie, as with the Garden of Eden, is a terrain of innocent felicity corrupted by desire into a topos of suffering. As with Eden, knowledge is invested with the power to damn: in this case, it is the knowledge Marcel gains of Swann's sorrows that seemingly induces his own. Later, he will attribute his suffering for Albertine to the knowledge he acquired of Sapphic desire at Montjouvain—as if Marcel's original sin was not the practice of profane desire, but the mere knowledge of it. He plucks the forbidden fruit of the tree of knowledge that is the tale of Swann's profane desire for a courtesan: a tale that deeply informs his profane desire for the mother insofar as it too recounts the sorrows associated with separation from the beloved: knowledge that comes to him in his own garden. The apple that is pastoral Combray, that is Marcel's family, that is youthful innocence is corrupted by the two-headed worm of profane desire or the knowledge of it. As Moss affirms, "[T]he relationship of Swann and Odette is the nourishing soil from which the emblematic tree of Marcel's life is to spring" (23). If Marcel's profane desire is the "original sin" of *Recherche*, then knowledge of profane desire is the "mortal sin," as evidenced by the near mortal effects it has upon Swann and Marcel respectively. Yet, the narrator's confession of incestuous desire in the novel is merely a transposition of the novelist's need to confess not only his knowledge, but his practice of homoerotic desires (a point I will develop at greater length in the next chapter).

Swann's amorous sufferings, more than his artistic sensibilities, are what he bequeaths to Marcel—and comprise (along with the maternal curse of the good night kiss) the source of the novel's determinism. In her penetrating work of Proustian criticism, *Time and Sense* (1996), Julia Kristeva observes that "out of Swann's excessive presence and his intrusive being (rather than through the photographs of Giotto paintings he generously gives the narrator . . .), an imagination, and therefore a narrator, is created" (23). The incestuous jealousy Swann incites in the narrator, by actuating his imagination, does far more to launch the careers of Marcel-the-lover and Marcel-the-artist than the narrator's mere perusal of masterpieces. For it is Swann "who ruins your evenings and leaves you all alone in your bedroom, torn between your desire to see your mother and the shame you would feel," as if the essence of that desire was discovered by he who has thwarted it. Kristeva continues: the narrator "could not have created his art without the sort of primordial suffering induced by Swann's actions," for "once the incisive imaginary is awakened, love becomes lethal, and jealousy becomes fiction"(22, 26).

This "black date in the calendar" signifies the conception of Marcel's creative soul, birthed in the psychic blood of separation anxiety. It connotes as well the birthday of his creative imagination, even if it is usurped by jealousy. No matter: the Icarian flight to the realm of the ideal (a realm of pure imagination) has been triggered. Psychic wings are flapping in the nest, animated by an epic migratory impulse.

The object of Marcel's desire is inherently fugitive, even when being kissed, which affords no "clearer idea of the taste of the rose of his desire" (979). Every attempt to possess the Other not only reinforces the Other's independence, but intensifies the self's dependence upon the Other. Possessive desire commences by seeking to increase the dependence of the Other upon the self, but ends by achieving the precise opposite: the increased dependence of the self upon the Other. Possessive desire defeats its own purpose—perhaps because its hidden agenda is not possession of the Other, but of the self; its real objective is not communion with the Other, but to either convert the Other into a function of the self, or to use the Other's rejection of the self as a further impetus to self-assertion through a deeper engagement of the self with the self. In either case (the fulfillment or the frustration of possessive desire), the effect is the same: the narcissistic assertion of the self.

The fall into the abyss of profane and possessive desire is, however, a fortunate fall for Marcel insofar as it awakens his creative imagination. And to the extent Marcel is Proust, perhaps those sufferings were willed, whether consciously or unconsciously, in an instinctive effort to awaken the ideal (artistic) self from its inward slumber. Perhaps here we discover as well the reason Marcel/Proust begins his narrative hovering in a realm of twilight psychology between wakefulness and sleep: an allegory, perhaps, of the artist who until this moment has slept (albeit fitfully) deep within the self. It is Absence that converts the absence of this ideal (creative) self into a presence: the absence of the beloved. This awakening of Marcel's imagination by desire is evidenced when he describes the "inconceivable, infernal scene of gaiety in the thick of which we had been imagining swarms of enemies, perverse and seductive, beguiling away from us, even making laugh at us, the woman whom we love" (SW 24). Marcel's yearning for the good night kiss is encoded with incestuous desire, as is the madeleine-flavored tea, which is "capable of awakening insatiable desires when placed on the tongue. And then the narrator discovers the forbidden pleasure of the mother's kiss" (Kristeva 11). When coupled to the allegory of incest in *Francois le champi* that his mother reads to him, Marcel's profane pleasure is redoubled—as is his subsequent guilt for thus profaning the maternal sublime. As Kristeva observes, a direct line can be traced from the madeleine to the "drame coucher": "[T]he 'madeleine episode' . . . openly invites us to restore the oral bond that attaches the narrator to a loved woman, who must nevertheless remain indifferent to him [and to his desire]" (13). The episodes of the madeleine, the "drame coucher," and *Francois le champi* are all metafictions of profane desire—as is Montjouvain.

Does the episode of the madeleine connote an erotic, incestuous desire to restore the "oral bond" with the mother? Is the illicit desire embedded in the tea-dipped madeleine brought to the lips merely a precursor of the illicit desires that underlie the good night kiss: to taste with the lips a forbidden maternal sexuality? The terrain of Combray is pervaded by the "oral disturbance around Mamma awakening desire and marked by readings performed and kisses sometimes withheld" (Kristeva 21). The symbiotic coupling of vice and genius is established early in the good night kiss tableau. There are undeniable oedipal overtones of incest in the narrator's love (and physical desire) for his mother, but to assert that a sublimated incestuous impulse is the sole source of his creative urge is to egregiously oversimplify the origins of creativity. It is not merely the repressed incestuous impulse, but the neurosis of separation anxiety associated with it that here informs the origins of the creative urge—and this it does in conjunction with a host of other factors. The will to form, the desire to eternalize the soul, to replace what has been lost, to free oneself from the oppressive effects of the creative urge itself are equally responsible for artistic production in general, and for the evolution of this work of art in particular.

Indeed, *Recherche* is not merely the developmental paradigm of an artist's initiation to art, but of a lover's initiation to those "cruel mysteries" whose unbearable pain becomes not only the object of his art, but the primary cause of it providing not only the material but the necessity for it. This too is immanent in the good night kiss, for the sweetness of that kiss has about it the savor of death: by virtue of the sorrows it incites, the separation it interrupts, and the innocence it ends.

THE AGONY OF THE ECSTASY:
THE SORROWS OF SEPARATION ANXIETY

In order to determine the relevance of a Rankian reading of *Recherche* it is first necessary to answer a fundamental question: does Marcel's suffering rise to the level of neurosis? The drama of the good night kiss suggests that it does. Further, it establishes the symbiosis between neurosis and creativity, as evidenced by the enervation of Marcel's "novelizing imagination" (Shattuck 77): a significant symptom of his pathology of the self. His own words repeatedly and poignantly evidence the morbid nature of his suffering and the root cause of it. He confides that the dining room that keeps his mother from him is the cause of his "mortal sadness" (SW 23) because of the pleasures she is experiencing, and from which he is "far away": a phrase that captures his sense of exile from the maternal sublime, and which contributes to his keen sense of maternal abandonment. The agony induced by his longing for the kiss is heightened by his fear that this "contrivance would make me ridiculous in Swann's eyes," and is surpassed only by the guilt that follows it.

Marcel's own words betray the violence of his torment, which he describes as "the agony through which I had just passed." Moreover, this "agony" is posited as the inevitable byproduct of all possessive love, not just the maternal, as evidenced by the fact the narrator equates it with "a similar anguish (that) had been the bane of [Swann's] life for many years." He continues:

> [A]nd noone perhaps could have understood my feelings at that moment so well as himself; to him, that anguish which lies in knowing that the creature one adores is in some place of enjoyment where oneself is not and cannot follow—to him that anguish came through Love, to which it is in a sense predestined. (SW 23)

He speaks, for example, of the "hours of anguish which I should have to spend, that evening, alone in my room, without the possibility of going to sleep," and of the "terrifying abyss that yawned at my feet"(SW 19). He writes of the "hateful staircase" he must climb, unkissed, as if to a dungeon or to a tower cell (21), and which reeks of a "special quality of sorrow," rendering it even "more cruel to my sensibility" (22). He speaks of an "anguish" that is "insidious and brutal . . . poisonous" (22): as toxic as the fresh varnish that invades his nostrils and lungs. Proust's imagery, filtered through Marcel's self-reflexive discourse, reinforces the morbid nature of his suffering. He turns down the covers of his bed, as if digging "my own grave, "and compares his nightshirt to a "shroud": images of death that reinforce the association of the kiss with death, which indeed make it a kiss of death. He speaks of "burying" himself in his "iron bed" and resorts to the stratagem of a "condemned prisoner." These images of morbidity underscore the neurotic nature of Marcel's conflict, even as they reinforce associations with the image of Geneviève de Brabant imprisoned in her feudal tower.

The solace of the magic lantern projections prefigures the psychic turn from the material to the immaterial realm, from the fleshly sorrows of the good night kiss to the idealizing adjustments of the imagination, which will invest the world of *Recherche* with its own fanciful projections from Paris to Normandy to Venice. Marcel's bedroom, awash in the fanciful projections of the magic lantern, becomes a surrogate topos for the creative self, as yet imprisoned within the self. This and "the little room at the top of the house" become his places of refuge, reserved for "reading or dreaming, secret tears or paroxysms of desire" (SW 10). Marcel's words evidence the fact that neurosis is the first master to which the creative imagination apprentices itself.

His imagination is fixated by those "inaccessible and torturing hours into which she has gone to taste of unknown pleasures" (24), a form of initiation into those "cruel mysteries," as a consequence of which his "heart began to beat more and more painfully as I increased my agitation, as I ordered myself to remain calm and to acquiesce in my misfortune" (25). Fears of maternal abandonment are as central to the birth of Marcel's creative imagination as fears of eternal damnation are in the birth of Stephen Dedalus's imagination. Both protagonists are plunged into a psychic hell of suffering that destabilizes the self in the act of fixating it, enervating the need to escape from the self into the illusory realms of the imagination. By objectifying a part of the self, art enables the remainder to cope with its neurotic imprisonment, which is no longer absolute inasmuch as it no longer totalizes the self. Art reduces neurosis from a totalizing to a partializing phenomenon with respect to the self—leaves a portion of the self to itself, and this difference makes all the difference in the world to the self: is the difference between madness and sanity, disease and health, mortality and immortality, self-destruction and self-regeneration. A touch of madness is beneficial to genius, which is enervated by it.

The good night kiss meta-drama also establishes the remedial effects of writing for Marcel, and by implication for the neurotic artist in general. Writing (the note he pens to his mother, and delivers through Francoise) converts her absence into a presence. Further, writing objectifies the sublimated desire to be the fixated object of the maternal gaze. It satisfies the "mirror-hungry" needs of the disordered self. If his physical being is denied the narcissistic pleasure of being the object of his mother's attention, then writing will, if only for a moment, bring the idea of him before the maternal gaze. The note Francoise delivers to his mother also reinscribes those urgent messages a lover sends via a servant to his beloved sequestered in a salon to which he has not been invited. It anticipates the desperate dispatches Marcel sends via Saint Loup to Albertine after her escape. The word is not passive, but protean: capable of projecting the self outside itself, of extending its domain beyond the boundaries of its own imprisoning flesh, of imposing its will upon the material world, of converting sorrow into joy and anxiety into repose. The word temporarily bridges the abyss between self and Other, as it will affect the eternal conjunction of mother and son in art. As an objectification of the self, the written word enacts the profane will of the self, insofar as each word will "pour into my intoxicated heart the gushing sweetness of mamma's attention while she was reading what I had written" (SW 23). This boyhood moment anticipates those dreamed of moments in adulthood when Marcel hopes she will be able to read "what I had written": a hope that will remain unfulfilled as long as the mother lives, insofar as she thwarts the impulse toward independence without which no artistic work can be achieved.

Writing consummates Marcel's profane desire for the mother. Writing is not only conscripted by desire, but consummates and consecrates it. The ideal self is corrupted by the profane self. Writing is a surrogate for possession insofar as it fixates the maternal gaze upon the abstracted self. Eventually, writing will liberate the ideal self from the profane self, by which it is profaned here, atoning for the sins of the profane self. The sadism of the profane self is purged by the figurations of an ideal self, as the sins of the son are expunged by the redemptive deeds of the artist. Each written word has for Marcel the redemptive power of a bead on a rosary. And *Recherche* is nothing if not a vast rosary that loops upon itself, a seventeen-year penance for sins committed against the maternal sublime, for the original sin of profanation which becomes for mother and artist alike a mortal sin, that contributes not only to the death, but to the immortality of each. *Recherche* is the eternal garden that the banished lovers (in this case, Marcel and his mother) regain through the redemptive power of the written word.

The written word produces the desired results: "[N]ow I was no longer separated from her" (23). Writing solves, if only temporarily, the central problem of his existence insofar as it effaces his separation from the mother. It replicates the ephemeral joining of the two-in-one enacted in the goodnight kiss. The word is a silken rope dipped in enchanted ink, lowered from the prison tower of his bedroom to the enchanted garden of the maternal sublime. Mother and son are temporarily united in a chain of signification—or, as Marcel states, "an exquisite thread was binding us" (SW 23): an emotional and psychic surrogate for the severed umbilical cord. He fashions an umbilical cord of ink. Ink, for Marcel is the "mother's milk" that restores the pre-oedipal, two-in-one symbiosis.

Significantly, writing becomes the vehicle not only for the resolution of neurotic conflict, but the means by which the maternal is first profaned, initiating the conjunction of vice and genius that recurs throughout *Recherche*. The longed-for kiss alas confers no pleasure because it "lasted too short a time," producing instead "the keenest sorrow" (SW 10). The tyranny of the transient haunts Marcel, even as the mother's presence is overshadowed by the awareness that some day she must die, is subsumed by the specter of maternal abandonment. Marcel speaks of his "wretchedness and agitation" (10). Instead of relieving his anxiety, the mother's kiss inaugurates a new round of suffering, induced by his acute sense of guilt. Marcel speaks of the "grave consequences" that "could follow only some really shameful fault" (SW 25). He speaks of the "anguish of mind" (25), of his "transgressions," the "rigor of punishment," comparing his behavior to "the same category as certain other sins for which I had been severely chastised, though infinitely more serious than they"; "I should not be allowed to stay in the house a day longer . . . so much was certain." As evidenced by his pangs of conscience, Marcel's crime is his punishment, the morbid cruelty of which anticipates the wounds inflicted by the sorrows of Sapphic desire: "Had I been obliged . . . to hurl myself out the window, I should still have preferred such a fate" (26):

> My heart was beating so violently that I could hardly move, but at least it was throbbing no longer with anxiety, but with terror and joy. . . . I threw

myself upon her . . . then her face assumed an expression of anger. She said not a single word to me; and for that matter, I used to go for days on end not being spoken to, for far less offense than this . . . a sin so deadly that I was waiting to be banished from the household . . . [h]ow wretched I was every evening. (27)

Marcel's guilt activates sado-masochistic impulses whose cruelties are directed outward toward the mother and inward at the self. As Deleuze asserts, "Freud assigned two fundamental anxieties in relation to the law [of love]: aggression against the beloved involves . . . a threat of the loss of love, and . . . a guilt caused by turning that aggression against the self. . . . Now, in Proust the theme of guilt remains superficial, social rather than moral, projected upon others rather than internalized in the narrator . . ." (126). I would argue that Marcel's guilt is both internalized and socialized. A sadistic impulse that commences with the personal and familial becomes social, finds its resonance in a social cruelty that is pervasive, which is institutionalized in the salons of the Faubourg St. Germaine, and in the salon of Mme Verdurin in particular. The sadistic impulse that is displaced across a spectrum of characters, from Francoise to Charlus, that pervades every social class in *Recherche*, is but the flip side of a cruelty directed at the self. This dream of social sadism mirrors the narrator's personal nightmare of sado-masochistic impulses inscribed in the rural "salon" of Combray: in the snobbery of Legrandin, in the middle-class snobbery of the narrator's family toward Swann, in the social banishment of Vinteuil, and in Francoise's overt sadism toward the chickens she strangles and the maid she persecutes (Giotto's Charity). If Marcel's willingness to profane the mother betrays a sadistic impulse, the even greater willingness to inflict pain upon himself underscores a masochistic impulse. The introduction of sado-masochistic tendencies in the "drame coucher" anticipates Proust's novel development of these impulses in other characters (Mlle Vinteuil and Charlus), which culminates in the meta-drama of Merovingian masochism mounted in Jupien's brothel.

As the one thing "upon which all his security and well-being depend" (Moss 21), the good night kiss exercises a disproportionate and deterministic influence over Marcel. His own words underscore the fugitive nature of felicity: "I ought to have been happy; I was not." The good night kiss simultaneously signifies the consummation and the frustration of Marcel's desire. The knowledge that he has profaned the object of his desire in order to obtain it, ruins his pleasure. To satisfy the desires of a profane self he has forever tarnished his ideal self: in his eyes, and worse, in his mother's. Hence, the narrator's accurate identification of himself with Golo, the cruel husband of Geneviève de Brabant, who plays the beloved false, and who rides fantastic circles about Marcel's tormented head, like an astral projection of his own sadistic impulse. Marcel's soul vacillates between Geneviève and

Golo, identifying now with the falsely imprisoned personification of the feudal ideal, now with the sequestering sadism of her mobile lover. As Moss notes, even these seemingly benign childhood memories (the magic lantern, *Francois le champi*) "contain a sexual secret" (Moss 54–55).

They comment on Proust's genius as well, adding an allegorical meaning that enriches the literal content of the "drame coucher." To the extent this medieval marriage is blighted by the specter of adultery it prefigures the real marriage of the Duc and Duchess de Guermantes (the feudal descendants of Golo and Geneviève). What is less apparent, but perhaps more significant, is that this feudal couple comments as well on the love of Marcel and his mother. A direct correspondence is established between his mother and Geneviève when he writes that the amorous "misfortunes of Geneviève de Brabant had made [his mother] all the dearer to me, just as the crimes of Golo had driven me to a more than ordinarily scrupulous examination of my own conscience" (SW 9). Why? Because of the manner in which he profanes his mother's love: by using his asthma to arouse her pity, by lying to secure a kiss, and perhaps by committing in adulthood, not the sin of adultery, but the even greater sin of homosexuality. As Marcel reveals in *Cities of the Plain*, he suffers the same pangs of conscience as that "race upon which a curse weighs and which must live amid falsehood and perjury . . . sons without a mother, to whom they are obliged to lie all her life long and even in the hour when they close her dying eyes" (CP 13).

The mother's kiss is not only fulfillment of a profane wish, but the product of a son's manipulation. Consequently, it leaves a bitter taste on the lips of his memory. As Moss observes "this 'involuntary' kiss seals Marcel's fate" by redoubling his sorrows: "[I]n ridding himself of one anxiety, he inherits others." Marcel's victory in this contest of wills comes with a terrible price insofar as it renews the cycle of sorrow. As Kristeva avers, "[F]rom the outset, this love was marked by confrontation and by a combination of violence and passivity and of desire and compunction. Indeed, as soon as the mother gives in and lets her son have the kiss he so desires, our budding narrator's victory turns into bitter regret, and pain begins to taint his pleasure" (175). The effect of his guilt is salutary, however, insofar as it becomes a further boon to creativity: if "the iridescent sensibility of childhood" is tainted "with violence," it is the violence of The Big Bang (Kristeva 180).

In *Recherche*, Proust shifts the locus of violence from the physical to the psychological realm. The pathological violence of an aggressive self is manifested in matricidal, suicidal, sadistic, masochistic, and possessive impulses that proliferate over the course of the narrative—an effect, perhaps, of his debilitating asthma which prevented the self from working off violent impulses in habitually masculine avenues: physical exercise, sports, warfare. These violent impulses are not only internalized, but enervated by their repression—surfacing in the form of matricidal and suicidal, in sadistic and masochistic tendencies, in the violent aggressions of a self: transposed to the realm of the personal and the social, in a pathological effort to re-masculinize the self. The violent impulses of the self are displaced from their normal arenas (the soccer field and the battlefield) to the privileged battlefields of a pathological self: the bedroom, the salon, and the garden. The violence that is everywhere turned on the Other (mother, Vinteuil, Albertine, Swann, Saniette, Giotto's Charity, Charlus) returns with a vengeance upon the self.

The crisis of the good night kiss underscores the impossibility of possession. As such, it sets the tone (and the course) for the entire novel. As Deleuze observes, "[T]he loss of love truly defines destiny or the law . . . and to stop loving, since the emptying of the worlds, the explication of the beloved, leads the self which loves to its death" (126). Desire is doomed to never obtain its object, or to perish in the act of possession. Consummation of desire, the thing wished throughout *Recherche*, comprises the death of desire. Desire cannot survive its fulfillment. And this tragic law casts a shadow over *Recherche* as deterministic as the law that sets the two apart. The two-in-one can never overcome the hyphen of differentiation. The dream of possessive desire dies the moment it ceases to be a dream—cannot withstand the dawn of reality. Fulfillment of desire is a contradiction in terms. The moment desire is fulfilled it converts to indifference. The moment of its consummation is the moment of its death. It exhausts its life in a consuming struggle toward its end, only to perish in the moment of gratification. Its resilient, questing flesh decays in the milk of its own sperm. The death of desire is executed by the gratification of desire—and this law is given in *Recherche* with the terrible grandeur of a New Testament of the heart, by one who has mounted a summit of introspection.

The self's aggressive explications of the Other not only does violence to the Other but to itself. The violence of *Recherche*, which is a self-violence as much as it is a violence upon the Other, derives from the efforts of the idealizing imagination to construct or deconstruct the Other. This volitional violence rebounds violently upon the self, in an endless sado-masochistic feedback loop. Deleuze is succinct in his analysis: each of these voluntary faculties "explicates a type of sign which does it particular violence" (165). The species of violence extant in *Recherche* is distinctly postmodern inasmuch as it shifts the locus of violence from the material to the immaterial world, from the violence of deeds to the violence of desire, from the collective violence of humankind's inhumanity to itself to the individual violence of the self on the Other, whose weapons of choice are an idealizing or jealousizing imagination and an interpreting intellect. The signs by which the self imposes itself upon the Other return upon itself, in a feedback loop of violence whose pathological circuitry is a sado-masochistic impulse. This is the sardonic irony of the sign's eternal return in *Recherche:* a sign with a double edge, which does violence in two directions, toward the Other and to the self, in the service of a sado-masochism whose inward violence turns outward and whose violence to the Other returns upon the self. As Marcel confides, "I felt that I had with an impious finger traced a first wrinkle upon her soul and made the first white hair show upon her head. This thought redoubled my sobs" (SW 30).

IS A KISS JUST A KISS? PSYCHOLOGICAL IMPLICATIONS OF THE "DRAME COUCHER"

What are the deeper psychological implications of this "black date in the calendar"? What implications does it possess for the novel as a whole? What myths does it reinscribe? The crisis of the good night kiss deeply informs neurotic as well as creative impulses. From a Rankian perspective, the "drame coucher" enjoins a contest of wills between mother and son and is significant insofar as it establishes the primacy of Marcel's will over his mother's, even as it evidences at an early age the presence of a strong inventive will, despite the narrator's assertion that a "weak will" is his Achilles heel. It is only through the persistent application of an "iron will" that Marcel is finally able to liberate the creative self from its captivity within the self. The heroic struggle of this will is metonymically inscribed in the labors of the "privileged moments." Sans the epic liberatory struggles of this will, the creative self would perish within the closed circle of the neurotic bind.

This "kiss of death" leaves Marcel an emotional orphan, even as it creates an emotional dependency upon the mother. The agony of the good night kiss plunges Marcel into a paradoxical limbo of unsatisfied dependency and emotional estrangement. The agony of the good night kiss is a symptom of a deeper disease—of a separation anxiety that produces a sense of maternal abandonment. Marcel's torment arises from two terrible sources: from the realization that his desire to possess his mother can never be realized, and that in contradistinction to their placental symbiosis, his being and hers are forever disjoined. His free-standing existence outside the womb is an unsatisfactory surrogate for the mother-son symbiosis within the womb—as if he never fully recovered from the shock of the severed umbilical cord. The narrator's trauma is in part the trauma induced at birth, as Rank asserts, by the severing of the umbilical cord: a severing the narrator has never been able to reproduce psychically or emotionally. Hence, the irreconcilable conflict of his existence in which psychic and emotional umbilical cords remain intact after the severing of the anatomical umbilical cord at the moment of birth. The fundamental dualism that generates the narrator's neurotic conflict stems from the irreconcilable fact of his physical separation from the mother and his psychic/emotional dependence upon her. This maternal dependence will bring him into direct and morbid conflict with a creative self, whose liberating autonomy is threatened by psychic dependence upon the mother.

Marcel's heart is still attached to his mother by an emotional umbilical cord he will not be able to sever until her death severs it for him, liberating him into the mothering embrace of art.

The self here and throughout *Recherche* is insufficiently differentiated from the maternal sublime to enable artistic production. Hence, the cruel duality of the narrator's condition, which is characterized by a yearning to create (to "mother" his own invention) and by an attachment to the mother which impedes creation. This is the deterministic bind at the heart of *Recherche*. As Doubrovsky observes, "[I]mpossible identification with the mother determines the long itinerary of the Narrator of *Recherche*"(72):

> [not only] the impossibility of rejoining being in the mother, but the reciprocal impossibility of finding any being in the self . . . the desire to have the self and the Other coincide, the obsession with the fusion of differences will establish at the narrative level the symbiosis of the two-in-one. (73–74)

Doubrovsky's interpretation reinforces the relevance of Kohut's theories regarding the personalities of the pathological self, and of the "merger-hungry" personality in particular. As Kohut observes, with this type of personality, "it is the need for merger that dominates the picture":

> Because the self of these individuals is seriously defective or enfeebled, they need selfobjects in lieu of self structure. . . . [T]he fluidity of the boundaries between them and others interferes with their ability to discriminate their own thoughts, wishes, and intentions from those of the selfobject. Because they experience the other as their own self, they feel intolerant of his independence: they are very sensitive to separations from him and they demand—indeed they expect without question—the selfobject's continuous presence. (380)

Kohut's analysis of the "merger-hungry" personality deeply informs the "separation anxiety" of Marcel, which comprises a fictional representation of it, as evidenced not only in the "drame coucher," but in the violent rupture with the mother that occurs when he first boards the train for Balbec. As Kohut asserts, the blurring of boundaries between self and other seriously impedes the project of self-differentiation. This passage informs Marcel's sensitivity to the mother's absence, the demands he makes on her to ensure her "continuous presence," which is thwarted in reality, but fulfilled on the plane of illusion: in art, wherein their mutual reading of *Francois le champi* prefigures the writing of *Recherche* insofar as it satisfies the wish for the two-in-one. The implications of Marcel's "merger-hungry" personality will be developed further in chapter 3, particularly as they relate to the "ideal-hungry" and "mirror-hungry" aspects of the pathological self.

Marcel's incestuous desire not only to be with the mother, but to be the mother, evidences an atavistic regression, is the manifestation of a desire to "return to the womb, already clearly glimpsed in the form of the 'quite thin partition' separating the narrator from his grandmother, upon which he has only to give 'three knocks' to have her come to 'give him milk'" (77). Writing becomes in the end a surrogate for the maternal sublime: "Ink is the resurrection of milk. In the fantasy's logic, the dying writer writes in a fetal position" (77). Doubrovsky continues:

> [T]he obsession with the two-in-one, with the 1 + 1 = 1, which the Narrator projects in all his relationships with others . . . is already nostalgia for an original fusion, for a lost age, where all difference is abolished . . . and where Proust's deepest desire to write originates . . . below the rivalries and the ambivalence that occur after birth . . . the serenity of the visceral enclosure is affirmed, the joy of the primitive circuit. (78)

Ink is his mother's milk.

This desire for an undifferentiated being is also the place where the desire for same-sex love originates. In all Proustian love, the Other is an ideal extension of the self. Hence, the ideal lover comes not from the opposite, but from the same sex. Doubrovsky even takes his analysis one step farther, linking "the original fantasy of fusion with the mother, the desire for non-difference" (81) to the original and recurring trope of the madeleine-flavored tea: "happiness of the embryo floating in its lime-flower-urine" (79).

The turn from the material to the immaterial, from the kiss withheld to the kiss imagined, the "gradual withdrawal from the world" that sets aunt Leonie's "model in place" and that culminates in the cork-lined sanitarium of the bedroom in Boulevard Haussmann, begins in this critical moment of a childhood trauma, arises from the conflicted material of a "dual relationship with the mother,"

> which you can never manage to leave behind or to go back to; from which you can neither free yourself nor separate yourself: insoluble conflict, producing contradictory behavior (adoration and profanation in sacrilegious gestures . . . and leading into a progressive inertia (bedroom-bed-paralysis). (Doubrovsky 77)

A double bind that paralyzes the will, that prompts a long delay to writing, which can only occur with the "murder" of the mother—which becomes, in essence, the vehicle of a matricidal impulse.

The desire for the mother is complicated by the desire to kill the mother, incestuous urges opposed by matricidal impulses. Marcel is torn in two by powerful opposing tendencies: the tendency toward maternal attachment and the tendency toward artistic independence. Though the two tendencies are incompatible, the conflict generated is essential not only to the conception but to the ultimate liberation of the artistic impulse. This first "black date in the calendar" signifies paradoxically the death and the birth of the ideal self.

If the original sin he commits slays the ideal self, then the psychological pathology this engenders eventually resurrects the ideal-self-as-artist. The mortal ideal of the self-as-good-son is replaced by a super-ideal (self-as-artist). An ideal self destabilized by profane desire is recuperated and sedimented as a super-ideal self by art. The origins of this impulse are dark indeed, belying the seeming Edenic, nostalgic terrain of Combray. Roger Shattuck, in his analysis of optical imagery in *Recherche* (*Proust's Binoculars* 1963), endorses this view: Like *Arabian Nights*, *Recherche* begins "by presenting a secure and happy life soon shattered by a revelation of infidelity and depravity. . . . Marcel's innocent vision of Combray collapses beneath the weight of vice and duplicity that reveal themselves in every character outside the immediate family" (137)—and within it as well, if we understand the mother's behavior in the context of the son's reaction: as an infidelity—which, moreover, extends from the material and maternal realms to the symbolic, as evidenced by Golo's accusations against Geneviève and by the incestuous theme of Sand's novel. Marcel's illicit desires and profanations reinforce the decadence and vice that inform the broader social landscape of Combray: as evidenced in the orgies of Uncle Adolphe, in the Sapphic trysts of Montjouvain, in Charlus's tête-à-tête with the courtesan Odette (the lady-in-pink). Hardly the landscape of Edenic innocence or orthodox piety suggested by the hawthorns and the spiritualized edifice of St. Hilaire, with its stained-glass windows, its biblical sculptures, and its heaven-reaching steeples. Like the microcosm of the bedroom/garden, the macrocosm of Combray reflects the superimposition of vice and virtue.

Marcel's mind and heart still dwell in a placental fluid outside the mother: as if the soul of a fetus is trapped within the body of a boy. Marcel's Otherness begins early, begins indeed at the moment of birth, which is nothing if not the birth of his otherness from mother: He never adequately adjusts to his sexual differentiation from the mother at birth. Moreover, Marcel's otherness is compounded in the author by his homosexuality and Jewishness. Consequently, the search may be posited as a quest to discover some means of adjusting to this a priori fact of life: Marcel's sexual differentiation from the mother—to which art is the ultimate adjustment. As Kristeva affirms, it is "the mother on whom the narrator must revenge himself in order to be separated from her so that sexual pleasure and writing may occur" (20).

The two-in-one communion of the womb engenders a need to surmount sexual differentiation in post-placental reality. Life after birth is a quest to enfold the self in the mother, which it finally does by immersing itself in the afterbirth of art. The self surmounts its differentiation from the mother by replicating the moment of pregnancy: by impregnating itself, by begetting a creative self: which then further replicates the birthing process by begetting itself in words. Writing is the self's means of rewriting the trauma of the birth experience—of closing the psychic wounds of sexual differentiation by objectifying them in ink, by differentiating the ideal self from its differentiated self. The self copes with its differentiation by displacing it onto art, which simultaneously fulfills its wish for communion with the mother, to eternalize the two-in-one. As Deleuze observes, "[T]he truth of love is first of all the isolation of the sexes. We live under Samson's prophesy: 'The two sexes shall die, each in a place apart'" (77)—symbolically inscribed by the separation of the "two ways," whose conjunction in the end reinscribes the narrator's primal wish for the "two-in-one." For Marcel, the knowledge that the two sexes must die apart is aggravated by the realization they must also live apart. Deleuze's observations are echoed by Samuel Beckett (*Proust* 1957), who argues that the narrator's separation anxiety is due not only to a fear of death (his own and his mother's), but to a fear of emotional death with respect to the mother—to a fear of indifference:

> [T]his reluctance to die ... explains also the horror at the idea of ever living without Gilberte Swann, of ever losing his parents, at the idea of his own death. But this terror at the thought of separation—from Gilberte, from his parents, from himself—is dissipated in a greater terror, when he thinks that to the pain of separation will succeed indifference ... when not only the objects of his affection have vanished, but that affection itself. (qtd. in Bloom 25–26)

The fear of death inherent in Marcel's separation anxiety is a precursor to an even greater fear, his fear of indifference—which in the Proustian universe is the locus of actual death, the final destination toward which everything in *Recherche* gestures, and whose governing determinism would be absolute were it not for art, for the possibility of eternalizing the objects of our affection in the abstract realm of signs.

Harold Bloom notes the Freudian implications of maternal separation anxiety, including its tendency to produce patricidal, masochistic, and homosexual impulses. As Bloom observes in *Modern Critical Interpretations* (1987), competitive jealousy "is compounded of grief, due to the loss of the loved object, and of the reactivation of the narcissistic scar, the tragic first loss, by the infant, of the parent.... Freud genially throws into the compound such delights as enmity against the successful rival, some self-blaming, self-criticism, and a generous portion of bisexuality" (Intro 1). Marcel's vice is the inevitable byproduct of his separation anxiety. Frustration of the desire to possess the mother prompts a desire to possess the self—and its idealized image, as embodied in the same sex (Saint Loup, Albertine/Alfred Agostinelli), even as it prompts the turn away from the material to the immaterial world. Separation anxiety leads to homoerotica and art. Unable to merge with the mother, the artist becomes a mother himself (impregnates himself, as it were), fulfilling the desire to be eternally enfolded in a maternal embrace by enfolding within himself the child of his own creation. The separation of the sexes is thus internalized in a hermaphroditic solution that characterizes the careers of the homosexual and the artist, and particularly of the homosexual-as-artist. Delueze's observations are instructive:

> But matters are complicated because the separated, partitioned sexes coexist in the same individual: "initial Hermaphroditism," as in a plant or a snail, which cannot be fertilized "except by other hermaphrodites." Then it happens that the intermediary, instead of effecting the communication of male and female, doubles each sex with itself: symbol of self-fertilization all the more moving in that it is homosexual, sterile, indirect. And more than an episode, this is the essence of love. (77–78)

The self-fertilizing hermaphroditic flower is a central trope for apprehending the deep psychological grammar of *Recherche*, and of the relation between sexual differentiation, homoerotica, and creativity in particular. Deleuze underscores the connection between this separation of the sexes and "initial Hermaphroditism, [which] is the continuous law of the divergent series; from one series to the other, we see love constantly engendering signs which are those of Sodom and Gomorrah" (78). Deleuze's reading is endorsed by Kristeva: "At the same time, the mother is absorbed by the homosexual, transmuted into a vice that is at once pleasure and eccentric discourse, and swept up by this detour into the accursed race. She vanishes inside 'the disease that devours' the 'smooth polish of a woman's belly'" (221).

This law of sexual desire has profound implications, for it establishes the parameters of the series of love. As Delueze asserts, "[T]he true generality of love is serial, our loves are experienced profoundly only according to the series in which they are organized" (79). The narrator's love for his mother establishes the pattern to be repeated in Swann's love for Odette, in Marcel's for Gilberte and Albertine, in Saint Loup's for Rachel, and in Charlus's for Morel. This initial separation of the sexes proliferates in these ensuing affairs, whose preponderance of homosexual, bisexual, or lesbian lovers would seem to dramatize the governing determinism between separation of the sexes and hermaphroditism. Marcel's two-in-one hermaphroditism is the internalized effect of thwarted desire, which objectifies itself in two principal signs: the homoerotic and the artistic. The ideal self seeks its object in the same sex and in writing, in flesh and blood and in ink.

Marcel intolerance of his mother's absence is but a symptom of his fear of her death, of her eternal absence. Her nightly abandonment prefigures her eternal abandonment in death. As Moss observes, "[T]he separation of the moment must, in the future, be permanent. . . . Painfully, her existence within him tells him that they are eternally separated" (103). Whatever joy Marcel finds in life is compromised by the realization that his mother must die. As Kristeva notes, "[H]e paints death casting a shadow over love. . . . Proust then quotes a line of Hugo: ['The grass must grow and children have to die']" (173). Present and future alike inscribe his separation anxiety; it inheres in the abstract as well as in the concrete—casts its shadow over the ephemeral as well as the eternal. *Recherche* owes its existence to the desire to alter this reality. It depicts the multiple strategies by which the self adjusts to its own sexual differentiation.

Maternal separation anxiety lies at the heart of the narrator's neurosis. It is the bitter root of his creative urge as well. "Writing is," as Kristeva asserts, "memory regained from signs to flesh and from flesh to signs through an intense identification (and a dramatic separation from) an other who is loved, desired, hated, and rendered indifferent" (245):

> The "vigorous and luxuriant" growth of a literary work requires death. Is it the death of a child? Which one? Albertine? Or is it perhaps the death of the narrator himself, who believes himself to have died many times over since his childhood, following each disruption, each separation, each bedtime drama that has taken him away form his parents, and especially his mother? And what if they were children only as long as a mother was present? In that case, the mother would have to die so that the child could separate himself from his childhood, turning it into a memory as well as the regained time of his past. Like the well-known Manet painting, the book will transform a graveyard of dead children into an outing and a snack of madeleines by relying on the ambiguous, loving, and vengeful memory of a mother who always loved too much though not enough and who thus made you into a child who never stops dying but who will come back to life and mature within the grassy growth of the book. (Kristeva 174)

Kristeva's interpretation reinscribes Rank's theories on the origins of the creative impulse insofar as it underscores the influence of an "ideology of sacrifice," the relevance of which for *Recherche* I will develop at greater length in the final chapter. Separation from the mother engenders a deeply ambivalent psychological terrain: it incites the neurosis that gives rise to the "merger-hungry" and "ideal-hungry" personalities, even as it produces the initial differentiation without which no artistic work can ever occur. *Recherche* narrates Marcel's love-hate relation to his own sexual differentiation, which is loathed by the son but loved by the writer, who succeeds in extricating the self from the neurotic bind by writing his way out of it. "What can be done about it?" Kristeva asks. "The narrator first detaches himself in the same way he detached himself from his parents to protect himself from the sexual difficulties they caused him" (253). This ability to detach the self from neurotic conflict distinguishes the artist from the neurotic. As Rank asserts, the artist is able "to detach the whole creative process from his own person and transfer it to an ideological abstraction" (41):

> This explains why hardly any productive work gets through with morbid crises of a "neurotic" nature; it also explains why the relation between pro-

ductivity and illness has so far been unrecognized or misinterpreted.... [A]s I have said elsewhere, the fundamental problem is individual difference, which the ego can interpret as inferiority unless it can be proved by achievement to be superiority. (41,42. My emphasis)

Unlike the neurotic (who being unable to objectify these conflicts is consumed by them), the artist is able to "detach the whole creative process from his own person and transfer it to an ideological abstraction" (41). For this type of artist, neurosis is not only a stimulus to creativity, but often becomes the theme of it—is not only a cause, but an effect of the creative urge. In contradistinction to the artist, the neurotic remains imprisoned in neurotic conflict: for which Mallarmè's swan frozen in ice is an apt emblem. An embryonic self whose maturation is arrested within the shell of its neurosis.

Rank's interpretation is significant because it not only informs the neurotic origins of the creative impulse, but informs Marcel's/Proust's conviction of Otherness, rooted in an uncomfortable consciousness of sexual differentiation, homoerotic desires, Jewishness, and artistic impulses. The artist's consciousness of difference relative to the putative "norms" of society incites a conflict that is yet another impetus to creativity. Conflicts of a neurotic order, insofar as they further individualize the artist, intensify this conflict with the collective ideology of society. Neurosis has a de-collectivizing effect on the would-be artist: as do Jewishness and homoerotic tendencies. In contradistinction to the neurotic, who is fatally fixated by the trauma, "the artistic reaction is thus distinguished . . . by an overcoming of the trauma. . . . This overcoming is only possible through will" (64).

Art, for Rank, is defined in terms of neurosis: "[P]roduction is the creative development of neurosis in objective form" (43)—is "forcible liberation from inward pressure" (51). Speaking of this modern, "individual-type" of artist, Rank concludes: "[W]e can thus understand the experience-problem of the individual type of artist also only by studying the nature of neurosis," which has to do essentially with the "problem of fear"(47)—and in Marcel's case, with fear of separation from the mother.

Marcel's ambiguity toward his sexual differentiation is projected onto the mother—one of the most ambiguous figures in *Recherche*. Kristeva's interpretation merits consideration: "Does the maternal breast save us from sin, or does its participation in sin make it even worse? What we do know is that purity no longer exists. The haven of infantile consolations that allowed us to imagine the budding girls . . . is itself contaminated by vice, betrayal, and jealousy" (76). The milk of vice and genius will flow from the maternal breast, feeding off one another, nurturing a bastard progeny tainted with vices deeply embedded in a cult of genius: the Vinteuil family; the Charlus-Morel-Jupien triad; Uncle Adolphe, Swann and Odette; Lea and Albertine, Saint-Loup and the Prince de Guermantes. Marcel's death to purity in the "drame coucher" coincides with his birth to impurity: as evidenced by the juxtaposition of the profane and the pastoral in Montjouvain and the Méséglise way—an allegorical reinscription of Eve's original sin in which vice corrupts virtue. If Aunt Leonie's garden is breached by the vice of incestuous desire, then the Garden of Combray is similarly penetrated by this variation on "the original sin of Woman." The metafictive contents of the magic lantern, of *Francois le champi*, of Montjouvain, and Marcel's "education" at his uncle Adolphe's are, as Paul de Man observes in "Reading (Proust)," "the first explicit example of his ritualistic initiation to the ambivalences of good and evil" (119). In the final analysis, it is the pure that redeems the impure in *Recherche*—the vices of character are redeemed by its virtues, as evidenced by Proust's novel interpretation of the sadistic impulse. In "Proust and Evil," Georges Bataille draws a significant distinction between the sadism of Proust and Sade:

> Impurity is only known by contrast by those who thought they could not do without its opposite, purity. The absolute desire for impurity, artificially conceived by Sade, led him to that sated state in which every blunted sensation, even the possibility of pleasure, ultimately escaped him. . . . He never knew the particular delight of that moral feeling that gives our sins that criminal flavour without which they seem natural, without which they are natural. Proust was more able than Sade. . . . [I]f he was virtuous, it was not in order to obtain pleasure, and if he obtained pleasure it was because he had first wanted to obtain virtue. The wicked only know the material benefits of Evil. If they seek other people's misfortune, this misfortune is ultimately their selfish fortune. We only escape the imbroglio where Evil lies concealed by perceiving the interdependence of opposites . . . happiness alone is not desirable in itself and would result in boredom if the experience of misfortune, or of Evil, did not make us long for it. The opposite is also true: had we not, like Proust . . . longed for Good, Evil would provide us with a succession of indifferent sensations. (qtd. in Bloom 59)

Evil in *Recherche* is not absolute, is everywhere mitigated by virtue: in Mlle Vinteuil, in Charlus, in Mme Verdurin, and in the narrator—a striking contrast to the portrait of absolute evil depicted by Sade. Proust's discovery of virtue in vice permits him to compose such a compelling portrait of vice. His moral judgments are tempered by the realization that vice and virtue are commingled, exist in a state of "perpetual alliteration." Everything in *Recherche* is permissible due to the good that exists in evil. There is no corner of the soul too evil to be objectified in art, for the simple reason that no soul in the Proustian universe is absolutely evil, is unmitigated by virtue. The result is a universe in which even the profane is poetic—in which every garden is a garden of good and evil.

Experience for Marcel is a landscape of exile, framed on either end by the Edenic gardens of pre-oedipal communion with the mother and of artistic creation. His exile is figured as the inevitable result of his "sin" against the mother, of his profanation of the pure. The sorrow and madness that ensue are figured as atonement for his original sin. His transformation into an artist is figured as the lasting redemption of a soul that has suffered for its sins. The narrative of *Recherche* inscribes the arc of a career that is quintessentially Catholic, if not at times, pagan—that is informed by the biblical allegories of Adam and Eve, Sodom and Gomorrah, *Paradise Lost*, Mary Magdalene, and *Faust*. Its central theme is the damnation of differentiation, and of the profane desires that arise from it: in which the sorrows of Swann for Odette are framed by the sorrows of Marcel for the mother and Albertine. *Recherche* is largely a landscape of damnation, exile, and redemption, whose external topoi are totalized by a psychological pathology rooted in the debilitating and liberatory effects of sexual differentiation. *Recherche* is Marcel's penance and atonement, in which he resurrects an ideal self sacrificed in the moment of profane desire, in which he objectifies and expiates his guilt in the confessional of art, in which he eternalizes the mother he has helped kill, and in which he eternalizes the maternal embrace sundered at birth.

THE RAVENS OF ST. HILAIRE:
THE MYTH OF THE PASTORAL SIGN

The locus of this pathology of the self extends far beyond the garden and the bedroom. Indeed, it corrupts the innocent pleasures extant in the broader gardens of Combray, casts its shadow over the pastoral pleasures of the Méséglise and Guermantes ways, totalizing the physical as well as the psychological landscapes of *Recherche* with the shadow of original sin. The pastoral is absorbed into the neurotic. No ground in Combray (nor in the novel at large) is free of its deterministic reach. What first appears as a free-standing signifier of the pastoral (the Combray countryside), and its beneficent effects upon the creative imagination, devolves into a sign of the neurotic which totalizes the landscape of Combray, if not the entire novel. All the pleasures of Combray, indeed of life itself (nature walks, dreams of knowing the Guermantes, fishing, drifting down the Vivonne), are pleasurable only insofar as they afford escape from the central traumatizing reality of Marcel's existence: the knowledge that when he returns to Aunt Leonie's he will have to go to bed alone, will be parted for the duration of the night from his mother—and if there was to be a visitor, without the consoling benediction of a good night kiss. The neurotic effects of Marcel's separation anxiety are evidenced not only by the symptoms produced in the bedroom, but by their ability to fixate his mind when far afield, when he has seemingly "escaped" into the pastoral, romantic, and social topoi of the "two ways." The psychic walls of his neurotic fixation with a mother's absence extend his prison from the bedroom to the encompassing countryside, totalizing the narrative terrain of Combray, as the circle of separation anxiety closes around the pastoral pleasures of the "two ways," in the process leaving Marcel no way out.

We gain a sense of this neurotic determinism when Marcel turns toward home after an enchanted apostasy into the realms of nature along the Méséglise or Guermantes way. His is the dread of a prisoner returning to his cell, of a Prometheus to his mythic rock, or of a Geneviève de Brabant to her prison tower:

> All day long, during these walks I had been able to muse upon the pleasure that there would be in the friendship of the Duchess de Guermantes, in fishing for trout, in drifting by myself in a boat on the Vivonne; and, greedy for happiness, I asked nothing more from life, in such moments, than that it should consist always of a series of joyous afternoons. But when, on our way home, I had caught sight of a farm . . . from which, to return to Combray, we need only turn down an avenue of oaks . . . then sharply, my heart would begin to beat, I would know that in half an hour we should be at home, and that there, as was the rule on days when we had taken the "Guermantes Way" and dinner was as a consequence served later than usual I should be sent to bed as soon as I had swallowed my soup, so that my mother, kept at table, just as though there had been company to dinner, would not come upstairs to say goodnight to me in bed. The zone of melancholy which I then entered was totally distinct from that other zone, in which I had been bounding for joy a moment earlier . . . (SW 140)

This alters critical perception of the pastoral sublime in Combray, whose poetic effects belie a deeper pathology of the self, and easily seduce the reader into a "reading" that is in reality a "misreading"—in which, as Homi Bhabha asserts, "signs are taken for wonders." The pastoral sublime of Combray is not a free-standing sign, but the other half of a metaphor that defines escape in terms of servitude, and nature in terms of neurosis. The "two ways" are satellites of the psychological black hole that is Marcel's separation anxiety, and around which revolves all matter (and all matters) in *Recherche*. The steps he takes along the Méséglise and Guermantes ways are not part of a healthy progression, but are coursed by forces beyond his control that inscribe an orbit that always and forever returns him to the dark gravitational field at the center of his universe: the sorrows of separation anxiety.

The eternal return of this neurotic fixation is effectively captured in the image of the ravens that return to the steeple of St. Hilaire from which they have been temporarily driven out. A second image of neurotic servitude underscores the first—again of a bird in flight that disappears into the horizontal gloom of night, "just as sometimes in the sky a band of pink is separated, as though by a line invisibly ruled, from a band of green or black. You may see a bird flying across the pink; it draws near the borderline, touches it, enters and is lost upon the black" (SW 140). These images of a bird "lost upon the black" and of ravens returning to their steeple roost at dusk trope on the self's servitude to neurosis. What Proust is inscribing in this "black date in the calendar" is his own "emergence motif": one that reinscribes pagan myths of origin, that evokes the Anasazi's mythical emergence from a black hole in the desert slick-rock. This first "black date" signifies nothing more nor less than the violent birth of the creative soul in the totalizing darkness of its own most primal fear: separation from the mother. It narrates the origins of a self birthed in the darkness of its own sexual differentiation.

The violence of this "immaculate" conception produces the fictional universe that is *Recherche*. In no work since Milton's *Paradise Lost* is the Luciferean gloom of original damnation so dramatically illumined with the shafts of redemption. In contradistinction to *Paradise Lost*, *Recherche* recounts not the collective salvation of humanity, but the personal redemption of genius—which nonetheless suffers like humanity for its sins.

THE LADY OF THE HOUSE OF SLEEP: AN ALLEGORY OF THE MOTHER

Recherche is not only informed by biblical allegories of damnation and redemption and by fictional allegories of adultery and incest, but by allegories of the femme fatale, of which "The Lady of the House of Sleep" is perhaps the most instructive. As Joseph Campbell observes in *The Hero With a Thousand Faces* (1949), this mythic female figure is

> the paragon of all paragons of beauty. The reply to all desire, the bliss-bestowing goal of every hero's earthly and unearthly quest. She is mother, sister, mistress, bride. Whatever in the world has lured, whatever has seemed to promise joy, has been premonitory of her existence—in the deep of sleep, if not in the cities and forests of the world. For she is the incarnation of the promise of perfection; the soul's assurance that, at the conclusion of its exile in a world of organized inadequacies, the bliss that once was known will be known again: the comforting, the nourishing, the "good" mother . . . who was known to us, and even tasted, in the remotest past. Time sealed her away, yet she is dwelling still, like one who sleeps in timelessness, at the bottom of a timeless sea. (111)

Campbell's observations further inform the "drame coucher." Marcel's mother is, for example, akin to the "Lady of the House of Sleep," whose house is reentered after a lapse of decades through the portals of sleep—even as the mother used to read him off to sleep from the pages of *Francois le champi*. The mother of the "drame coucher" is a threshold guardian to the realm of sleep, a goddess who confers the bliss of sleep (as concretized in the good night kiss) and who protects the child while he sleeps. She is, alas, the maternal siren who still beckons to him from the "deep of sleep," whom he encounters while voyaging through the realms of sleep.

Marcel's mother is similarly figured as the ideal of ideals, as the "paragon of paragons" (not of beauty, but of love)—the "bliss bestowing" embodiment of the maternal sublime, the "reply to all desire." She too is the goal of Marcel's "earthly and unearthly quest" as evidenced by his desire to possess her in life and to eternalize her in death. It is evident that to Marcel she is the "incarnation of perfection," the embodiment of the maternal and the artistic sublime. As such, she is imbued with a nostalgic enchantment, with an innocence connoting a blissful, pre-oedipal, Edenic moment that contrasts with every subsequent moment of his existence "in a world of organized inadequacies." She signifies a moment the narrator hopes "will be known again . . . even tasted, in the remotest past," as indeed it is when he brings to his lips the cup of tea. Time has indeed "sealed her away," and it remains for him to rescue her from Oblivion. Geneviève imprisoned in her tower is also a sign for the mother imprisoned in the past. The mother is the goddess in the garden of the maternal sublime, The Lady in the House of Sleep.

There is, however, a dark side to this goddess figure. As Campbell observes, this "remembered image is not only benign," for the "bad" mother too . . . persists in the hidden land of the adult's infant recollection and is sometimes even the greater force. She is at the root of such unattainable great goddess figures as that of the chaste and terrible Diana—whose absolute ruin of the young sportsman Actaeon illustrates what a blast of fear is contained in such symbols of the mind's and the body's blocked desire. (111)

Perhaps it is this dark figure of femininity who returns to haunt Proust's vision on his deathbed, whose presence in the room he confides to Celeste Albaret. The passage is significant insofar as it posits the maternal sublime as the origin of the unattainable. Marcel's desire for the unobtainable ideal incites his vagabond quest to obtain surrogate sublimes, to incessantly scale, Sisyphus-like, the slippery slope of the ideal—only to be denied and defeated by the "organized inadequacies" of reality time and again.

Campbell's reading of this myth informs the matricidal impulses and other "aggressive fantasies" of the mother-son dyad of *Recherche*. Like the Lady in the House of Sleep, Marcel's mother is not only positively figured as the "goddess" and "the reply to all desire," but negatively figured as the "absent, unattainable mother"

> against whom aggressive fantasies are directed [incest, injury, murder] . . . the hampering, forbidding, punishing mother . . . the desired, but forbidden mother (Oedipus complex) whose presence is a lure to dangerous desire"— perhaps transposed in the narrator's case to the illicit desire for courtesans, prostitutes, and bisexual girls. (111)

The frustration of Marcel's desire in the "drame coucher" deeply informs his obsessive need for the ideal, ubiquitously projected onto objects throughout The Search. As J. C. Flugel observes in "The Psycho-analytic Study of the

Family," "it seems very probable that a good many of the more pronouncedly idealistic tendencies in philosophy may owe much of their attractiveness in many minds to a sublimation of this reaction against the mother" (145n, Campbell 113). The mother's denials of the good night kiss are significant not only for inciting Marcel's neurotic fear, but for engendering as well the idealizing constructs of his imagination which herald the birth of his art. This turn toward the realm of the ideal is Marcel's primary response to a thwarted desire for the maternal ideal: a turn that establishes the presence of absence and the relative absence of the material.

This "black date in the calendar" establishes the antithetical correspondence between the material and the spiritual world in *Recherche*. As Campbell notes, "[T]here exists a close and obvious correspondence between the attitude of a young child toward its mother and that of the adult toward the surrounding material world" (113). Nevertheless, this "black date in the calendar" is not an "event" in the sense in which events are normally ficted in novels. Richard Terdiman, in his essay "The Depreciation of the Event," observes that "Proustian events diffuse through the texture of his narration. They hardly ever 'occur'":

> [T]he subjective effects of such an event are only understood over the long term, and it is fair to say that for Marcel this particular event does not "occur" until three thousand pages later, when with infinitely greater lucidity he recalls it in the Princess de Guermantes' library on the afternoon of his revelation. Its "occurrence" in the early pages of Swann might almost be called fictitious, a pure anticipation by retrospective memory of something not realized until many years later. . . . These "pre-revelations" are one of the principal means Proust employs to diffuse the facticity of the event over time, space, and even the less measurable dimension of memory. (qtd. in Bloom 140)

This "event" enacts Proust's conception of time. It is not simply a "black date" on the calendar; it *is* the calendar. This metonym of time is always and already a metaphor of time insofar as every "date" in the "calendar" of *Recherche* inheres in this "black date in the calendar."

chapter two

The Art of Sapphic Desire: The Curse of the Little Phrase

> And it is perhaps from another impression which I received at Montjouvain . . . that there arose long afterwards, my idea of that cruel side of human passion called "sadism."
>
> —SW 122

PART I: SWANN AND THE SORROWS OF THE SAPPHIC SUBLIME

PROUST'S NOVEL TREATMENT of Vinteuil's "little phrase" provides a case study on the Rankian origins of the creative impulse. While criticism has expended much ink interpreting the privileged moments of Montjouvain and the "little phrase" separately, it has not sufficiently developed the implications of their interrelationship. Yet, the deeper grammar of the Montjouvain seduction and the "little phrase" epiphany deeply inform the plot of *Recherche*. These two moments of the artistic bildung develop the series of profanation, transposition, and transfiguration introduced in the "drame coucher," revealing this progression as one of several narratological "engines" (or series) that power the search. In the first half of this chapter I will explicate the meta-dramatic content of the Montjouvain vignette, for it not only reveals Proust's novel "take" on sadism, but deeply informs his interpretation of the origins of the creative urge.[1]

THE ARTFUL SADIST: THE META-DRAMATIC MISTRESS OF MONTJOUVAIN

Mlle Vinteuil's sadism toward her father is "artful" in a dual sense: it not only gives rise to Vinteuil's sublime music, but is itself "artful," a displacement of the creative impulse. There is about Mlle Vinteuil's cruelty in these scenes a strong suggestion of role playing, a redemptive touch of pretense, of impersonation. Her sadism is an affectation of evil, not evil incarnate. Further, this performative nature of her cruelty is not only evidence of a creative personality, but of a creativity that is hereditary. The lesbian love scene that profanes the patriarch is a scene she scripts, sets, stages, directs, and performs. Before her scene-partner enters, Mlle Vinteuil frantically dresses the set, moving her father's photo from the mantelpiece to the end table which she "drew close beside her" (*SW* 123). Her "dressing of the set" reinscribes the behavior of her father who once "had 'placed' beside him the piece of music which he would like to play over to my parents" (123), evidencing the influence of a hereditary determinism that pervades this profane meta-drama. She disguises her indiscreet desire by "pretending" to "make room" on the sofa for her friend while lying down, then disguises this indiscretion with a pretense of being tired (she yawns), "so as to indicate that it was a desire to sleep, and that alone, which had made her lie down there" (123). Proust underscores the hereditary nature of her "performance": "I could recognize in her the obsequious and reticent advances, the abrupt scruples and restraints which had characterized her father" (123).

Her friend, too, recites lines as if reading from a script, "like a lesson prepared before hand, which she knew it would please Mlle Vinteuil to hear. 'And what if they are? All the better that they should see us'" (124). At this juncture of the "scene," Mlle Vinteuil has difficulty remaining in character. She "goes up" in her lines: "[S]he was ignorant of what words ought to flow spontaneously from her lips, so as to produce the scene for which her eager senses clamored" (124). The character she is trying to play comes into conflict with her own character.

> [She casts herself as] a vicious young woman . . . but the words which she imagined such a woman might have uttered with sincerity sounded unreal in her own mouth. And what little she allowed herself to say was said in a strained tone, in which her ingrained timidity paralyzed her tendency to freedom and audacity of speech. (124)

Mlle Vinteuil is unable to assume the role she has scripted for herself. Her performance consequently lacks credibility, is too transparent to suspend Marcel's disbelief that he is indeed watching a "vicious young woman." The view that her sadism is performative as opposed to inherent is reinforced by the fact that she needs an audience to derive pleasure from it, needs to be watched while in the act of acting sadistic. Thus, M. Vinteuil and Marcel, watching respectively from a photograph and through the window, play the part of spectators in this theatre of lesbian sadism whose metafictive material comments not only on the performative nature of the sadistic impulse, but on the sadistic nature of love, as well as on the psychological origins of the artistic impulse.

Mlle Vinteuil's reticence and ambivalence prompt an overt display of desire from her friend, from which Mlle Vinteuil flees in a pretense of displeasure only to allow herself to be captured on the sofa: a playful duet that will be reinscribed in the musical coitus of the piano and violin. She pretends to notice her father's portrait for the first time, her vice giving rise to sadistic impulses that redouble the pleasure of it:

> This photograph was, of course, in common use in their ritual observances, was subjected to daily profanation, for the friend replied in words which were evidently a liturgical response: "Let him stay there. He can't trouble us any longer . . . the ugly old monkey. . . . Do you know what I should like to do to that old horror?" she said, taking up the photograph. (125)

Cued by Mlle Vinteuil's dare, the friend spits upon the photograph: a gesture that succinctly and effectively physicalizes the sadistic impulse.

The curtain falls, so that this violence is enacted offstage, is left to our imagination, and more significantly, to Marcel's. For the narrator's imagination is the principle locus of possession, the means by which he takes possession of objects in general, and the most precious of all objects in particular, the self. What commences as a strategy of possession whose destination is a given object in the material world ends by becoming a "strategy of self-possession" whose primary vehicle and effect is a "novelizing imagination" that performs the preliminary work of artistic production (97). As Leo Bersani notes: Marcel's is "a world where imaginative fantasy is no longer a sign of helplessness, but rather an instrument of ideal control and possession" (*Marcel Proust: The Fictions of Life and Art* 97). Both strategies are, moreover, part of a twofold pattern that recurs throughout the novel in which the desire to possess when frustrated gives rise to a desire to possess the self—in a narcissistic infatuation with a projected image of the self. Mlle Vinteuil thus comprises a profane objectification of Marcel's hidden same-sex desires, projected in reality onto Saint Loup. Mlle Vinteuil is the surrogate for a profane self that Marcel cannot objectify, the fantasy fulfilling object of a profane desire fixated by his possessive gaze. Whereas the sacred ideal of the self is crystallized in the image of the writer, the profane ideal of the self is concretized in the fetishized images of same-sex desire that proliferate throughout *Recherche*: Mlle Vinteuil and her friend are the first actors in a notorious cast of characters whose freedom to enact the scenes of same-sex desire excite Marcel with vicarious and voyeuristic pleasures: Charlus and Jupien, Albertine and a series of Sapphic loves (Andre, Mlle Vinteuil, Lea), Charlus and Morel, Charlus and Maurice in the brothel. All contribute to the carnivalesque theatre of the profane, which comprises a collective transposition of the author's own homoerotic desire, as well as the origins and effects of it.

ART AND ANALYSIS OF ART: A STRATEGY OF SELF-LIBERATION

At Montjouvain, Proust shifts from a presentation of the melodramatic nature of the sadistic impulse to an interpretative explication of it. Having "shown" us this impulse in action, he then comments upon it, like a director treating an audience to his interpretations of a play after its performance. The actor yields the stage to the critic, the spectator to the commentator, and the artist to the scientist: "And yet I have since reflected that if M. Vinteuil had been able to be present at this scene, he might still . . . have continued to believe in his daughter's soundness of heart . . ." (SW 125). It is Proust's novel view of the sadistic impulse that redeems Mlle Vinteuil insofar as the evil associated with it is performative, not inherent, is the "antic" evil of Hamlet not the "motiveless malignancy" of Iago, is the byproduct of a melodramatic rather than a malevolent impulse. For example, after the spitting scene, Mlle Vinteuil again drops out of character, lapses into herself: "Mlle Vinteuil, who now seemed weary, awkward, preoccupied, sincere, and rather sad, came back to the window and drew the shutters close" (125). There is redemptive value in Mlle Vinteuil's gesture and in her attitude, which is now more truly her own. Proust calls our attention to the performative aspect of her cruelty, deploying an array of meta-dramatic imagery to underscore the intimacy of the sadistic and the artistic impulse:

> when we find in real life a desire for *melodramatic* effect, it is generally the "sadistic" instinct that is responsible for it. . . . A "sadist" of her kind is an *artist* in evil, which a wholly wicked person could not be, for in that case the evil would not have been external [as it is here] it would have seemed quite natural to her, and would not have been distinguishable from herself. . . . "Sadists" of Mlle Vinteuil's sort . . . endeavor to *impersonate,* to assume all the outward appearance of wicked people. (125–26, my emphasis)

Underscoring the redemptive quality of Mlle Vinteuil's cruelty is the fact that every time Proust deploys the signifier "'sadism'" it is bracketed with quotes, which qualify and ironize its meaning, which beg the question: Is this truly sadism?

The scene suggests there is indeed artistry in her cruelty—and more: heredity. That her cruelty assumes artistic expression should come as no great surprise inasmuch as she is the daughter of one of the greatest geniuses in the novel: the composer Vinteuil (an analog for Proust, the artist). Indeed, Proust concludes this Montjouvain scene by noting the daughter's redemptive similarity to the father:

> At the moment when she wished to be thought the very antithesis of her father, what she at once suggested to me were the mannerisms, in thought and speech, of the poor old music-master . . . what remained between them . . . was the likeness between her face and his, his mother's blue eyes,

which he handed down to her, like some trinket to be kept in the family, those little friendly movements and inclinations which set up between the viciousness of Mlle Vinteuil and herself a phraseology, a mentality not designed for vice.... (126)

The difference between the artful sadism of Mlle Vinteuil and the genuine sadism of Iago is that the latter is, in essence, cold-blooded—his actions unimpeded by pangs of conscience. And herein lies the distinction between the Proustian sadist and his or her counterparts in literature and history: between the performative and redeemable cruelties of Mlle Vinteuil and Charlus and the authentic cruelties of Iago and Ivan the Terrible. This is not evil for the sake of evil, but an affectation of evil, which is in turn a byproduct of the creative urge. The novelty of this scene derives from the contrasting species of sadism with which Proust presents us, as well as from the peculiar intimacy of vice and virtue, immorality and genius, whose cross-contamination throughout the search is metonymically reinscribed at Montjouvain.

The most significant effect of the Montjouvain seduction and its profanation of paternal love, however, is not the premature death it inflicts on the composer Vinteuil, but the genesis of his deathless music. At Montjouvain, Proust not only presents us with a dramatic and meta-dramatic scene of Sapphic seduction, but this same-sex tête-à-tête sustains the theme of parental love profaned, first taken up in the "drame coucher" and here given an even more sadistic twist. Even more significantly, Montjouvain comprises a useful case study on the origins of the creative urge which can be usefully "read" from a Rankian perspective. If Montjouvain explicates the origins of the sadistic impulse, then Vinteuil's "little phrase" deeply informs the origins of the creative impulse.

Swann and the Sirens of the Sapphic Sublime

Mlle Vinteuil's sadism is artful in another sense, for it not only arises from an artistic impulse, but gives rise to M. Vinteuil's own art: is both an effect and a cause of the creative urge. This not only has deep implications for the careers of both Swann and Marcel, but comments metafictively on the creative process that brings the entire work into existence. The same heartbreak that gives rise to Marcel's romanticizing imagination, and hence to his literature, is here transformed into music—reinforcing a psychological law of invention that posits art as the byproduct of "morbid crises of a 'neurotic' nature." The creative inventions of Marcel and Vinteuil are part and parcel of the same process. Whereas Marcel's sorrows are mitigated by the projections of the magic lantern, by the imaginary realms of *Francois le champi*, by his own fanciful projections of Balbec, Venice, and the Guermantes, and ultimately by the book he writes, Vinteuil's sorrows are absorbed into his music.

Proust explicitly situates the origins of Vinteuil's sonata in F sharp for piano and violin in the suffering induced by the daughter's scandalous behavior. Indeed, this music seems to comprise a sonorous transformation of the illicit caresses of Mlle Vinteuil and her friend, as Mme Verdurin observes to her Sapphic partner, Odette: "[N]ow it is you that are going to be caressed, caressed in the ear; you'll like that, I think" (SW 159). The seductive and transformative quality of this music is difficult to overstate. The ear becomes the medium of musical "caresses" in the Verdurin salon as it is the conduit for the rhetorical and physical seductions enacted at Montjouvain. It may even be argued that the duet between violin and piano represents the flirtations of the Sapphic pair, the playful pursuit and capture, the tensions between their dissonance and harmonizing, separation and commingling: as if Vinteuil transformed into music a Sapphic seduction, as well as the heartbreak it engenders.

The signifiers Proust deploys reinforce this transposition, for sounds are not merely made by these instruments, but "secreted" like bodily fluids: "[T]he violinist seemed to wish to charm, to tame, to woo, to win [the piano phrase]," which is depicted as lying "below the narrow ribbon of the violin part," as if under a "delicate" supple female partner. The piano part begins to "surge upwards in a flowing tide of sound . . . breaking everywhere in melody like the deep blue tumult of the sea, silvered and charmed into a minor key by the moonlight" (270, 159). The "wetness" of feminine desire is replicated in the water imagery that predominates throughout the passage: "submersion," "molten liquidity," "to plunge again and disappear and drown," "firm foundations beneath the tumult of the waves," "emerged . . . from the waves of sound." These water images also connote the fugitive flux of the feminine.

The sexual and the creative, the erotic and the artistic are conjoined here as elsewhere in The Search, in a manner that paradoxically reinforces Freudian theory while subverting it, even as it sustains the coupling of vice and genius. If the sexual engenders the artistic, as for example when the illicit caresses of Mlle Vinteuil and her friend inspire Vinteuil's sonata, then similarly the artistic excites the sexual, as for example when a similarity between a Botticelli portrait and Odette excites Swann's desire to "fling himself upon this Botticelli maiden and kiss and bite her cheeks" (183), even as the "caresses" of Vinteuil's music excite the caresses between Swann and the piano-playing Odette. In contradistinction to women, however, artworks can be owned, possessed, their secrets fathomed, their images fixed. Odette, by contrast, is a Botticelli in motion, a woman who must be studied on the run, an object in perpetual flux, like the water imagery associated with the feminine throughout Recherche—with a feminine sublime that is always and forever fugitive.

Vinteuil's musical inscription of Sapphic desire is strengthened by the personifications associated with it: "stealing forth from underneath that resonance, which was prolonged and stretched out over it," "secret, whispering"(160–61). The redeployment of flower imagery in relation to this "little phrase" further reinforces the connection between this music and the profane, between femininity and creativity: "[H]e had tried to treasure in his memory the phrase . . . that had just been played, and had opened and expanded his soul, just as the fragrance of certain roses, wafted upon the moist air of evening, has the power of dilating our nostrils" (159). Flower imagery is here associated with Swann's spiritual regeneration, though it still evokes a whiff of the erotic: of the cattelyas fastened to Odette's bodice, of the flower imagery invoked by the Jupien-Charlus seduction, of the pink hawthorns reincarnated in Gilberte's cheek or which evoke the mother, the "lady-in-pink": the courtesan, Odette.

The sexual imagery reinforces the connection between Montjouvain and the "little phrase," which extends to Swann "an invitation to partake of intimate pleasures, of whose existence . . . he had never dreamed, into which he felt that nothing but this phrase could initiate him." Indeed, the "encounters" of Mlle Vinteuil, Marcel, and Swann have about them the feel of an "initiation," of a "rite of passage" ambiguously coded with profane and sacred implications. All three are initiates into a cult of vice and genius, for which this music comprises a deterministic threshold. Upon hearing this music, Swann is filled with "a new and strange desire" (SW 150). The "little phrase" is yet another incarnation of the "two-in-one" insofar as it conjoins the profane desires of the flesh and the sacred impulses of the soul—is a metonym of degenerate pleasures and regenerative spirituality. It is deeply inscribed with the myth of the femme fatale, for within this music Swann perceives a feminine figure as alluring as it is fugitive: "as though he had met, in a friend's drawing room, a woman whom he had seen and admired, once, in the street, and had despaired of ever seeing her again" (SW 161).

The "slow and rhythmical movement" of the piano and violin reprises the coitus of the Sapphic lovers on the couch, building toward its own ecstatic climax: "more rapid . . . incessant, sweet, it bore him off with it toward a vista of joys unknown. . . . He was like a man into whose life a woman, whom he has seen passing by, has brought a new form of beauty, which strengthens and enlarges his own perception" (160). Again, perception is masculinized— to the extent it becomes the locus for possession, enlarging like the male sexual member when aroused, to penetrate and possess the object of its desire: in this case, the secrets of the "little phrase." For Marcel and Swann, perception becomes the locus of conquest, virility, and action, for a reconfigured masculinity in which the higher orders of the self (intellect and imagination) are sexualized by baser, possessive instincts, foregrounding the ego's need and desire to dominate the world around. The aggressions of the self toward the Other throughout *Recherche* evidence a masculinity displaced from its normal realms of aggression.

The association of the "little phrase" with the feminine in general and with the feminine bisexual in particular illustrates yet another aspect of Rankian theory: the bisexual nature of the creative process itself, of which these figurative women are projections. As Rank observes, "[T]he artist not only uses this introverted world as protection, but as material; he is thus never wholly oppressed by it—but can penetrate it by and with his own personality and then again thrust it from him and re-create it from himself. This extrusion is a process both of begetting and bearing"(377). Rank's observation has important implications for understanding the creative process in general, and the deeper grammar of the "little phrase" in particular. Not only is the process of artistic production inherently bisexual, but "the artist tends to project on to the beloved woman his bisexual creative urge—of begetting and of bearing" (378). This casts the association of three bisexual women (Mlle Vinteuil, Odette, and Albertine) with the "little phrase" in an entirely new light. From a Rankian perspective, Proust's foregrounding of the Sapphic sublime may be interpreted not only as a cause of creativity but as an effect of it—as a figurative projection of a creative process which is bisexual in essence, involving both the begetting and the bearing of the work. The three sirens of the Sapphic sublime associated with the "little phrase" are not only projections of Proust's own bisexuality, but of the inherently bisexual nature of all artistic production. Rankian theory thus proffers an alternative interpretation of the Sapphic caresses of Montjouvain, which critics have traditionally viewed as a transposition of Proust's own homosexual tendencies and the profanation of maternal love. These illicit caresses represent not just a transposition of the artist's own sexual tendencies, and the conflicts associated with them, but a projection of the creative impulse itself, of its innately bisexual nature. If the "little phrase" is an effect of the sorrows of Sapphic desire, then it is equally true that the sign of the feminine bisexual is a projection of the bisexual nature of all artistic production.

The turn inward may be construed as a compensatory adjustment to the given conditions of Marcel's existence: one which makes a virtue of a weakness and which masculinizes the imagination and the perception instead of the body, using these as the preferred vehicles of possession. The higher orders of the self are infused with the sexual energy of the lower orders, hence the predominance of sensual images (flowers, water, and food) and phallic images (steeples, trees, hymenoptera) when representing the self-other dyad. The penetration of a series of exotic Others by Marcel's possessive imagination may be viewed, at least in part, as a surrogate for the sexual act itself, as the working off of repressed sexual desire. The discourse of these privileged moments climaxes in a kind of sexual ecstasy, as if Proust's rhetoric of possession is energized and sexualized by libidinous impulses—evidencing the usefulness of Freudian theory regarding the origins of the creative urge. Freud's mistake was to totalize those origins under the sign of sublimation. To gain a more nuanced appreciation of those origins, something beyond Freudian theory is required.

Indeed, Proust's representation here not only subverts but inverts Freudian assumptions regarding the origins of the creative impulse. As often as the sex impulse gives rise to creativity, as in the case of Mlle Vinteuil's performative sadisim, the creative urge leads to sexual arousal, as evidenced by the proliferation of sexual images in association with Vinteuil's "little phrase," and even more explicitly in the arousal of Albertine's Sapphic desires by her metafictive description of the "ices" (LP 469).

This conjunction between femininity and creativity is given an ingenious twist when Swann induces Odette (the author of his heartbreak) to play the "little phrase" of Vinteuil to him. The "little phrase" is both an effect and a cause of sexual impulses. It not only replicates the seduction of Mlle Vinteuil and her Sapphic lover, but stimulates the caresses of Swann and Odette. As Proust observes, "[H]e would make Odette play him the phrase again, ten, twenty times on end, insisting that, while she played, she must never cease to kiss him. Every kiss provokes another." The flirtatious repartee of Odette and Swann reprises that of Mlle Vinteuil and her friend: "Am I to play the phrase or do you want to play with me?" (SW 182–83). Thus, the phrase that was inspired by the Sapphic love of one woman is played by another who shares the same predilection, which incites the anguish that becomes not only the central theme of *Swann's Way* but of *Within a Budding Grove, La Prisonnière, and La Fugitive*. Lisa Appignanesi's interpretation is instructive: "For Proust, the essence of the feminine is somehow inextricably linked to the essence of creativity"—usually through the suffering it induces. "Throughout the novel, creativity is connected directly or indirectly with femininity" (*Femininity and the Creative Imagination* 205).

Swann's encounter with the "little phrase" retrospectively informs the material of Montjouvain in other ways. For example, "the recreative influence" that the music has on Swann reinscribes the transformative influence that these Sapphic sorrows have on Vinteuil, from which this music emerges (SW 161). Swann's bracketing by Mme Verdurin and Odette when he is introduced to the "little phrase" further reinforces the association of this music with the illicit pleasures of Sapphic love. These sirens of same-sex desire are never far removed from the fatalistic strains of the siren-like music. The "little phrase" is a narrative bridge to the novel's past and future, reinscribing the sorrows of Vinteuil and heralding the heartbreak of Marcel—comprises the eternal return of a curse rooted in profane desire and visited on three generations of male lovers.

The Art of Madness: Rankian
Implications of the "Little Phrase"

Swann's initial encounter with the "little phrase" precipitates a quest to possess its secrets, to discover its biographical origins. This search leads to

Montjouvain and the profane pleasures of a beloved daughter: "Then he asked for some information about this Vinteuil . . . and at what period in his life he had composed the sonata;—what meaning the little phrase could have had for him, that was what Swann most wanted to know" (SW 162). Knowledge, for Swann (as it is for Marcel), is not only a vehicle of the possessive self, but a lightning rod for the damnation of the self. A little knowledge of the wrong things precipitates the catastrophic declines of Swann and Marcel. The taste of the madeleine is only redemptive because it has been preceded by the bittersweet taste of forbidden fruits in the form of profane desires (incestuous, Sapphic, homoerotic, matricidal, suicidal, sadistic, and masochistic).

Master Biche (Elstir) provides the critical clue that establishes the Rankian origins of Vinteuil's music when he reveals the link between this music and the sorrows of Sapphic desire. As Proust observes, "[T]he painter had heard, somewhere, that M. Vinteuil was threatened with the loss of his reason. And he insisted that signs of this could be detected in certain passages"(SW 164). Upon further hearings of the little phrase, "Swann thought that he could now discern in it some disenchantment. . . . It seemed to be aware of how vain, how hollow was the happiness to which it showed the way" (167). As he plumbs the depths of the "little phrase" in quest of its psychological and biographical origins, Swann (Proust) leads us farther from a Freudian reading and nearer to a Rankian interpretation of those origins, which have little to do with sublimated sexual urges and everything to do with the objectification of morbid sorrows:

> He began to reckon up how much that was painful, perhaps even how much secret and unappeased sorrow underlay the sweetness of the phrase; and yet to him it brought no suffering. What matter though the phrase repeated that love is frail and fleeting, when his love was so strong! He played with the melancholy that the phrase diffused. He felt it stealing over him, but like a caress. . . . (182)

The observations of Elstir and Swann are significant insofar as they endorse Rank's assertion that art is often the result of the artist's successful attempt to "detach the whole creative process from his own person, and transfer it to an ideological abstraction . . . to shift the creative will-power from his own person to ideological representations of that person, and thus to render it objective. . . . This explains why hardly any productive work gets through without morbid crises of a 'neurotic' nature" (41). Appignanesi underscores the significance of Vinteuil and his sonata for the entire work, even as she sheds light on the conflicted origins of the "little phrase":

> The relationship Proust depicts between Vinteuil's art and his women is more central to Marcel's development than that of the other two artists in

A la Recherchè. Vinteuil's music reverberates throughout the work and it is the leitmotif of Swann's love of Odette as well as the prime example for Marcel of what can be achieved in art. Yet the great composer Vinteuil is, in reality, the little music master of Combray who dies of a broken heart when his beloved daughter enters into a Sapphic relationship. The agony of Vinteuil's life is what permits him to produce the overpowering Septuor wherein pain gives way to an "ineffable joy which seemed to come from paradise." . . . Vinteuil suffers through women and creates out of his suffering a work which surpasses his agony. (206)

Swann then pierces the veil that has cloaked the origins of Vinteuil's composition, establishing beyond doubt the symbiotic, cause-and-effect relation between suffering and creativity:

And Swann's thoughts were borne for the first time on a wave of pity and tenderness towards that Vinteuil, towards that unknown, exalted brother who alas must have suffered so greatly; what could his life have been? From the depths of what well of sorrow could he have drawn the god-like strength, that unlimited power of creation? (SW 267)

The narrator's descriptions of the broken-hearted composer leave no doubt regarding the cause of his suffering, further reinforcing the generative link between it and his music. The cruelty of Mlle Vinteuil's behavior is evidenced by the magnitude of the effects it produces in the doting father who is changed "in a few months into an old man, engulfed in a sea of sorrow, incapable of any effort not directly aimed at promoting his daughter's happiness . . . he was dying of a broken heart . . ." (113). Proust writes of the "still more cruel renunciation to which M. Vinteuil had been driven," of "the utter and crushing misery" that had come upon him (123). The situation is given a grimly ironic twist by the old music master's failure to perceive the true nature of his daughter's Sapphic "friend," who he believes to be a "superior woman, with a heart of gold," while remaining oblivious to the fact it is "not music that she is teaching his daughter." As a consequence of this scandal, the doting composer pays the ultimate price: his heart broken and his reputation ruined, his life comes to a premature and "sad end" (122).

In contradistinction to Freud, Rank views artistic production as the working off of a matrix of conflicts, the most protean of which are neurotic in nature. He defines "neurotic" as nothing other than "those morbid reactions of a psychic and bodily nature" or again as "morbid crises" (43). It is evident from an analysis of their enfeebling effects and from the imagery Proust uses to describe them, that the "morbid crises" of Vinteuil, Swann, and Marcel as depicted in the episodes of Montjouvain, the "little phrase," and the "drame coucher" are neurotic in nature. The trio are useful examples of "the individualistic artist type of today with his 'neurotic' psychology"(3): a type that Rank refers to as the "artiste manqué" (27). The genesis of Vinteuil's sonata attests to the procreative power of a "morbid crisis," to the "interdependence between production and suffering . . . production being a creative development of neurosis in objective form" (43). Proust's depiction of its origins illustrates Rank's theory that "artwork is rather a forcible liberation from inward pressure" (51) for it is through creation that the artist "finds relief from the inner conflicts, which would otherwise compel him to create for himself some ideology for the objectification of his psychic tensions" (370). Rank concludes that "a certain measure of conflict is, of course, necessary to creative work, and this conflict is, in fact, one of the fields in which an artist displays his greatness, or psychologically speaking, the strength of his creative will-power."

Vinteuil's ability to transform his heartbreak into art establishes the pattern that is sustained and brought to transcendent closure by Marcel. It further evidences his strong creative will, which distinguishes the artist from the neurotic, which identifies the artist as a "productive neurotic type." As Rank affirms, "[B]y means of it he is able to work off a certain measure of his inner conflict in his art. . . . [W]hat distinguishes the neurotic from the artist is that the latter constructively applies his will-power in the service of ideological creation" (58–59). Hence, the "little phrase" is a metonymic fragment in which the entire *Recherche* inheres, in which one can indeed apprehend the universe in a drop of rain—even as Vermeer's genius is inscribed in "the little patch of yellow light," and as society inheres in the "little clan" of Mme Verdurin. The whole is in the part, which nonetheless stands apart from the whole. This "little phrase" is but one of a series of free-standing fragments in *Recherche*, by which the entire work, including its neurotic origins, is informed.

The music master's humble existence further illustrates Rank's theories on the origins of the creative impulse, insofar as it underscores the limitations of looking to the artist's outward life to explain his work. This calls into question the project of biography, and reveals yet another theoretical consonance between Proust and Rank. The little music master of Combray anticipates Elstir's humble seaside studio, even as Marcel can find no evidence of Bergotte's genius in the little man with the red face and the funny nose. As Rank observes, "[I]t is significant that many of the greatest artists . . . have a strong bourgeois tinge . . . genius needs a touch of conventionality. Many whose work is of the highest value and who live wholly in their art lead a very simple, ordinary life" (379). Consequently, instead of looking to the artist's life to explain his or her genius, the critic should do the precise opposite: look to his work to explain his or her life. Rank's observations are to the point: "[T]here is thus an influence of personal experience on creation [Vinteuil's sorrows on his music] and a reciprocal influence of creation on experience, which not only drives the artist externally to a Bohemian existence, but makes his inner life a picture of his art-ideology." Consequently, "his life is invented to suit his work" and the artist's "personal life is an ideological expression of his artistic production" (382). Rank's theories bear a strong affinity to those Proust enunciated in *Contra Sainte-Beuve* and subsequently dramatized in *Recherche*. Rank concludes: "We do look in his life for the experiences that would explain his work. But we never find it" (383).

Rankian Implications of Swann's Damnation and "Redemption"

The "little phrase" courses through the entire novel like a dark undercurrent, uniting the diverse landscapes through which it sweeps: the troubled loves of the three men. Yet, it is a fortunate curse insofar as the sorrows associated with it are redemptive, lead to artistic or intellectual rebirth. The heartbreak it induces in Swann prompts his discovery of the "deep well of sorrow" from which Vinteuil drew this music, even as it triggers his rebirth to life, and to his true intellectual self, after a lapse into a world-weary, jaded indifference which he mistakenly assumed to be life's final, if not inevitable condition, and which prefigures Marcel's penultimate disenchantment with life, concretized by his confinement in a sanitarium.

The anxiety aroused by the "little phrase" is but a harbinger of the anguish aroused by the sorrows of Sapphic desire, which return to break Swann's heart as they broke Vinteuil's. The "little phrase" is a temporal metaphor which by virtue of its ability to juxtapose a happy past with a tormented present induces Swann's heartbreak. Many critics have commented on the role of metaphor in *Recherche*, but few have explicated the significance of the temporal quality to Proustian metaphor as effectively as Rank. These metaphors "associate the past and present, either spatially or temporally." Rank continues:

> In fact, the temporal quality of Proust's metaphor is typical not only of his famous similes but of his whole work, which one might take as a single gigantic metaphor (*Le Temps Retrouvé*).... [T]his fact, [is] characteristic of Proust's metaphors, that they dominate not only his language but his whole work. (222)

The little phrase, like the madeleine, resonates backward and forward in time, deeply informs the career of Marcel, as well as those of Vinteuil and Swann. Art's implication in vice throughout The Search exerts a governing determinism on the careers of all three. The musical daemon announces its eternal return by the heartbreak it engenders in Swann:

> [H]ow small a thing the actual charm of Odette was now in comparison with that *formidable terror* which extended it like a cloudy halo all around her, that *enormous anguish* of not knowing at every hour of the day and night what she had been doing, of not possessing her wholly, at all times and in all places [and whose address] is printed in letters of fire that seared his heart. (SW 265, my emphasis)

The sonata in F sharp engenders in Swann a heartbreak akin to Vinteuil's. It converts Odette's absence to a presence, transforms a soothing forgetfulness into a wounding remembrance, by virtue of its cruel ability to resurrect the past: "[this music] tore him with such anguish that his hand rose impulsively to his heart" (SW 264). The violin rises like the blade of a guillotine "to a series of high notes, on which it rested as though expecting something, an expectancy which it prolonged," and then at the moment the little phrase appears, like a woman entering a room, the memories that are triggered descend with the force of a guillotine:

> "It is the little phrase from Vinteuil's sonata. I mustn't listen!" All his memories of the days when Odette had been in love with him, which he had succeeded . . . in keeping invisible in the depths of his being . . . had awakened from their slumber, had taken wing and risen to sing maddeningly in his ears without pity for his present desolation. . . . (SW 264–65)

Vinteuil's sorrow is now finally and fully Swann's, as if in the brokenhearted connoisseur of art, the composer has been reincarnated. Involuntary memories sing like the violin, casting their siren spell in what comprises a diabolical flip side to the redemptive memories revived by the madeleine. Involuntary memory is invested with the power to damn or redeem: Swann's damnation by the "little phrase" of the sonata heralds Marcel's damnation by the septet, even as it contrasts with the narrator's redemption by the madeleine. Like Marcel, Swann is reunited with a past as empirical as it is immortal. Each detail, each metonymic fragment, each piece of poetic empiricism strikes a blow at his defenseless heart: "[H]e now recovered everything that had fixed unalterably the peculiar, volatile essence of that lost happiness; he could see it all: the snowy curled petals of the chrysanthemum which she had tossed after him into his carriage, which he had kept pressed to his lips . . ." (265). Swann's involuntary reunion with the past is the dark inverse of Marcel's, the "little phrase" the flip side of the "petites madeleines": two fragments of time immortalized in serendipitous epiphanies as masterful as "the patch of sunlight" in Vermeer's *View of Delft*.

Proust's imagery underscores the fatalism of the "little phrase," even as it reinforces the fatal conjunction of femininity and creativity:

> There are in the music of the violin . . . accents which are so closely akin to those of certain contralto voices, that one . . . is tricked by the deceiving appeal of the *Siren*; at times, too, one believes that one is listening to a captive spirit, struggling in the darkness of its masterful box, a box quivering with enchantment, like a *devil* immersed in a stoup of holy water. (266)

This proliferation of deterministic signifiers ("siren," "captive spirit," "darkness," "enchantment," and "devil immersed in a stoup of holy water") explicitly and figuratively invest the "little phrase" with a governing fatalism that is Zola-esque—an influence on Proust insufficiently noted by criticism. The eruptive force of the "captive spirit" imprisoned in the music tropes on the ubiquitous captives of *Recherche:* Geneviève in her tower, the house arrest of Albertine *(La Prisonnière),* the "captive" selves immured in the madeleine, the steeples of Martinville, the trees of Hudimesnil, the paving stones et al., the feminine imprisoned within Charlus, and last, but not least, the artist imprisoned within Marcel. All are invested with an eruptive impulse that threatens the tenuous control of the imprisoning self. Proust's association of involuntary memory and art with a governing fatalism is as surprising as it is provocative in a novel that on the surface seems nothing if not a monument to the cult of genius and the bohemian credo, "art pour l'art." His treatment of the "little phrase," however, is as distinctly unromantic as his treatment of possessive love. The fatalism of both operates in direct proportion to the romantic idealism they annihilate. The miracle of *Recherche* (and the true measure of Proust's genius) is its ability to regenerate the wished-for fusion of idealism and realism after the catastrophic decline of Swann and Marcel, and the catastrophic defeat of idealism, precipitated by the fatalistic conjunction of art and profane desire. The eternal return of the curse of the "little phrase" is only broken by the novel's final redemptive turn, in which vice is finally and forever absorbed into art.

The fatalism of the "little phrase" is reinforced by its association with the composer's death. Vinteuil is entombed in his music. Rank's theories on the fatalistic connotations of art are instructive insofar as they not only inform the narrator's long delay to writing, but the fatalistic connotations of the "little phrase":

> But the retardation or refusal to complete some work may have another, deeper reason. The restraint which holds the totality tendency in check is basically fear, fear of life and of death, for it is precisely this that determines the urge to eternalize oneself in one's work. Not only has the completed work the value of an eternity symbol, but the particular creative process, if it involves an exhaustive output, is by the same token a symbol of death. (386)

Art is a sign of death as well as an emblem of the soul's immortality. Art's tendency to threaten the ego and the very life of the artist incites one of the gravest conflicts the artist experiences, touching off a struggle between art and artist. How the artist resolves this conflict is one of the more interesting aspects of the psychology of invention, a discussion I will take up in the final chapter. Proust's treatment of the "little phrase" comprises a useful case study of the fatalistic and redemptive effects of art.

The "little phrase" is not only a talisman of damnation and death but of regeneration. Having incited Swann's heartbreak, it now authors his rebirth to life. Swann's redemption begins with his recognition of the music's deeper thematic material. Beneath the music's ineffable sorrow he detects something else: the sufferer's release from sorrow, effected through "the charm of a resignation that was almost gay" (SW 267). This resignation becomes the inspiration for Swann's release from those same sorrows, "of which the little phrase had spoken to him . . . which were now become his own, without his having any hope of being, ever, delivered from them, it seemed to say to him . . . 'What does it all matter; it is all nothing'" (SW 267).

Swann's bittersweet wisdom anticipates Marcel's amorous epiphany with respect to Albertine's association with Mlle Vinteuil, where "'the joy of a great discovery" not only attends our keenest sorrow, but has the power to detach us from it (*Cities of the Plain* 367). If Swann had on first hearing the "little phrase" "divined an element of suffering in its smile," now he hears something else, something deeper, more profound, and truly transformative: a philosophic resignation that absorbs into itself all sorrow and by so doing, transcends it.

The passage is significant not only because it foregrounds the generative and redemptive power of suffering, but because it also establishes the correspondence between Swann and Vinteuil, here for the first time signified as an "exalted brother": a brother in love, in the sorrows of the Sapphic sublime, in art, and now in the transformative release from suffering through a transcendent resignation. Swann, like Vinteuil, discovers in his sorrow "a sweetness in that very wisdom . . . those graces of an intimate sorrow." The "divine sweetness" that he tastes is as transformative for him as the madeleine is for Marcel, through a "little phrase" that has "discovered to him many of the riches of his own soul."

The language and actions of rebirth celebrate this transformation of Swann, even as they anticipate Marcel's transfiguration in the novel's climax. In and through the "little phrase," Swann is reunited with lost realms of the self, in whose existence he had ceased to believe. Through Vinteuil's music Swann discovers "what richness, what variety lies hidden, unknown to us, in that great black impenetrable night, discouraging exploration, of our soul, which we have been content to regard as valueless and waste and void" (SW 268). Proust revives the image of the garden, in this case the Garden of Eden, to capture the redemptive quality of Swann's rebirth through art: "[I]t was as at the first beginning of the world, as if there was not yet but these twain upon the earth . . . the world of this sonata" (SW 269).

The end of *Swann's Way* reinforces the redemptive turn of the "little phrase," even as it anticipates the climax of *Recherche*. Swann's liberatory rebirth is indicated by his departure from Paris by train (a symbol of the self's liberation), by the recuperation of his ideal self, as evidenced by his desire to begin writing the essay on Vermeer, and by the entombment of his love for Odette in marriage. As evidenced by Proust's novel treatment of the "little phrase," the origins of the creative impulse are often rooted in morbid suffering. In *Recherche* that suffering not only leads to the rebirth of Swann's artistic sensibilities, but to the birth of Vinteuil's music and Marcel's literature.

PART II: MARCEL AND THE SORROWS OF SAPPHIC DESIRE

The Spectator and the Spectacle: Profanation, Transposition, and Transfiguration

The Montjouvain scene not only has profound implications for Swann, but deeply informs the amorous and artistic careers of Marcel. The profanation of the maternal sublime in the good night kiss scene foreshadows a similar profanation of parental love in the Montjouvain vignette, in which a daughter profanes the love of a father during a lesbian love scene. The correspondence between this scene and the good night kiss scene is sustained on several levels—and represents the author's transposition of his own feelings of guilt and shame for the suffering inflicted on his mother by a similar tendency toward same-sex desire. The gender of parent and child have merely been transposed from the "drame coucher."

The link to the author's own conflicted experience is reinforced by the presence of Marcel observing the illicit tryst between Mlle Vinteuil and her friend through the window. His proximity to Mlle Vinteuil reinforces his close identification with the parent-profaning daughter, who is a projection of his "mirror hungry" personality: an objectification of a pathological self. As Marcel confides, "[S]tanding in front of me, and only a few feet away from me, in that room in which her father had entertained mine. . . . I could watch her every movement without her being able to see me" (122). The final words are instructive. This scene reinscribes the artist's conflicted negotiations with homosexuality, evidencing his close personal identification with it ("a few feet away") as well as the necessity to distance himself publicly from it ("without her being able to see me"). The scene dramatizes the narrator's dual need to "be seen" as a homosexual and to conceal his close identification with same-sex desire. Mlle Vinteuil is a "mirror" for Marcel's own profane fantasies (to "act out" similar same-sex desires), and consequently a projection of his "mirror hungry" personality. The association of this sitting room with memories from his own childhood further reinforces his identification with Mlle Vinteuil's profane desire. The narrator's presence at the window satisfies the conflicting needs for disclosure and detachment—underscores his simultaneous presence and absence from the scene of sin, establishes his literal innocence and his figurative complicity. Marcel's voyeuristic stance evidences the artist's complex negotiations with homosexuality and satisfies multiple needs: the artist's need for truth, the neurotic's need to objectify an agonizing conflict, and the individual's need for self-preservation. Proust can "confess" his own profane desire in a way that enables him to distance himself from it—in a way that satisfies the conflicting demands of art and life: to objectify the immortal and to protect the mortal self. Deleuze notes the ubiquity of this "theme of profanation so dear to Proust":

> Mlle. Vinteuil associates her father's photograph with her sexual revels. The narrator puts family furniture in a brothel. By making Alerbtine embrace him next to his mother's room, he can reduce his mother to the state of a partial object (tongue) contiguous to Albertine's body. Or else, in a dream, he cages his parents like wounded mice at the mercy of transversal moments that penetrate them and make them jump. Everywhere to profane is to make the mother (or the father) function as partial objects, that is, to partition her, to make her seem a contiguous spectacle and even to participate in this spectacle she can no longer interrupt and no longer leave. . . . (126)

Marcel's conscription of the mother's participation in the projects of the profane self (homosexuality) reinscribes Proust's, who in addition conscripted his mother's participation in the projects of the ideal self (the Ruskin translations)—which may be viewed as an attempt to satisfy the "merger hunger" needs of both the profane and the ideal self for the two-in-one. Marcel's presence at the window manifests his need to participate in the "spectacle" of profane desire. The drama of the "drame coucher" is prologue to the spectacle of Montjouvain, in which his role as participant or spectator evinces a need to profane the parent with illicit desires. The mother participates in the spectacle of Marcel's profane desire when he conscripts her into reading *Fancois le champi*, an allegory of incest—prefiguring her complicity in the spectacle of Albertine's sexual house arrest in *La Prisonnière*. This spectacle of parental profanation is reinscribed when Marcel "dresses the set" of Jupien's brothel with his aunt's sofa: an emblem of seduction. The mother-as-spectator of the son's profane desire is reinscribed by the profaned and fixated gaze of Vinteuil watching from the photo, which the daughter positions to heighten her sadistic pleasure in this meta-theatre of profanation.

This tendency to profane the maternal sublime, arising from separation anxieties and frustrated oedipal desires, constitutes a displacement of a sadistic impulse toward the mother onto other characters (Mlle Vinetuil and her lover). It is, moreover, an impulse with a double sheath, which turns upon the self as guilt and shame in the service of masochistic tendencies. The implications of profane desire in *Recherche* cannot be overstated insofar as they totalize Proust's depiction of love. As Deleuze asserts,

> To be harsh and deceptive to what one loves, since it is a matter of sequestering the beloved, of seeing the beloved when she can no longer see you, then of making her see the partitioned scenes of which she is (an actor) in this shameful theater or simply the horrified spectator. To sequester, to see, to profane—summarizes the entire law of love. (126)

Marcel's voyeuristic presence here prefigures those scenes in which he spies on the same-sex encounter between Charlus and Jupien and is a witness to the sado-masochistic flagellation of Charlus in the brothel:

> I noticed that this room had a small round window opening on the hallway... and there, chained to a bed like Prometheus to his rock, and being beaten by Maurice with a cat-o'-nine-tails, which was studded with nails, I saw before me M. de Charlus, bleeding all over and covered with welts. (PR 955)

The spectacle of profane desire is a mobile meta-drama mounted on diverse sets, as evidenced by the spectacles of the "drame coucher," Montjouvain, and Jupien's brothel—all of which testify to the daring invention of Proust's genius, which seemingly reinvents itself whenever it mounts one of these spectacles of profanation, in which the self strategically distances itself from the profane while objectifying itself in it.

There is a redemptive element in these spectacles that conditions our final judgment of them. For example, Proust redeems Charlus's sado-masochism in the brothel, even as he redeems Mlle. Vinteuil's sadism at Montjouvain. Profanation is contextualized within a performative impulse that mitigates evil. If Mlle Vinteuil's sadisim masks a desire to act evil, Charlus's masochism similarly betrays meta-dramatic impulses arising from the need to assert his masculinity, to prove his virility in a manner worthy of his feudal heritage, that conforms to his ideal of Merovingian manhood. To pass this ritual of feudal virility, Charlus scripts, stages, and performs his own sado-masochistic spectacle, inventing his own medieval torture chamber in the basement of Jupien's brothel. As Proust writes:

> At the bottom of [this sado-masochism] was to be found M. de Charlus' dream of virility proven by brutal tests... and all the rich store of medieval scenes, crucifixions and feudal tortures which his imagination treasured.... [A]nd he pretended to dread the Gothas... with vague dreams of dungeons and subterranean chambers of the middle ages. In short, his desire to be chained up and beaten, for all its ugliness, betrayed in him a dream as poetic as does in other persons the desire to go to Venice. (PR 972–73)

This brothel scene is not merely an affirmation of Charlus's vice and cruelty, but of his creativity and noble lineage. Like the vignette of vice at Montjouvain, it underscores Proust's novel treatment of the sadistic impulse, in which vice is redeemed by virtue. Proust's depiction of the sadistic impulse subverts traditional representations of it as innately evil. The meta-dramatic impulses that underlie the profane desires of Mlle Vinteuil and Charlus reaffirm the hereditary determinism by which the sadism of each is redeemed.

In a provocative departure from traditional readings, Margaret Gray calls into question the seeming innocence of Marcel's voyeurism, arguing that it entails a "failure to respond, particularly acute in his voyeuristic observations of the intimate and scandalous scenarios of others" (50). Gray indicts Marcel's passivity:

> [A]ll effect seems to be missing—no shock or sympathy for the pathos of Vinteuil's death. . . . This "spectacle" of Montjouvain, witnessed by a narrator who remains an indifferent, unengaged onlooker. . . . But such fascination remains . . . unengaged, for there is otherwise no affective response— no visceral response of surprise, shock, desire. (52)

Gray similarly indicts the narrator's absence of response in the Charlus brothel scene, where the "same contemplative distance will be maintained. . . . Rather than registering astonishment, the narrator's account continues to document action . . . Jupien's brothel fails to provoke affect or response in him" (53)—all evidence of an "absent narrator." Yet, the only other responses available to him (overt approval of the vice he observes or explicit censorship of it) would betray the very vice he needs to keep secret on the one hand, or would place the narrator (and by implication, the author for whom he more than occasionally speaks) in a moral position that is not only inconsistent with his fictional nature, but hypocritically so. To condemn as vice in others the profanations he himself is guilty of would seriously call into question his own credibility. Similarly, to openly embrace them would deprive the writerly self of the protective screen it requires for its own preservation. Sans condemnation or complicity, what other responses are available to the narrator? He therefore treads a middle ground between the two, ambiguously negotiating the conflicting needs for truth and freedom: the two greatest imperatives of the artist's spiritual life. Marcel's censorship of vice would dishonestly condemn the very impulses Proust is disclosing. Whereas the first response is blatantly dishonest, the second has negative survival value. Marcel (and by implication, Proust) finds a third way that reconciles the conflicting needs of art and life for truth and privacy respectively. His voyeurism is at once a presence and an absence, enacted in response to the conflicting mandates of fiction and reality. This "fiction" of spectatorship affords the privacy of a confessional in which the narrator/author can objectify neurotic conflict without surrendering the freedom essential to the survival of both the creative and the living self.

Given Marcel's confidences of the "drame coucher," we can hardly expect him to rise up in condemnation of profane desires. Further, the response of condemnation is predicated on a false assumption: that these vices are absolutely evil and therefore warrant his condemnation. However, the narrator's realization that these vices are mitigated by virtues, by the performative impulses from which they arise, cancels the very response whose absence Gray faults in the narrator: the need to condemn. Further, Gray contends that Marcel's passive voyeurism in these scenes "flatten[s] them to the indifference and remoteness of spectacle, of a mise en scene" (54). If so, I would argue this "spectacle" is the very effect Proust is anxious to achieve insofar as it reinforces the performative impulses of the principal players, who are themselves anxious to participate in this "spectacle" of evil without themselves being completely evil. Despite their contrasting roles as participants and spectators in these spectacles, the experiences of Mlle Vinteuil, Charlus, and Marcel are essentially the same: the self of each is redeemed by a moral distance that buffers the self from the profane desire with which it identifies.

Marcel's "neutrality" in these voyeuristic scenes preserves the moral ambiguity and detachment necessary for his creator to simultaneously "confess" without confessing, thereby satisfying the conflicting demands of fiction and reality. Therefore, I feel Gray's ethical indictment of the narrator's "failure to respond" is unwarranted, is not indicative of a flawed passivity. It is rather an effective, if not inevitable, solution to a conflict between the demands of art and life that places the artist in a peculiar and difficult bind. Inward pressures compel the artist to objectify neurotic conflicts in the interest of his own psychic health, if not survival. Social pressures similarly forbid the disclosure of these very impulses, posing an external threat no less intimidating than the inward threat of psychosis. A closer identification with vice would undermine the protections the self requires in a society that persecutes the practitioners of it, as the career of Proust's contemporary, Oscar Wilde, sadly evidences. The moral intolerance evidenced in the critical reception of *Cities of the Plain* suggests that Proust's concerns were well founded. D. H. Alden, for example, asserts that "with Sodome, he went even further with this grovelling into the slime of human nature . . ." (qtd. in Hodson 23).

Trapped between this "rock and a hard place," the creative impulse resourcefully negotiates a middle way, displacing the need to objectify neurotic conflict onto characters (Mlle Vinteuil, Charlus) while displacing the need to protect the self onto the narrator. The self divides itself between these two objectifications of itself, thereby escaping the double bind posed by the mutually opposed imperatives of fiction and reality.

Far from signifying a "failure to respond," Marcel's voyeuristic presence at these windows on vice is itself a response. Moreover, it is the only response available to the artist and the human being. How much honesty can he risk? How much can he disclose, given the prevailing attitudes of society and his lofty position in it, without compounding his sorrows—or those of his mother (fictional or real)? He must satisfy both the demands of art and of his ego, which requires a certain measure of privacy in order to create, a certain distancing from the truth he desires to divulge. These voyeuristic scenes do not, as Bersani asserts, connote "his own absence from the world" (401), but his simultaneous presence and absence in events, by a division of the creative ego between participant and spectator, in which participation is displaced onto Others, while observation is confined to the self. Far from constituting a "mode of disappearance," or of "involuntary transparence," as Beaudrillard writes, the narrator's detachment is not only deliberate, but symbolic of the ego's detachment from suffering: an essential precondition for objectifying and abstracting those sufferings in art. Thus, Marcel's presence at the window reinscribes the gaze of the self directed inward toward itself, commenting on its own vices by abstracting them, by displacing them onto others. This fictional subject position is, moreover, entirely consistent with Rankian theory regarding the origins of the creative impulse, which partially situates those origins in neurotic conflict.

The self is eternally present in its own abstractions of itself.

Therefore, I cannot agree with Gray's hypothesis that "the narrator's voyeurism might thus be an index of his own departure . . . [of] Beaudrillard's absence of engagement, the melancholic fascination of a failure to engage selfhood" (51). If anything, the narrator's voyeurism is an index of the dynamic tensions between neurosis and creativity, suffering and art, repression and abstraction, driven by the contradictory needs for disclosure and privacy: a conflict resolved on the plane of illusion by dividing the self between a participant and a spectator both of which are surrogates for itself. The self escapes totalization by neurosis by partializing itself on the illusory plane.

These scenes of voyeurism inform the very complex tensions and conflicts that characterize art in the modern and postmodern era, with its emphasis on subjectivity, confession, disclosure—an emphasis at times incompatible with the ego's need for privacy, preservation, and illusion. If Gray asserts that "perhaps the narrator is absent from the scene of his own sufferings as he is from those of others" (55), we may respond that this is not only as it should be, but as it must be for the artist, for without this singular ability to detach himself from his or her own sufferings, s/he could not create. Without the artist's ability to absent himself from his own suffering, there would be no art—only neurosis.

Gray is correct when she observes that "the narrator's incessant analysis of his jealousy as an entity of its own eventually distances both himself and us from it," though from this she draws the wrong conclusion: "[I]n making jealousy an object of study, the narrator saps the pathos of jealousy's suffering" (55). Through analysis of jealousy, as through analysis of art, the narrator is able to distance himself from its enfeebling effects, but not in a sense that is deadening, but liberatory—in the sense that the truths he discovers set him free. To the degree he illuminates the operation of jealous tendencies that are common to us all, he liberates the reader as well from their mystifying effects. This is not the distance of indifference, but the distance of liberatory struggle. Marcel's separation from the spectacle of profane desire reinscribes the psychic independence from neurosis that creativity achieves.

Gray deflates Marcel's tendency toward analysis, and the maxims its produces, asserting that it further evidences an "absent" self. Grey writes, "Marcel has always already contemplated the world as the theatrical spectacle of his own absence—an absence indexed by increasingly futile hypothesizing, and ultimately certified by maxims which, by ontological 'fiat,' elevate his own helpless distance from the world by ascribing to it the indisputability of universal truth" (65). I would argue that, by contrast, the distance he achieves from the internal, far from being "helpless," is enabling: is the liberatory detachment of the self from its own self-destructive, undifferentiated absorption in itself: a distance that signifies not an absence but a regenerative presence that enables the self to move beyond a neurotic fixation with itself into an active, mobile reengagement with itself and the material world. The abstraction of inward conflict not only allows Marcel to escape the neurotic, fixating tyranny of that conflict, but to indeed contemplate it as "theatrical spectacle." It is not, however, the spectacle of his own absence, but the spectacle of his own suffering from which he has creatively absented a part of the self. It is not the self that is eternally absent from suffering, but suffering that has been "absented" from the self through creativity—thrown off in productivity, objectified in fiction. The neurotically fixated self regenerates itself by differentiating itself from suffering. If Marcel is contemplating the "theatrical spectacle of his own absence" it is from the perspective of a regenerated and liberated presence: a presence recuperated through language, representation, abstraction, and meta-dramatic impulses which by creatively differentiating the ego from that which negatively totalizes it, revitalizes and magnifies it. If anything, the self is amplified, not absented in these meta-dramatic spectacles of vice. Montjouvain, like the "drame coucher," and Jupien's brothel are critical topoi for apprehending the self's complex relation to neurosis and creativity. As spectacles of a pathological self, they constitute paradoxically a compelling indictment of profane desire (as evidenced by its effects on both the profaned object and the profaning subject) as well as a redemptive view of it.

What is significant about Marcel's habitual voyeurism is not its passivity, but its detachment from what is being observed. Marcel's "innocent" presence at these windows is as close to a "confession" of vice as the artist can go. The window at Montjouvain is his confessional: a small frame that opens on vice, through which the self and vice communicate, disclose their intimacy, but in a manner that protects the self from public persecution even as it confers the blessings of catharsis. The artist negotiates the very problematic terrain of homosexuality by transposing it to a Sapphic seduction and by dividing the self amongst the participants and spectators. His role as spectator reinscribes the confessional presence of the priest who bears witness to sin. The social persecution engendered by a more explicit identification with this vice would pose a threat to the ego, and by extension to the creative self, the protection of which is the artist's a priori concern. At Montjouvain, as in the Guermantes courtyard and Jupien's brothel, "truth" is negotiated between the conflicting demands of art and life for disclosure and protection.

Marcel's voyeuristic tendencies reveal other aspects of his character, which can be apprehended from a Freudian perspective. Gray observes:

> [A]s understood by Freud in his argument for the vicissitudes undergone by instincts, voyeurism involves its apparent reversal, a vicarious exhibitionistic pleasure in which the observer imagines him—or her-self in the position of the observed. . . . [T]he Freudian gaze is thus, implicitly, also its own reversal, the desire for passivity—to be gazed upon, to be "objectified" by a new gaze. (50)

Marcel's gazing through the window is the expression of a desire to bring his own hidden vice into the open, to be gazed upon, objectified, abstracted. Marcel the spectator is a would-be participant. The ego can always tell itself (and those who raise a moral eyebrow over these scenes), "Well, such things do go on in the world, and after all I was just an accidental observer. A mere recorder. No blame." However, the stance of objective neutrality is modified in favor of the Sodomites and Gomorrheans when he confers upon the practitioners of these vices an exculpatory virtue of pretense: a meta-dramatic impulse by which his own vice (or so we are left to infer) was not only motivated but redeemed. In forgiving their vice he is attempting to exculpate his own, to grant a pardon on the level of fiction that he denied himself in reality. These meta-dramatic spectacles of vice enact the self's need to expatiate deeply rooted neurotic conflicts—and the redemption they confer on Mlle Vinteuil and Charlus prefigures the narrator's own redemption in the novel's dramatic denouement, which is not only a redemption to art, but from vice: is not only an elevation to the realms of the sacred, but a liberation from the depths of the profane.

The author is "present" in this scene in more ways than one, not only in the persona of a voyeuristic narrator who is his namesake, but in dual gender transpositions that mediate between reality and fiction, and between fiction and metafiction. Proust's transposition of gender in *Recherche* has been the subject of much debate. Justin O' Brien's article, "Albertine the Ambiguous: Notes on Proust's Transposition of Sexes," argues that the feminization of character (Gilberte and Albertine) is merely another instance of the author attempting to resolve the dualities inherent in the desire to write about homosexuality. While criticism has duly observed the implications of gender transposition in the loves of Marcel, it has not sufficiently developed the implications of the transpositions that inform the Montjouvain vignette. To my knowledge Lisa Appignanesi is one of the few critics who observes the significance of gender transposition in this scene, yet she observes it merely in passing. In *Marcel Proust: Femininity and Creativity*, Appignanesi writes,

> In the scene which describes Mlle Vinteuil and her lesbian friend spitting on the dead Vinteuil's portrait, for example, we find not only a transference of sexes, but an equally profaned parent. . . . Profaned by his daughter's les-

bian relationship (just as Proust defiled his mother through homosexuality), he [Vinteuil] ultimately dies because of it, as did the mother in "La confession d'une jeune fille." (174)

I want to develop more fully the implications of gender transposition at Montjouvain, for the sadistic impulses associated with it not only inform Marcel's relation to his mother, but the more fundamental relationship between neurosis and creativity. A strong "alliteration" exists between the characters of the mother and M. Vinteuil, similarly profaned by a child's illicit desires. The narrator's admission that his mother was deeply offended by Mlle Vinteuil's vice (SW 122) further evidences the artist's attempt to work out deeply rooted feelings of guilt and shame related to the anguish his own homosexuality caused his mother. Proust, like Mlle Vinteuil, was the child of a doting mother who similarly was "incapable of any effort not directly aimed at promoting his . . . happiness," yet who no doubt suffered on account of the rumors regarding his same-sex love affairs. Vinteuil's circumstances reinscribe those of both the fictional and real-life mother:

> [Vinteuil] knew, perhaps even believed what his neighbors were saying. There is probably noone, however rigid his virtue, who is not liable to find himself . . . living at close quarters with the very vice which he himself has been most outspoken in condemning. (SW 113)

The phrase "living at close quarters" reinscribes the domestic intimacy of the profane desires associated with the "drame coucher" and with the "house arrest" of Albertine, both enacted with the mother's complicity, under her modest, Catholic nose. The very proximity of the vice, transposed in *La Prisonnière* to cohabitation with a homosexual woman under the mother's roof, redoubles the cruel effects of it, "so as to wound and to make him [her] suffer" (SW 113–14). The affinity between the two profaned parents is reinforced by the unconditional nature of their love for the sadistic child: "And yet however much M. Vinteuil may have known of his daughter's conduct, it did not follow that his adoration of her grew any less" (SW 114). The very immutability of the mother's love, even in the face of vice, not only redoubles Marcel's love for her, but intensifies his guilt for the suffering he has inflicted upon her— even as the mother sets a saint-like standard of self-sacrificing love beside which the self-serving desire of all other loves in the novel will be found wanting. The transposition of gender is further evidenced by the fact M. Vinteuil had to "play both mother and nursery maid to his daughter": a role identical to that fulfilled by Mme Proust toward her son, and by the mother toward Marcel. Vinteuil is not only completely absorbed in this role, but in "the suffering which she had caused him; she could see the tortured expression which was never absent from the old man's face in those last terrible years" (122). His self-sacrificing love for his daughter reinscribes the mother's suffering indulgence of Marcel's every need, even as it reinscribes an ideology of sacrifice which, like neurosis, also informs the artistic impulse. The construction of a work of art, like the "construction of the world" in pagan mythologies, "apparently demands a living sacrifice," whose creation justifies and in some cases eternalizes the individual that has been martyred to it—a notion I will develop more fully in the final chapter. The immortalization of Vinteuil years later through the publication of his compositions by the daughter's lesbian lover establishes another correspondence between Marcel's love for his mother, whose soul he will similarly eternalize in art.

Georges Bataille succinctly explicates the "alliterations" of the profane between Montjouvain and the "drame coucher," between fiction and reality effected through the transposition of gender:

> Vinteuil's daughter, whose father dies of grief at her behavior, made love, in her mourning clothes, a few days after the funeral, with a lesbian who spat on the dead man's photograph. Vinteuil's daughter personifies Marcel, and Vinteuil is Marcel's mother. Mademoiselle Vinteuil's invitation to her lover to stay while her father was still alive is parallel to the narrator's inviting Albertine (in real life the chauffeur Albert [sic] Agostinelli) to stay in his apartment. (57)

Marcel's pleasure, like Mlle Vinteuil's and Charlus's, is rooted deeply in the profane, in incestuous and sadistic tendencies toward the mother that mask matricidal impulses. The masochistic effects of profanation, however, are Marcel's alone. In the development of those effects, Proust establishes a keen affinity between reality and fiction, between himself and Marcel. As Bataille observes, "[S]ensual pleasure depended on his feeling of horror":

> At one point . . . Marcel writes of his grandmother: "Comparing my grandmother's death to that of Albertine, I thought that my life was branded by a double murder." To the stigma of assassination was added another, a still deeper stigma: that of profanation [in which] "sons not always resembling their father, fulfill the profanation of their mother in their faces." (56)

Bataille's interpretation reinforces the symbiosis between the profanation and the murder of the mother—displaced onto the grandmother, whose cause of death is given as a stroke, but is treated as a murder. Kristeva notes the deeper psychological implications of the Montjouvain profanations for the scene recounting the death of the narrator's grandmother, observing that "the blasphemous scene . . . contains the 'seed' or 'albumin' of the pivotal episode that will become the death of the narrator's grandmother, a scene inserted directly into *Sodom and Gomorrah*":

> Hence, Mlle. Vinteuil profanes the father within the context of the childlike sensuality that pervades Combray. . . . [T]he narrator preserves the secret garden of his childhood at the very heart of his inversion. Mlle. Vinteuil and the narrator. The dead father—the grandmother—the dead mother. Reverbera-

tion and secret confession. The pain felt by Vinteuil . . . is offered to us in exchange for the description . . . of the sorrows experienced by the narrator's mother when Albertine (or Albert) enters the picture. (184)

Profanation thus becomes a critical survival strategy for differentiating the self from the maternal sublime—and as such a critical step in Marcel's effort to become an artist. Of the many influences in his "apprenticeship to signs"(and to the artistic sign in particular) profanation of the maternal sublime is perhaps the most significant inasmuch as it mitigates emotional dependency upon the mother which retards the evolution of an independent, figuring self. Profanation helps the self differentiate itself, helps liberate it from undifferentiated communion with the maternal sublime. Profanation is part of an aggressive strategy the self deploys to assert the differentiation it simultaneously abhors and requires (in order to become an artist). The impulse to profane is rooted in the deeper impulse to write, which it ironically enervates by virtue of its ability to wound. Separation anxieties of a neurotic order are the inevitable price that is paid for this liberating differentiation, in which the neurosis of profane desire for the mother is replaced by the neurotic effects of profaning the mother with illicit desires of a homoerotic nature: desires that not only mask sado-masochistic tendencies, but matricidal and artistic impulses. Kristeva's observations are instructive:

> The idealized object, which is invariably maternal, is so scrupulous and coercive that escaping it requires profaning and debasing it in the inhuman world of pleasure. . . . A son who is one with his mother punishes himself by profaning her, and he punishes her by profaning himself. (185)

Profanation leads to a protean differentiation, which is purchased at the price of profound guilt—a guilt that becomes a further impetus to creativity. Thus, profanation not only produces the differentiation that is essential for creativity, but the guilt which catalyzes the creative impulse as the only means of escaping from it. Marcel is trapped in a classic double bind that produces contradictory desires: a desire to differentiate the self from the maternal sublime and a desire for a self that is undifferentiated from the mother. The paradox comprises a conflict that stimulates both homoerotic and creative impulses. He escapes the bind of differentiation through same-sex love, and on the plane of illusion, by abstracting it in art. Art is born, at least in part, of this sublimation of conflict and pain. "Ideas," as Proust's narrator affirms, "take the place of sorrows; when the latter are transformed into ideas, they at once lose part of their noxious effect on the heart and from the very first moment the transformation itself radiates joy" (PR 1021).

The most significant effect of this displacement (or abstraction) of sorrow into art is that it "releases [or "radiates"] a little joy." As Kristeva notes, "[T]he enigma of the form of sublimation that characterizes artists . . . is perhaps bound up in displacement of this tempting wound, this highly pleasurable bite into the flesh of the tongue itself . . ." (186). Sublimated pain is not only displaced in artistic urges, but in sadistic impulses as well—the wound giving rise to a desire to wound. Kristeva's interpretation reinforces the relevance of sublimation to the creative process, as long as we understand sublimation in a broad sense: as the repression of neurotic conflicts, and not just in the narrow, more traditionally Freudian sense as the sublimation of sexual impulses.

The profanation of the mother is more explicitly associated with the narrator, as evidenced by his profanation of Aunt Leonie's sofa. The aunt, as Kristeva observes, "offers a derisive version of the maternal image":

> In *Within a Budding Grove*, the profane nephew goes so far as to bequeath his aunt's sofa to a brothel (the sofa on which he claims to have had his first sexual thrills). . . . [H]e admits to the pain . . . he experienced following what he consciously believes to have been the rape of a dead woman: "Had I outraged the dead, I would not have suffered such remorse." If we add that, in reality, the furniture in the mother's home experienced a similar fate, it becomes clearer that Aunt Leonie assumes the role of the mother on whom the narrator must revenge himself in order to be separated from her so that sexual pleasure and writing may occur. . . . On two occasions, then, a growing degree of disparaged maternity—first simply distanced, then explicitly desecrated—guarantees the narrator's sense of time. . . . In the end, putting the flavor of the madeleine into words and climaxing while seeking revenge require the same logical process and serve as the two indissociable sides of Proustian experience. (Kristeva 19)

If as Freud asserts, the creative urge is a manifestation of sublimated sexual impulses, the reverse may also be asserted: that sexual desires comprise a displacement of the creative impulse—as evidenced by this little theatre of profanation that Marcel stages on Aunt Leonie's sofa. "My imagination," as Kristeva affirms, "is my repeated vengeance. Without becoming literally 'indifferent,' imagination turns itself into style . . . the substance of metaphor" (20). Marcel derives pleasure from profaning the maternal sublime not only by acting out sexual desire on his aunt's sofa, but by donating it to a brothel. His meta-dramatic impulse to "act out" profane desires resincribes the antic sado-masochism of Mlle Vinteuil and Charlus. The aunt's sofa is a surrogate for Vinteuil's photograph in this mobile theatre of profane desire, in which parents are profaned by children in same-sex trysts under their own roofs or through the desecration of family heirlooms in brothels—all prefigured by the initial spectacle of profanation scripted, directed, and staged in the little black box of Marcel's bedroom.

In the final analysis, sexual, sadistic, matricidal, masochistic, homoerotic and artistic impulses share a common, incestuous heritage, are implicated in a chain of cause and effect. Profane (incestuous) sexual impulses beget sadistic, matricidal, and homoerotic impulses, whose aggressions turn inward, begetting masochistic and suicidal tendencies, which in turn enervate the creative urge, transforming it into a liberatory compulsion. The artist is impelled to create in order to save himself from the destructive impulses he has unleashed in order to awaken the very artistic urge upon which his entire salvation depends.

It is not entirely clear whether neurosis begets creativity, or is itself begotten by a latent creative impulse seeking to enervate itself, to wound itself into existence. Hence the notion that masochistic tendencies and creative impulses are inseparable. The latent creative urge compels the self toward neurotic destruction to activate its own liberatory struggle. This motif of imprisonment and emergence is the central, dominating trope of The Search, as a dormant creativity resorts to every pathological impulse conceivable (from incestuous and homoerotic desires to sadistic, matricidal, and masochistic tendencies) in order to flagellate itself into existence—and once liberated, narrates the epic struggle of its self-liberation, which is essentially a movement from the profane to the sacred, in which even the profane is redeemed by virtue: and by its greatest virtue, the art to which it gives rise. The profane's implication in the sacred is evidenced from the outset in the episode of the tea-soaked madeleine. As Kristeva asserts, the orality associated with the madeleine connotes the desecration of the Holy Eucharist during "communion." Kristeva's reading is provocative: "This is enough to desecrate not only Mamma and the madeleines, but the Eucharist itself. Each of them is summoned, adored, and degraded" (20). Hence, the incestuous communion of the sexual, the sadistic, and the artistic—of vice and genius, of the sacred and the profane. The madeleine that redeems Marcel's wasted and vice-ridden life is itself profaned with illicit connotations. The Eucharist of his spiritual redemption resonates with fantasies of fellatio—the spiritual devolving into the sensual, as if a holy Eucharist was transfigured into one of Albertine's "ices."

The good night kiss scene begs the following question: did the impossibility of love in its purest, most ideal state (the maternal sublime), incite, if not justify, the quest for "impure" forms of love, even as it incited the narrator's sado-masochistic tendencies? Since virtuous love is an impossibility what point is its cultivation or pursuit? Given the impossibility of a moral love, what choice remains but to pursue love in all its immoral manifestations? The impossibility of the sacred frees the lover to indulge in the profane: an indulgence that perhaps has as its ulterior motive the infliction of pain upon the mother who has caused pain, and upon himself for the pain he caused the mother—produces as its primary effect, matricidal and suicidal tendencies, instigates both sadistic and masochistic impulses which are displaced onto others in the course of the novel. Desire's divorce from virtue in the "drame coucher" begets its deep implication with vice in *Recherche*—and through the sorrows of vice, its protean influence on the creative impulse.

Marcel and the Curse of the "Little Phrase"

The dramatic reappearance of the "little phrase" in Vinteuil's septet reinforces Marcel's association with Swann as a victim of romantic heartbreak induced by Sapphic desire. The "little phrase" reinforces as well his association with Mlle. Vinteuil, as the sadistic agent of a parent's premature death. Whereas Mlle Vinteuil's vice is redeemed by its meta-dramatic motive, no such exculpatory gesture is extended to Marcel, whose suffering is not only unmitigated by virtue, but is intensified by masochistic tendencies. Marcel flagellates himself for his "vice" no less mercilessly than Maurice administers the cat-o'-nine-tails to Charlus. However, Charlus's vice is redeemed by its motive: to undergo a rite of Merovingian manhood, whereas Marcel's masochism is unmitigated by any redeeming virtue. Redemption, in his case, is deferred until the novel's end, until the moment of his transfiguration into an artist: a metamorphosis engendered equally by his crucifixion on the cross of Sapphic desire and by the serendipitous resurrection of involuntary memories.

Marcel's fatal association with Vinteuil's sonata in F sharp is revealed in a confidence to Albertine that he

> must remember to ask Mme. Verdurin about something that may prove of great interest to myself, provide me with a subject of study, and give me pleasure as well . . . that Mme. Verdurin should let me hear some things by a musician whose work she knows very well. I know one of his things myself, but it seems there are others I should like to know if the rest of his work is printed, if it is different from what I know. (366)

He is cursed by the same desire to know the music's secrets that precipitated Swann's sorrows: knowledge of the wrong things being invested with the power to damn. In contradistinction to Swann, who apprehends the music only in terms of his desire for Odette, Marcel seeks to know the septet on its own terms—as a free-standing work of art. Marcel's attitude not only establishes the primacy of art over love, but represents the primary distinction between himself and Swann whose career evidences the reverse: art's servitude to desire. The sorrows incited by Vinteuil's septet have an even more transformative effect on Marcel than did the sonata on Swann insofar as it converts his relative indifference toward Albertine into an obsessive desire (this section is after all titled, "The Need for Albetrtine"), even as it compounds a neurosis that increasingly mandates objectification in art as a means of relieving inward pressures that border on madness. Mme Verdurin, as the elder "sister" of Sapphic desire and as a variation of the femme fatale, functions not only as the gatekeeper to Vinteuil's music, but as the gatekeeper to its sorrows as well. Her association with the "little phrase" reinscribes her watchful stewardship of it during Swann's sorrows for Odette. Referring to the determinism of the little phrase, Harold Bloom observes, "[W]e are in the elegy season, ironically balanced between the death of jealousy in Swann and its birth in poor Marcel, who literally does not know that the descent into Avenues beckons.... Into that metaphor, Marcel moves like a sleepwalker, with his obsessions central to *The Captive* and insanely perverse in *The Fugitive*" (Intro 10).

On this fateful occasion, Marcel discovers that Albertine is on intimate terms with both Mlle Vinteuil and her Sapphic "friend" ("with whom I spent the happiest years of my life at Trieste" [CP 366]):

> At the sound of these words . . . so far from Combray, so long after the death of Vinteuil, an image stirred in my heart, an image which I had kept in reserve for so many years that even if I had been able to guess, when I stored it up, long ago, that it had a noxious power, I should have supposed that in the course of time it had entirely lost it; preserved alive in the depths of my being—like Orestes whose death the gods had prevented in order that, on the appointed day, he might return to his native land to punish the murderer Agamemnon—as a punishment, as a retribution . . . for my having allowed my grandmother to die, perhaps; rising up suddenly, like an Avenger, in order to inaugurate for me a novel, a terrible, and merited existence, perhaps also to making dazzlingly clear to my eyes the fatal consequences which evil actions indefinitely engender, not only for those who have committed them, but for those *who have done no more than look on* at a curious and entertaining spectacle, like myself, alas, on that afternoon long ago at Montjouvain, concealed behind a bush . . . where I had perilously allowed to expand within myself the fatal road, destined to cause me suffering, of Knowledge. (CP 366–67, my emphasis)

Evil deeds alone are not enough to explain the "fatal consequences" Marcel suffers. The mere act of acquiring forbidden knowledge condemns him, as it does Faust or Adam, to "a novel, a terrible, a merited existence." Marcel's knowledge of vice, if not the actual practice of it, is enough to ensure his damnation. The scene is significant insofar as it "alliterates" with the transposition of vice at Montjouvain, but represents an even closer identification with it, an even bolder gesture toward disclosure. Unable to "cop to" the sin of same-sex desire himself, Proust substitutes the crime of matricide for it, which in reality was an effect of the author's profane desires. It is this sin which is substituted for the "original sin" of homoerotic desire, so that the author is simultaneously able to objectify his pain and maintain his privacy, in a scene that strikes a novel balance between identity with and distance from a vice. If the vice itself is projected onto others, as at Montjouvain, the damnation associated with it is owned up to—and dramatically rendered. The crime of matricide is "copped to" in order to bridge the disconnect between crime and punishment, to reconcile the conflicting demands of art and life for truth and self-preservation. As at Montjouvain, Marcel is prepared to "cop to" the knowledge of this vice, but not its practice—an understandable position given the social intolerance of the times. Proust transfers his suffering to Marcel without transferring his sin—which requires a greater displacement, onto fictional third parties (Albertine, Charlus et al.) in order to satisfy the imperatives of reality, which in this instance supersede those of art.

More significantly, these proliferating inhabitants of Sodom and Gomorrah are the fragmentary analogs of a homoerotic self that grows more assertive the deeper it gets into *Recherche*, as if actuated by an impulse to "out" itself despite the powerful constraints imposed upon it by fears of social persecution. This tension between disclosure and survival, between the mutually opposed imperatives of art and reality, is in play throughout the narrative and represents one of the deepest conflicts underlying the work's creation. Proust's ability to work off this conflict on the plane of illusion no doubt mitigated suicidal impulses—of the sort depicted in "La Confession d'une jeune fille."

Recherche is not a search, but a confession—or rather a search for absolution: for crimes committed against the mother, for profane desires and the "matricide" they engendered. This, more than involuntary memory, is the dark wellspring of Proust's inspiration insofar as it produces the conflict that fuels the search engine, that powers it for seventeen years, through seven volumes—an inexhaustible reservoir of narrative energy.

The House of Vinteuil is the origin of a curse, embodied in the "little phrase," reincarnated here in the septet, that visits heartbreak on those male lovers curious enough to possess its secrets or the secrets of Sapphic desire. The pervasive, if not deterministic influence of this musical fragment is reinforced by the imagery Proust deploys in this critical passage. Its "noxious power" reinscribes Greek myths of the femme fatale, of the siren whose alluring song tempts the curious and desiring male to his doom. Marcel's heartbreak is a function of his differentiation from the Sapphic pair, of his status as Other relative to a female rival's privileged status as "same." The original wound of "differentiation" from the mother is opened anew through differentiation from the Sapphic Other, as Kristeva observes: "[F]emale homosexuality . . . precedes sexual differentiation. It enraptures the narrator through a luminous purity that masks an out-and-out depravity" (75). Sexual differentiation is the dark wellspring of Marcel's sorrows, separation anxiety, and neurosis. Sapphic lovers enjoy a state of undifferentiated sameness, of oneness with the feminine, which has been Marcel's governing desire since the "first black date in the calendar" of Combray. The grim irony of his suffering is difficult to overstate: a boy desires a girl, as a surrogate for thwarted communion with the mother, only to be wounded anew by the same reality: his sexual differentiation. Moreover, his sorrows are compounded by the realization that a female rival enjoys the pleasures denied to him, by virtue of her sexual sameness with the object of his desire.

Albertine's "merger-hungry" personality trumps his own. Implicit in Marcel's jealousy of Albertine's Sapphic loves is envy for the "two-in-one" merger that has been his governing, if futile, desire since the "drame coucher." The consummation of her "merger-hungry" desire redoubles the bitterness induced by the spectacle of her infidelity, authoring a species of sorrow unique in the annals of literature. The voyeurism of Montjouvain prefigures the spectacle of Sapphic desire that will fixate Marcel's inward gaze through the volumes of *La Prisonnière* and *La Fugitive*. The "sins" he witnesses there return as spectacle with a fourfold capacity to wound for the very reason that the spectacle occurs "offstage"—in his imagination. As evidenced throughout *Recherche*, Marcel's imagination exerts a governing determinism over The Search insofar as it not only incites his quest for the ideal, but his possessive desire as well. His madness is largely imagined, which is to say, is rooted in the disease of the imagination. He is victimized by his inability to imagine anything aside from the spectacle of Sapphic desire, which undermines his reason with the destructive spell of an "idée fixe." The gaze fixated on the imaginary ideal (Berma, Balbec, Venice, the Duchess de Guermantes et al.) is now fixated by the fugitive spectacle of Sapphic desire. His condition indeed replicates that of Narcissus, fixated on an image he desires but can never possess, which wastes away the intellect and the memory: the two greatest weapons of Marcel's possessive consciousness. All other faculties fade amidst the fixating glare of the imagined Sapphic sublime. Indifference alone can shatter the spell, liberating him from his fixated imagination—like a stone tossed into the narcissistic pool of the pathological self, whose ripples efface the image that fixates.

Indifference is a necessary precondition for the liberatory discoveries of the involuntary memory insofar as it frees Marcel from the neurotic bind of possessive desire. However, there is yet another intermediary stage in which his indifference to Albertine is totalized: becomes indifference toward all reality. Albertine's death heralds the death of his soul to life. Only when death is totalized as a cosmic indifference toward all does Marcel's redemption occur—evidencing what Rank describes as the artist's tendency toward totality, his or her gravitation toward experiences that totalize the self: neurosis, possessive desire, and eventually creativity itself—which ironically inaugurates a new round of struggles: to free the self from the totalizing fixations of art (ch. 5).

The "same-different" binary that so darkly informs the landscape of the good night kiss is resurrected here through the medium of Vinteuil's "little phrase" (working now through the septet) to author even greater suffering. Marcel suffers the damnation of differentiation, and The Search is largely the long tale of this woe. Further, Marcel's need to overcome his sexual differentiation from mother and woman informs his own latent homosexuality (projected onto Saint Loup, and to a lesser degree, Charlus and Morel). Saint-Loup comprises an idealized objectification of the self who satisfies the need for undifferentiated communion with an Other. As Rank asserts, this type of artist deals with the problem by "personifying a portion of his own ego in another individual (52)." Rank continues:

> [H]e will find his truest ideal in an even greater degree in his own sex . . . this glorification of a friend is, fundamentally, self-glorification, just as was Greek boy-love. . . . [T]his impulse is, at bottom, directed to the creator's own rebirth in the closest possible likeness, which is naturally more readily found in his own sex; the other sex is found to be biologically a disturbing element except where it can be idealized as a Muse. But the likeness to himself will not only be found in the bodily form of his own sex . . . and in this regard the youthfulness of the beloved stands for the bodily symbol of immortality . . . his spiritual ideal, the symbol of his vanishing youth. (56)

The character of Saint Loup can be usefully interpreted as a personification of the narrator's idealized self that satisfies the need for a sexually undifferentiated intimacy with an Other: a desire thwarted by the mother and by the Sapphic feminine. Moreover, the frustration of this need enervates it, even as Marcel's same-sex friendship with Saint Loup represents an attempt to satisfy the need and to solve the problem. Hence, incestuous desire, Sapphic desire, and homoerotic desire constitute a profane progression that shapes The Search from its earliest phase to its liberatory culmination, in which these three profane desires are absorbed into the creative impulse, which finally fulfills the self's desire for the "two-in-one," harmonizing the conflicts between self and other on the plane of illusion.

If desire for a woman represents a displacement of desire for the mother, intended to satisfy the neurotic needs of a "merger-hungry" personality, then the homoerotic impulse constitutes a displacement of heterosexual desire in a quest to satisfy the same need. The need to escape the prison of sexual differentiation into undifferentiated communion with an idealized projection of the self is the protean desire that drives The Search, that subsumes and consumes its proliferating contents, that initiates, unifies, and concludes the progression of profane desires in which a self seeks to lose itself in an Other that is in reality a projection of its idealized self, whether mother, girl, or boy, whether the object of incestuous, heterosexual, or homoerotic desires. The creation of Saint Loup signifies the solution to a problem deeply rooted in sexual differentiation with which the narrator has been wrestling since the "drame coucher." The Albertine volumes dramatize a failed attempt to resolve the same problem.

This need for communion with an idealized Other is also displaced onto places (Balbec, Venice, and the Faubourg St. Germain) which arise in response to the self's need for communion with an idealized topos of the self, whether this be the gardens of Aunt Leonie, Combray, or the Faubourg St. Germain, of the familial, the natural, or the social. To the extent a given place is a topos of the ideal self, Marcel desires to possess it.

The narrator's latent homoerotic impulse for an Other-as-self is deeply narcissistic. This narcissism is also displaced onto the objects of the "privileged moments," which are similarly colonized as fragmentary projections of the self, and whose assimilation into the self satisfies the same need for an undifferentiated communion of self and other. The metaphors that proliferate throughout *Recherche* also represent an effort to solve this problem of sexual differentiation. In other words, the deep psychological conflicts engendered by sexual differentiation are resolved on the level of art in general and through the figurative device of metaphor in particular, which is deployed ubiquitously throughout The Search to efface the differentiation of any two given signifieds, whether it be a present that is undifferentiated from the past, a materiality undifferentiated from spirituality, a woman who is naught but the projection of a man, or an object of the "privileged moments" undifferentiated from the self. The metaphoric conflation of these disparate signifieds (which is further signified by the metaphors it generates) operates in stark contrast to the ineffaceable differentiation of the self from the mother and the feminine Other.

The sorrows of sexual differentiation not only determine the plot of The Search, but its heavily metaphoric style as well. The recurring conflict that inheres in the plot is resolved on the level of figuration, of style: in metaphor. Metaphor satisfies the pathological need for the two-in-one: is at once a symptom and a cure of this self-pathology. The conflicts associated with sexual differentiation not only give rise to the series of stories within the story, but to the style with which it is told. The novel coherence of *Recherche* derives from the alliteration between form and content, theme and style. The two-in-one impulse thwarted on the narrative level is realized on the figurative level, through metaphor. Hence, the style of *Recherche* fulfills the wish of its contents, reinscribing the wish-fulfilling tendency of all art. Mataphor mitigates the sorrow of tragically disparate signifieds—is the healing balm for a self-pathology rooted in differentiation from the Other. Metaphor effects the harmonization of signifieds, whose tragic disconnect the narrative so compellingly depicts. Metaphor is not only the prevailing aesthetic strategy of the creative self, but the dominant psychological strategy of the neurotic self. Each metaphor is also a metonym for the two-in-one, repeatedly fulfilling on the figurative level the wish repeatedly denied to Marcel on the fictional level, as it was presumably denied to Proust on the literal.

The writerly ecstasy of metaphor is reincribed in the narrative whenever Marcel encounters an object of the "privileged moments" (the madeleine, the steeples, the trees, the paving stone). Why? Because, like metaphor, these object embody the two-in-one. It is the exhibition of the self-in-the-Other that thrills him. It is the self's ability to transcend itself, to exist in two places and in two moments at once that thrills. It is the alliteration of the self across time and/or space that occurs in these "privileged moments" and that triggers its joy. Seeing the self redoubled in the Other produces a narcissistic pleasure, satisfies both his "ideal-hungry" and "merger-hungry" needs. Like Narcissus, his pleasure stems from gazing on the self outside the self, stems from the sudden realization that there is after all a deep correspondence between the world and the self, between the material and the spiritual, between the Other and the same. He realizes in fact that the Other is same.

The liberation of the ideal self from itself, which is the narrator's governing desire throughout The Search, and which is symbolically objectified in the "privileged moments," also reinscribes the desire of the homosexual self to "out" itself: a desire enervated by its repression. This latent desire is displaced onto the objects of the "privileged moments," whose "outing" of the self Marcel joyously, if vicariously, celebrates. These serial "outings" of the self contrast with the perpetual incarceration of the sacred and profane self within Marcel, even as they signify the possibility of liberation. This liberation of the ideal self into a two-in-one symbiosis leaves him singing along the Méséglise way and writing at Martinville—even as it will effect the climactic liberation of the ideal self-as-writer through the metaphoric and transformative effects of the "uneven paving stone."

Walter Kasell in his penetrating analysis underscores the centrality of metaphor in Proust, and of one metaphor in particular, "whose structure describes the literary project on which he is about to embark" (3, 4). The image is encountered during a "fishing expedition" to the Vivonne (SW 129) and possesses a "deliciously elusive quality": it is, of course, the image of the bottles "suspended in the stream." Kasell continues:

> The stream and carafes exchange their respective properties.... Marcel's image initiates a play of container and contents.... [T]he delicious irritation that Marcel feels in response to the image will be shown to be an exemplary Proustian reaction.... The carafes which separate the two waters ... are able to transcend their difference and resemble, in this respect, the language which creates the image of inaccessibility. (4–5)

I would argue that the image of the carafes in the stream not only "describes the project on which he is about to embark," in which a novel embodies the experience in which it is immersed, but informs the primal conflict that is at once the cause of the novel and its principal effect: the sorrows of sexual differentiation, which are here thrown into dramatic relief by the "'perpetual alliteration' between the flowing water ... and the carafes which ... are able to transcend this difference." The image of the bottle in the water becomes a trope for Marcel's deepest desire and most conflicted self. The bottle immersed in the water is an alliteration of the two-in-one self. Its immersion in the current not only reinscribes the madeleine's immersion in the tea, but the pre-oedipal immersion of the fetus in the placental fluid of the womb. This is the source of his "delicious irritation." The bottle in the stream is a metaphor for the self in communion with the Other—signifies the wished-for destination of the self, which is throughout The Search always and forever in the problematic process of becoming one with the other, of "outing" its ideal self from itself.

Marcel's chains are undone, if only briefly, through the chains of signification, which convert his dissociation into an association, if only through vicarious identification of a differentiated self with the undifferentiated dyad of bottle and stream. The "perpetual alliteration" of bottle and water frees the self from the claustrophobic bottle of its own sexual differentiation. The bottle hints at the possibility of liberation from conflict into the "delicious flowing water" of harmony (5), whose temporary effects here prefigure the permanent harmonizing of conflict in the "delicious flowing water" of Proustian prose. Kasell continues:

> The two elements in Marcel's image combine into a new and complex unity. . . . The rhetorical figure has introduced a new "ground" of possibility, in which the elusive flow can be seized. . . . [S]uch attempts reveal the force and attraction of metaphor, for the possibility of seizing the *fraicheur* exists only on the level of language. (5)

This "new space . . . created by the juxtaposition of incompatible elements, a 'middle distance' between them, within which the activity of fiction can take place," heralds the conjunction of the formerly disjoined "two ways": "unaware of each other's existence, in the sealed vessels . . . between which there could be no communication" (SW 104). This marriage of the two ways through the matrimony of a Swann and a Guermantes (Gilberte and Saint Loup), similarly opens "new space" in which the "activity of fiction can take place." Kasell writes:

> [This] interchange . . . maintains the ground of fiction by preserving the tension in which it can exist. The language of fiction continually generates the play between similitude and difference, recreating the transformation which forms the image. Simile . . . exists . . . in the tension between identity toward which it is moving and the difference. . . . (5)

Metaphor, by virtue of its ability to efface difference, accomplishes what the series of profane desires (incestuous, Sapphic, homoerotic) fails to achieve: fulfilling the wish for the two-in-one. The real fugitive of *Recherche* is the two-in-one. Metaphor alleviates the pathological effects of spatial, temporal, and sexual differentiation. Kasell's conclusion is instructive: "Proust's transparent carafes offer the reader an image of identity which is simultaneous with the difference it is always in the process of overcoming" (6).

Nowhere in The Search are these sorrows or their effects more prominent than in the revelations of Albertine's Sapphic desire, and the "perpetual alliteration" of this desire with Vinteuil's music. Gray observes a correspondence between the "seepage and exchange" of these contexts and Lacan's theory of "transference":

> [S]uch a dynamic model of the power of context in metonymic disconnecting and reconnecting, seepage and exchange, in many ways finds further resonance in the dynamics of transference, as understood by Lacan. Transference is the ever-present context within which the psychoanalytic exercise is played out. (88)

Lacan's theory of transference usefully informs the governing determinism of the "little phrase," and the "transference" of its heartbreak from Vinteuil to Swann to Marcel. The curse of the music is the "ever-present context" within the disparate contexts of the trio's sorrows. This "seepage and exchange" also occurs within the context of the subject-object dyad. Gray continues: "The observed, for Lacan is 'pulled,' determined by the observer, who in turn is pulled and shaped by the object of observation—in Felman's metaphor, the working of 'contradictory gravitational pulls'" (89). I will revisit the implications of Lacanian "transference" for the subject-object dyad at greater length in the next chapter, for it is an aspect of *Recherche* that deeply informs the aesthetic strategies of its invention, and as such merits further interpretation. In obedience to Lacan's theory of transference, Vinteuil's little phrase is both the effect and the cause of the sorrows of Sapphic desire, arising from the Sapphic caresses of Mlle Vinteuil and Lea, giving rise to the sorrows that ravage the souls of Swann and Marcel. As Kristeva observes,

> An innocent Albertine was introduced to "music" by Mlle. Vinteuil's perverse friend . . . who revealed to her the secrets of the composer. . . . The fluid Albertine is thus perfectly vicious; she has a "vice parallel" to Charlus. . . . Contaminated with eroticism and weighted down with jealousy, betrayal, and death, music expresses the communication of souls that occurs before language. (76, 265)

The music communicates its sorrows directly to the souls of those who, like the composer, have suffered heartbreak in the gardens of Sapphic desire. *Recherche* subverts the traditional "romantic conception of music," as it subverts the traditional romantic conception of love, "by flooding it with the intensity and absurdity of sexual drama" (265)—and more, by investing it with the fatalism of a curse. Gray underscores the intertextual determinism of these contexts: "In a prescient observation, the narrator even implies that his own contextual association with Swann's story, the very proximity of listening to it, may generate its recontextualization as his own; thus, the entire mystery of Albertine's surreptitious activities might be produced by a fearful and unfounded analogy with, or recontextualization of, Odette" (88). Marcel's own words reinforce this view:

> I thought then of all that I had heard about Swann's love for Odette, of the way in which Swann had been deceived all his life. In fact, when I think of it, the hypothesis that made me gradually construe the whole of Albertine's character and painfully interpret every moment of a life that I could not control in its entirety, was the memory, the conviction of Mm. Swann's character, as it had been recounted to me. These accounts *contributed* towards the fact that . . . Albertine might . . . have had the same immorality, the same capacity for deceit as a former prostitute, and I thought of all the suffering that would in that case have been in store for me if I should ever have loved her. (qtd. in Gray 88, my emphasis)

The story of Swann, like the allegories of incest and adultery embodied respectively in *Francois le champi* and the magic lantern, is invested with a determinism whose influence extends far beyond the volume that contains it. Each is an allegory whose subsequent influence on Marcel belies the seemingly innocuous, free-standing nature of its first impression: a determinism that only emerges in time. Marcel's descent into vice, madness, and heartbreak not only replicates the decline of Swann and Charlus, but unites their atavistic regressions in a plot of decline whose torment is "perfectly vicious," and whose climactic reversal of fortune contrasts powerfully with the catastrophic closure that culminates the careers of his romantic and social precursors.

Deterministic images proliferate amidst the eternal return of the "little phrase." The allusion to Orestes, an allegory of vengeance, reinforces the fatalism of the "little phrase": "to punish the murderer of Agamemnon," "as a punishment, a retribution for having allowed my grandmother to die," "striking like an Avenger," "the fatal consequences which evil actions indefinitely engender." Marcel clearly perceives this transformative moment as a Day of Judgment, of retribution for the "matricidal fantasy hinted at in this passage" (Bersani 258n). Kristeva develops a similar interpretation:

> Orestes, who avenges Agamemnon's murder by killing Clytemnestra, has become the classical image of an anti-Oedipus. This passage shows that the narrator takes responsibility for the sins of Mlle. Vinteuil and for those of the friend who profaned her dead father. To these women, the young man links Albertine and the composer's death, which is transformed into a "murder" of the mother. (76–77)

Consequently, "the feeling of guilt and sin indelibly marks Proust's representations of eroticism" (77).

Marcel's self-punishment revives masochistic tendencies, elsewhere transposed onto Charlus. The question arises: Is the real offense (for which this appears to be a fictional transposition) not the sin of matricide or homoerotic desire committed against the mother, but the sin of artistic dishonesty, the betrayal of the artistic imperative for truth, committed against the creative self? Is this the "sin" that unleashes the wrath of a vengeful masochism already aroused by feelings of guilt for matricidal and homoerotic impulses? Whatever the underlying origins of the masochism evident in these passages, it represents a strategic compromise between the conflicting demands of fiction and reality for truth and protection. Hence, this passage reinscribes the spectacle of Montjouvain in more ways than one. It signifies the artist's desire to move one step closer to the profane truth, comprises an even more explicit confession of profane desires than is signified by Marcel's seeming innocent and accidental presence at the window of Montjouvain. For here, Marcel directly takes upon himself responsibility for vice, as well as the psychic sorrows reserved for its practitioners. The blame he assumes is tantamount to a confession—satisfies the artist's need to confess the vice that the man does not dare confess. We here see the artist negotiating with the same problem of homosexuality, mediating the problematic terrain between fact and fiction, arbitrating between the conflicting needs to objectify and to protect the self. Both are essential to the preservation of the self. To what extent is he willing to compromise the integrity of the artistic self to ensure the protection of the self's ego? How much truth can he risk? At what point does disclosure of the truth have negative survival value? Which are more immediate: the imperatives of the artistic or the egotistic self? Again, he finds a novel middle way: accepting the blame and the punishment of vice (through Marcel) without copping to the vice itself. Like many criminals, Marcel cops a plea bargain: confessing to a lesser crime (involuntary matricide) to avoid persecution for a less exculpatory sin (homosexuality).

The suffering that is posited as an effect of the voyeuristic acquisition of profane knowledge is in reality a transposition of the secret sorrows the author endured from the practice of vice. The mere acquisition of profane knowledge, as in his mere presence at the window of Montjouvain, at the brothel of Jupien, at the spectacle of Albertine's vice, is a "sign" that encodes a deeper implication in vice, that indeed signifies his membership in a "race upon which a curse weighs." As evidenced by the heartbreak of Vinteuil and Swann, and even more explicitly by the sorrows of Marcel, the "little phrase" is the vehicle for this curse, whose eternal return is visited upon those who love the practitioners of profane desire, who are punished for their "knowledge" of this vice. Not content to merely describe their "race" as accursed, Proust expends a significant portion of *Recherche* dramatizing the curse of the "little phrase," whose effects are brought violently home (literally and figuratively) upon his narrator.

Transfiguration: Sorrow's Silver Lining

Having developed the psychological and aesthetic implications of profanation and transposition, I wish now to turn to the last aspect of this progression: transfiguration, developing its implications for The Search. The curse of the "little phrase" precipitates Marcel's descent into the madness of jealousy: an atavism compounded by the degeneration of his reason, memory, and morals, which culminates in the sanitarium and in the living death of a spiritual sterility. The self of the sanitarium is totalized by indifference (to life and love, to art, nature, and society). The existential gloom of this living death would signify the catastrophic closure of Marcel's career, as it did for Swann and Charlus, if not for the transfiguration that redeems him. As it was for Adam and Eve, Marcel's fall into sin (and into the sorrows associated with it) is fortunate insofar as it constitutes a descent into the self, which awakens the creative self. Even more so than Swann, Marcel is rewarded for his suffering with the "grace of a particular wisdom," which first assumes the form of a liberatory resignation to fate, in which suffering is mitigated by acceptance of it. Embedded in the sorrows of the Sapphic sublime is the silver lining of a redemptive wisdom that transfigures the self into an artist. Fortunately, the spiritual gloom of Marcel's sorrow is offset by the ray of a "great discovery":

> And at the same time, from my bitterest grief I derived a sentiment almost of pride, almost joyful, that of a man whom the shock he has just received has carried at a bound to a point to which no voluntary effort could have brought him. . . . It was a terrible terra incognita this on which I had just landed, a fresh phase of undreamed-of sufferings that was opening before me. . . . And the most terrible reality brings us, with our suffering, the joy of a great discovery. . . . [B]ehind Albertine I no longer saw the blue mountains of the sea, but the room at Montjouvain where she was falling into the arms of Mlle Vinteuil with that laugh with which she gave utterance to the strange sound of her enjoyment. (CP 367–68)

The pain of this terrible truth is mitigated when he discovers it is part of a larger pattern into whose wisdom his heartbreak is absorbed—even as this wisdom will be absorbed into language, as sorrow resolves itself into a chain of signification, by which the self ascends from the abyss of itself, as if by a spiritual rope: by which he is "carried at a bound" (and quite by chance) into the immortal pastures of the past, "to a point to which no voluntary effort could have brought him." The sorrows of the present are absorbed into the patterns of the past, before both are assimilated into the signs of art, which by novel's end loom in a future as immediate as it is transcendent.

The sorrows of the "little phrase" visited upon Marcel return him to the "terrible terra incognita" of Montjouvain, even as they anticipate the redemptive topoi of the novel's climax: the paving stone, the Guermantes library, St. Mark's baptistery et al. The career of Vinteuil's "little phrase" unfolds like an allegorical fugue of damnation and redemption, enacted between the poles of Sapphic sorrow and art. The "little phrase" metonymically signifies the redemptive power of all art, in whose company death is "less bitter, less inglorious, perhaps even less certain" (SW 269). Art not only has the power to overcome death by eternalizing the soul of the deceased artist, as it does for Vinteuil, but has the power as well to transform a living death into life, as it does for Swann—and as it will for Marcel. Like Hamlet, Swann and Marcel are freed from their paralyzing sorrows by an awakening to the governing determinism of fate, to the "concatenation of necessity" (SW 292). In the dramatic tableau of Montjouvain and the "little phrase" Proust not only develops the intimacy of Sapphic desire and artistic production, of damnation and redemption, but provides a second case study on the neurotic origins of the creative impulse. Vinteuil's "little phrase" is a metonym for the entire *Recherche*, a fragment that informs the whole, whose origins and effects evidence the art of madness.

NOTE

1. A portion of this chapter appeared in *College Literature* 30.4 (Fall 2003): "The Curse of the Little Phrase: Swann and the Sorrows of the Sapphic Sublime."

chapter three

The Hymenoptera of Self and Other: The Making and (Un)Making of Knowledge

---

> The psychology of the self is to be found in the Other.
> —Otto Rank, Beyond Psychology

A STRATEGY OF SELF-POSSESSION: PENETRATION, CONVERSION, AND ASSIMILATION

PROUST'S GENIUS IS to a significant degree inscribed in the dynamics of the self-Other dyad. Writing occurs in the space between self and Other—is the effect of the self's sexual differentiation from the mother and all Other, and the principal means by which the self surmounts its differentiation. Writing is the ultimate cure for the pathology of the fictive self, fulfills the series of pathological desires rooted in differentiation: ideal-hungry, mirror-hungry, and merger-hungry. This dyad further evidences strategies of possession that on occasion (Albertine) enact the dispossession of the self. For the most part, however, the Other is possessed as an extension of the self; the possession of the Other is in reality a strategy of self-possession. Nevertheless, when confronted by a fugitive Other, the violent aggressions of the self return upon itself. The burrowing wasp of the self, instead of evacuating the essence of the Other, empties the essence of the self, which is defined in terms of the Other. Possession gives way to dispossession: the desire to possess the Other devolves into a desire to be possessed by the Other.

Further, the dynamics of the self-Other dyad evidence the operation of yet another series (or progression): penetration, conversion, and assimilation. Operating in the service of a pathological possessive desire, this series constitutes yet another "search engine" of the narrative. *Recherche* is as deeply informed by this tripartite strategy of self-possession as it is by the series of profanation, transposition, and transfiguration. After the Other is penetrated by the self, it is redefined in terms of the self, after which it is assimilated into the self. The medium for this "exchange" between self and Other is metaphor. If the series of profanation, transposition, and transfiguration objectifies the conflicts associated with sexual differentiation, then similarly the series of penetration, conversion, and assimilation (transference) comprises a second strategy by which the self attempts to objectify itself: by selectively asserting itself in violent aggressions against "privileged" Others. Metaphor is the weapon of choice in both strategies. Profane desires rooted in differentiation inaugurate the deterministic series of profanation, transposition, and transfiguration as evidenced in the incestuous, Sapphic, and homoerotic relationships of The Search. Differentiation similarly initiates the deterministic series of penetration, conversion, and assimilation associated with Marcel's possessive desire, whether this desire is displaced onto persons, places, or things, onto Albertine, Venice, or the Martinville steeples.

The narrator of *Recherche* subjects a series of "privileged" Others to the violent aggressions of a pathological self, using metaphor to bridge the moat between self and Other, to crack open the "sealed vessel" of the mystifying Other, in order to evacuate its essence as a precondition for objectifying its own in the Other. This "seepage and exchange" between self and Other fulfills the ideal-hungry, mirror-hungry, and merger-hungry desires of the self. Moreover, the aggressions associated with this progression evidence a self that is not only pathological but violently masculine. Its masculinity is pathological, however, insofar as it is displaced from the body to the mind by the asthmatic attacks that enfeeble the body, and hence the self's masculinity. The self reclaims this lost masculinity in violent aggressions against the Other, including the mother. In *Recherche*, the imagination, not the body, becomes the locus of masculinity. And the aspect of the imagination that does most of the heavy lifting in the self's aggressions against the Other is a muscular metaphor. The physical infirmity (asthma) that feminizes the body by rendering it passive is overcompensated by a masculinized imagination whose weapon of choice is a rapier-like metaphor—or more appropriately, the burrowing wasp of metaphor.

Whereas Saint Loup mitigates the self's aggressions by virtue of his sameness, all other Others kindle its violently masculine aggressions by virtue of their differentiation from the self: whether it is a trio of steeples, a trio of trees, a tea-soaked madeleine, or a "little phrase" of music. This desire to possess the Other is intimately associated with the need to possess (or repossess) the self that is immanent in the Other.

The process of transference is preceded by a process of transposition, in which the Other is first converted into a metonym of the self—even as one fraction must be converted before it can be added to another. Metaphor is the medium for this conversion, and the fragmentary self into which the Other is converted becomes the common denominator that enables the "merger" of the two-in-one. Initial differentiation between self and Other collapses into undifferentiated sameness. A self-Other dialectic evolves into a self-self alliteration, in which a self "squares" itself in the Other, multiplies itself across a fictional time-space, discontinuous-continuum.

The last two phases of this progression, conversion and transference, are preceded by an equally violent initial phase of penetration. Metaphor is the hypodermic by which the pathological self first penetrates and immobilizes the Other. The dynamic of the self-Other dyad is particularly informed by one of Proust's more memorable metaphors: the hymenoptera:

> [T]he burrowing wasp, which in order to supply a fresh store of meat for her offspring after her own decease, calls in the science of anatomy to amplify the resources of her instinctive cruelty, and having made a collection of weevils and spiders, proceeds with marvelous knowledge and skill to pierce the nerve center on which their power of locomotion . . . depends, so that the paralyzed insect, beside which her egg is laid, will furnish the larva, when it is hatched, with a tame and inoffensive quarry, incapable either of flight or resistance, but perfectly fresh for the larder. . . . (SW 93)

Though deployed as a sign of Francoise's predatory cruelty toward the "poor kitchen maid," the burrowing wasp is an apt trope for the aggressions of a pathological and creative self that preys upon the essence of a series of "privileged" Others. These "essences" of the Other become the essence of the self insofar as they comprise the select diet upon which the parasitic self subsists. The self of *Recherche* bloats itself on a rich diet of "essences." Further, its gluttony prompts the regurgitation of the self-as-Other. Art is the regurgitated self embodied in signs. And the proliferation of the Proustian sign across the empty pages of space and time signifies the insatiable and narcissistic desire of the self to regurgitate itself, symbolically. Once ingested, the "essence" of the petite madeleines is regurgitated in ink. The ingestion of the Other is thrown off in the self. The creative impulse, with respect to the self, is liberatory; however, with respect to the Other, it is parasitic. Indeed, it is as a parasite of the Other that the creative impulse liberates the self.

The Search dramatizes the proliferation of the self through a discontinuous series of Others—is essentially a quest by the self to re-colonize the lost and scattered fragments of itself: a Humpty Dumpty shattered by time, piecing together the fragments of itself. The fragments for which it searches, a few of which it fortuitously finds, are the immortal metonyms of the self, randomly immured within a series of Others. Because the Other imprisons a fragmentary self, its autonomy is an impediment that must be overcome, and which is ultimately sacrificed to the reunion of the self with itself. Metaphor is the tilting lance that ensures the triumph of Marcel's Quixotic quest, that enables him to penetrate the seemingly invincible shields of a host of Others. With each penetration, a captive self is freed, is reunited with its host: a liberation that is commemorated in a ritual explosion of figuration, in a rhetorical fireworks whose most luminous trajectories are inscribed by the proliferating metaphors that announce and celebrate each liberation of an imprisoned self. Metaphor mediates the reunion of the self with these lost fragments of itself. Consequently, metaphor is both medium of this exchange and the principal effect of it.

The Other that mediates between the self and itself is put under erasure by metaphor, which brings the self back into unmediated alliteration with itself, fulfilling the wish for the two-in-one, displaced from the son-mother dyad to the son-Other dyad. Metaphor is the medium that converts the Other into a metonym of the self. The reunion of the self is also a communion, as evidenced by the self's ingestion of the fragment of itself embodied in the host of the petite madeleine. The Search thus commences with a rite of communion, in contradistinction to (and in atonement for) the sins of differentiation committed by the self against the mother (incest, matricide, sadism, and same-sex love).

The climactic events of *Recherche* signify the transformative evolution of the self-Other dyad from a state of generative, if volatile, disequilibrium in which the essence of the self is absorbed by the Other as often as the reverse, into a harmonized stability in which the Other is finally and forever assimilated into the creative self. The moment of the two-in-one absorbs time, along with every other moment in The Search—even as both time and The Search are absorbed into signs: into a realm beyond time and the sorrows of differentiation, in which ironically the self's differentiation from all others is signified for all time.

The narrator's redemption to art is largely achieved on the angel wings of metaphor, which by decoding the mobile, differentiated, material sign, opens it up, makes possible its assimilation into the possessive self—makes possible the liberation of the self that is immanent in the material sign. Marcel's struggle to liberate the ideal (creative) self from within himself metonymically reinscribes the struggle of every artist. A sculpture by Rodin or Michaelangelo might dramatize this epic struggle with a Herculean figure laboring to liberate a captive soul from its marble block with an upraised sledge hammer—though Mallarmé's image of a swan encased in ice poeticizes the imprisonment of the creative impulse within the self just as succinctly.

The violence and insistence of this protracted struggle is crystallized in the "privileged moments." If the sorrows of sexual differentiation denote the "first black date on the calendar" then the liberation of the self into undifferentiated communion with itself on the Icarian wings of metaphor is what the last luminous date in the calendar of *Recherche* celebrates. If the first "black date" connotes the death of the ideal self then the last series of "privileged moments" on this fictional calendar signifies the rebirth of the ideal self in art.

The Other is first immobilized in metaphor, in a chain of figuration that "encloses it in a style," as a precondition for its assimilation by the self. The centrality of language to the meaning-making process in *Recherche* is what invites interpretation from postmodern perspectives, as evidenced by Deleuze's analysis of "signs," by Kristeva's interpretation of rhetorical tropes, by Gray's focus on a "feminine ecriture," and by Doubrovsky's assertion that subjectivity is a function of language formation: "[T]o be yourself is to invent your own language" (36). Ironically, as Derrida's analysis evinces, signs are themselves grounded in difference. Doubly ironic then that signs signifying difference should be used to efface the self's difference from the Other. However, if the sign signifies its difference from other signs, its meaning only derives from its presence in a chain of association with other signs, and it is this associative faculty of the sign in general, redoubled in metaphor, that makes it the ideal medium for satisfying the self's desires for eternal correspondence with the Other.

The Proustian sign reverses the historical function of language, which is to effect the self's differentiation from the world, as birth signifies its sexual differentiation from the mother. In its prelinguistic state, the ego exists in a state of undifferentiated domination by the world. By naming it, the ego frees itself from the world: objectifies the world from itself. Language creates and guarantees the autonomy of the ego, liberating it from a condition of undifferentiated domination by the world to a state of differentiated independence from it, from a determined servitude to the world to a self-determining objectification of the world through the word. As Rank observes, language "helped the ego to magnify itself and to dominate its world around" (240). More significantly, metaphor is the primary means, the defining process by which language effects this differentiation of the self from the world, and its re-association with the world through metaphor. Language, in fact, is "one vast metaphorical comprehension of the world . . . no word has any but a metaphorical meaning" (236–37). Rank continues: "[M]etaphor, which is the means of language growth, may perhaps have been its actual source, in the sense that metaphor may once have linked concepts of time and space . . . to notions of sound" (237). Metaphor is not only an effect of language, but a cause of it. Similarly, in *Recherche* metaphor is not only an effect of the self's association with the Other, but the primary means by which this association occurs, first through the literal association of two fragments of the self across time, and subsequently through their figurative association in language, through metaphor.

Proust's project reverses this process, undoes the sexual and linguistic differentiation of the self by collapsing the self back into the world—

through language. The language-driven differentiation that normally signifies the self's autonomy signifies its isolation within the context of Marcel's pathological maternal dependency. Marcel uses language to undo what birth has done, to collapse his sexual differentiation into a state of undifferentiated communion with the Other. The Other is explicated as the self and the world is converted into a vast sign of the self, by a "world creation in words" (Rank 220). Marcel's linguistic project (and Proust's) satisfies the self's dual needs for "merger" and differentiation: it merges the Other with the self as a means of reasserting the domination of the self. The role of language is paradoxically reversed and reiterated: it effaces the self's differentiation from the Other in order to assert its dominion over the Other. As Doubrovsky observes, the governing desire in *Recherche* is a "desire for language"—because it comprises the sole means of differentiating the self from the Other, and in particular from the mother (37). In Doubrovsky's succinct formulation: "Identity is the authentic—that is, the singular—production of a language" (35).

The linguistic project of *Recherche* is radically subversive. If language reinforces the sexual differentiation of the self from the Other, then Proust deploys language to unwrite the self's differentiation from the Other. The self surrenders its differentiation but not its ability to signify. The self, instead of imploding into the world, explodes through language, subsuming the world in itself. The universe outside the self is absorbed into the linguistic nebulae of the self that is *Recherche*.

PENETRATION: THE BURROWING WASP OF METAPHOR

The possession of the Other begins with the possessive gaze of the self, which when thwarted by the fugitive, impenetrable nature of the Other, turns to metaphor to crack the safe, as it were: to convert the Other into a quantity familiar to the self (in some cases, a prior incarnation of the self), which facilitates its assimilation by the self. Marcel accesses the desired essence of the Other indirectly, through the side door of metaphoric transposition. Figuration brings the "sealed vessels" of self and Other into direct communication—even as the bedroom wall in the Grand Hotel at Balbec became the medium for Marcel's communication with his grandmother.

Metaphor aborts the false pregnancy of the Other, impregnating it instead with the self. The Other becomes a surrogate womb for the self—is, indeed, a surrogate for the womb of the mother, to which Marcel has been yearning to return since the violent expulsion of birth. The womb signifies an Edenic, pre-oedipal moment of the two-in-one: the self immersed in the placental fluid of the womb, for which the cork-lined bedroom is yet another surrogate: a topos for the perpetual two-in-one alliteration of mother and son in the placental ink.

The Other is the surrogate womb into which Marcel has been trying to inject himself since the "first black date on the calendar." The "trauma of birth" is the inciting violence that forcibly expels the self from the womb, into an involuntary and unwanted differentiation from the mother. Marcel's neurosis can be comprehended as a species of "post-traumatic stress syndrome." Life is one long "post-traumatic stress syndrome" in which the self is pathologically fixated by the wound of differentiation inflicted at birth, to which it never adequately adjusts and for which it futilely tries to console itself by injecting itself into a series of surrogate "wombs" (or Others). Because the self cannot reimpregnate the mother with itself, it tries to impregnate the Other with itself. The self's promiscuous attempts to impregnate a series of "privileged" Others is a means of reasserting its masculinity, even as its metaphorical "penetrations" of the Other is laden with phallic connotations. The self renounces the masculinity imposed upon it by birth, rejecting its sexual differentiation from the mother. Its masculine impulses, however, are enervated by their repression, and work themselves off in violent aggressions against the Other, working largely through a libidinized imagination that impregnates through figuration. The violence of birth is thrown off in the violence of possessive and profane desire. The violence of the mother-Marcel dyad begets the violence of the Other-Marcel dyad, in which expulsion from the womb incites the desire to return to the womb, which is displaced in the violent desire to penetrate a series of surrogate "wombs" (Others). The self-Other dyad is, however, characterized by a "mutual interpenetration" (Brady 72).

The self's aggressions against the Other is not just a question of penetration, but of mutual parasitism and "mutual torment." As Doubrovsky affirms, "[I]t is not a question of symbiosis but, strictly speaking, of parasitism. Such is clearly the biological model, the final nourishment that Proustian fantasy gives itself" (22). Metaphor revives the mother in the Other: "Metaphor is, in writing, the place of the mother's resurrection (46)":

> Through radical incestuous possession, which is not satisfied with the bliss of a banal Oedipal complex, he does not have his mother; he is his mother. He becomes himself by becoming—in the beyond which is death. With the same stroke, metaphor comes into being; the "two" terms or "objects" are now "one." (Doubrovsky 50)

Marcel's conversion of the "essence" of others into an image of the self through metaphoric assimilation reinscribes the parasitic strategy of the hymenoptera, the wasp that burrows into its victims, converting their deep tissue into a food source for itself and its offspring. Marcel's encounter with the triad of steeples bears closer scrutiny insofar as it dramatizes a prevailing strategy of self-possession and informs the series of penetration, conversion, and transference. Patrick Brady underscores both the significance of this Proustian "privileged moment," as well as those elements of it neglected by critics:

> [P]revious critics appear to have imitated the Proustian narrator in skating over this "hidden meaning" without ever penetrating it. . . . We need to rethink both the meaning of these various triads and the function of their literary transposition, for these elements shed a precious and apparently neglected light on the psychological makeup of Proust's fictional narrator, and consequently on the deep structure of the work as a whole. (91)

Criticism, insofar as it covets the deeper grammar of the "privileged moments," and of *Recherche* itself, reinscribes the aggressions of the narrator's possessive self—in an effort to surmount its own alienation from the text, to convert the text into an objectification of the critic. Conversely, in its relation to the Other in general, but particularly in the "privileged moments," the possessive self reinscribes the alienated, desiring subject position of the critic. This mutual parasitism of the creative and the critical impulse is evidenced in the privileged moment of the Martinville steeples, as is the series of penetration, conversion, and assimilation.

THE STEEPLES OF MARTINVILLE: DESIRE AND DIFFERENTIATION

> In Proust, the steeples of Martinville and Vinteuil's little phrase, which cause no memory, will always prevail over the madeleine and the cobblestones of Venice, which depend on memory and thereby still refer to a material explanation.
> —Deleuze

As with so many objects that comprise the "privileged moments" of *Recherche*, Marcel launches his campaign to free the steeple-captive with his possessive gaze. Shortly, however, metaphor is deployed to breach the "sealed vessel" of the desired object. The task is compounded by the fact that unlike objects in an ordinary material world, those in the Proustian universe are not fixed, but moving targets. The mobility of the Other engenders a threefold strategy of immobilization through a fixated and fixating male gaze, followed by a conversation of the Other into a function of the self via metaphor, as a precondition for its assimilation into the self, which thus objectifies itself in the Other. The Other, in other words, is converted from an object into a subject. That which appears to be different is, in reality, the same. The exhibition of the self in the Other prompts Marcel's joy at the beginning of this privileged moment. The objectification of that self in writing redoubles his joy at the conclusion of this significant encounter. The word effects the two-in-one, bridging the habitual abyss between the self-in-the-Other and its ideal mate imprisoned within the self.

Patrick Brady notes the significance of this and other "triads" in *Recherche*, arguing that they reinscribe the nuclear triad of mother-father-son, which is more stable than the simple "dyad" of a mother-son relationship. Whereas Brady attributes Marcel's joy to this symbolic stability of the triad as embodied in the steeples, I attribute it to an entirely different source, whose psychological implications inform the entire work, and the self-Other relationship in particular. I endorse Brady's assertion that the dyad is an unstable relationship, and the self-Other dyad the most unstable of all. Whereas Brady assigns a negative value to this instability, however, I prefer to see that volatile disequilibrium as a protean dynamic that produces the Proustian universe, and that evidences the laws of its genesis. Self and Other dwell in a combustible, unstable, disequilibrium, which signifies the life or death of the self. This self-Other dyad is the site of a violent struggle for possession, whose outcome is totalized in the absolute servitude of the self to the Other or the absolute dominion of the self over the other. Essence are exchanged between self and Other in a duet of mutual parasitism, in which each plays host to the predatory impulses of the other. This protean disequilibrium predominates throughout The Search, until precipitated in the stable compound of the two-in-one in the realm of the symbolic, concretized in ink—where the Other is assimilated into the ideal self it helped liberate. Art stabilizes the self-Other combustion, synthesizing both under the sign of an ideal self, liberated and fused in a binding compound inscribed in a chain of signification.

The steeples of Martinville are, as Brady avers, "associated with a mysterious pleasure and a hidden meaning . . . and its central significance in the *Recherche* as a whole is indicated by . . . his writing-up of the experience" (84). Although I endorse Brady's assessment of the scene's significance, I disagree with his interpretation of it, and in particular with his conclusions regarding the cause of Marcel's joy and the implications of his "writing up." Brady calls into question Proust's failure to "'explain' the hidden meaning of the scene of the bell-towers":

> One has the impression that he is right in sensing a hidden meaning; one does not have the impression that he has discovered just what that hidden meaning is. . . . This question, the essential one (as he appears to realize), remains unanswered. (87)

I disagree with Brady's assessment. Marcel does not explicate the "hidden meaning" or "essence" of the steeples because it possesses none. What it does possess is a hidden self—and this he brilliantly explicates in imagery. Brady's objection foregrounds the assumption that the steeples are free-standing signifiers, invested with a hidden essence. As Proust's treatment of this "privileged moment" evinces, however, the steeples can only be explicated in terms of the self. The "hidden meaning" is that the steeples have no meaning in and of themselves; their meaning derives solely from their alliteration with the self—and this Marcel/Proust does explicate. The three steeples and Marcel's soul are kindred spirits of isolation, abandonment, and captivity. It is not a question of a subject-object differentiation, nor even of "the difference . . . between subjects" (Deleuze 42). It is a question of a false differentiation between subject-object that vanishes altogether because of a simple reality: the object subjectivizes. Deleuze writes, "[I]t is not the subject which explains essence, rather it is essence which implicates, envelops, wraps itself up in the subject. Rather in coiling round itself, it is essence which constitutes subjectivity. . . . Essence is not individual, it individualizes" (43). Moreover, this symbiotic relation between essence and self "is all the more important in that Proust sees it as the only possible proof of the soul's immortality" (43)—it is these essences alone that unite the disparate fragments of the self over space and time, that reintegrate the mortal and immortal fragments of the self arbitrarily and deterministically partitioned by time.

Involuntary memory, chance, and figuration recompose the self after its decomposition by time. Hence the ubiquity in Proust of images that connote division and reintegration, that reinscribe the generative tension between the fragment and the whole: the magic lantern, Vermeer's "patch of yellow light," Vinteuil's "little phrase," the various prisms and fountains that capture his attention—all are tropes for a self that is forever fragmenting into its component selves or reconstituting itself into a whole: of a self that longs to be as divine in its totality as it is in its immortal fragments.

It is a lost fragment of the self that Marcel's rediscovers in the steeples of Martinville, imprisoned like Geneviève in her feudal tower. This captive self reinscribes the fragmentary selves imprisoned within the madeleine, the trees of Hudimesnil, the uneven stones of the Baptistery steps et al., even as it tropes on the novel's real captive: the creative self chained within Marcel. Until differentiated in language (in writing) this self remains imprisoned within the Other and the self. When Marcel finally "names" the joy associated with the steeples, he is literally naming himself. The self, originally fragmented and divided from itself is reunited with itself through language (writing), which converts the Other (the steeples) into a sign of the self. Writing occurs in the space between self and other, and its principal effect is to efface this space, to erase the self's differentiation from the other.

The self proliferates across time and space, becoming a transcendent signified, stabilized in writing. The sorrows of its mortal differentiation are absorbed into the ecstasies of its immortal differentiation, which simultaneously solves the conflicting need for the two-in-one and for the one that arises from the fusion of the two. The antithetical sorrows of the self's differentiation are harmonized in the synthesis of the artist. Marcel's joy is not the result of apprehending a "hidden meaning" in the steeples that is never named, but the joy of finding and freeing a captive self. It is the joy of alliteration between self and Other, the joy of a differentiation temporarily transcended—and most significantly of all, it is the joy of an ideal self (the writer) rediscovered. Having repeatedly despaired of ever realizing this ideal self, whose liberation is fundamental to his redemption insofar as it alone can atone for the sins of profanation, Marcel is overjoyed by its sudden revival. The steeples rekindle the creative impulse, whose flame has all but been extinguished within Marcel. And this too rekindles his spiritual exaltation:

> At the moment when . . . I had finished writing it, I found such a sense of happiness, felt that it had so entirely relieved my mind of the obsession of the steeples, and of the mystery which they concealed, that as though I myself were a hen and had just laid an egg, I began to sing at the top of my voice. (SW 140)

The full throat Marcel gives to his singing voice reinforces the rediscovery of his writerly voice, which had all but vanished. The hen-egg imagery is significant insofar it posits creativity as a surrogate for the birth process, even as it symbolizes the rebirth of the ideal self, which has been and will remain Marcel's governing desire since the death of the ideal self to profane desire in the "drame coucher." The hen-egg dyad reinscribes the two-in-one, mother-son dyad inasmuch as the self becomes the mother of its own inventions. It also resurrects the creative parasitism of the hymenoptera, which having bloated itself on the "essence" of a host, propagates itself. Further, not only have the steeples impregnated Marcel with a creative self, but the steeples are pregnant with one of his lost selves, completing the narcissistic feedback loop between a self and itself.

The self is fixated by a mobile Other until it immobilizes the Other in words, in the process regaining its own mobility. Mobility passes from the Other to the self, through metaphor. The initial paralysis of the self gives way to the paralysis of the Other through figuration. Art enables the narrator to capture that which has captured himself, in the process freeing a series of selves while capturing a multiplicity of objects. The selves that are captured by time are liberated by art—for all time.

The correspondence of the steeples with the madeleine and other imprisoning objects is explicitly stated by Proust:

> Whether objective impressions such as I had received from the sight of the spires of Martinville, or subjective memories like the unevenness of the two steps or the taste of the madeleine, I must try to interpret the sensations as the indications of corresponding laws and ideas. I must try to . . . bring out of the obscurity what I had felt, and *convert it into a spiritual equivalent [which is to say, to make it a part of the self]*. Now this method, which seemed to me the only one, what was it other than to create a work of art? (PR 1000–1001, my emphasis)

Art completes the translation of the Other into the self. The word *corresponding* is significant insofar as it establishes the affinity between these three experiences (the madeleine, the steeples, and the paving stone). Moreover, the effort to "bring out," to "convert" this material to a "spiritual equivalent" signifies a dyadic differentiation between self and Other, which when the process is complete leaves the self entirely free of the Other, whose essence has been "brought out," converted into signs that can be assimilated by the self, that establish a spiritual equivalency with the self—that have subjectivized the objective and spiritualized the material. It is not simply a matter of decoding the sequestered "essence" of an object, as Deleuze infers: "To learn is first of all to consider a substance, an object, a being as if they emitted signs to be deciphered, interpreted. There is no apprentice who is not the 'Egyptologist' of something. . . . [W]e discover no truth, we learn nothing except by deciphering and interpreting" (4–5). Deleuze continues,

> [W]hatever the example—madeleine, steeples, trees, cobblestones, napkin, noise of a spoon or a pipe—we witness the same procedure. First, a prodigious joy, so that these signs are already distinguished from their preceding ones by their immediate effect. Further . . . the necessity of mental effort: to seek the sign's meaning. Then the sign's meaning appears, yielding to us the concealed object. (11–12)

I would qualify Deleuze's interpretation as follows: the "sign" of the Other only has meaning as an aspect of the self. The "object" it yields is not some hidden essence of itself, but an essence of the self. The "sign's meaning" can only be explicated in terms of the self. Having decoded the object, Marcel finds it is in reality a subject; having deciphered the material Other he discovers himself in possession of a dematerialized and rematerialized self—as if the Egyptologist upon deciphering the hieroglyphics, discovered that they inscribed his own past. The object is merely a fugitive subject in disguise—the Other merely a lost self, whose immortal fragment is restored to the mortal self who, like the Egyptologist, has been searching for its hidden tomb: a lost self that habitually hides in plain sight, in those nondescript objects that voluntary memory has forgotten, but which time randomly hides about us—like so many Easter eggs awaiting our serendipitous discovery.

THE OTHERING OF THE SELF:
MOVEMENT, METAPHOR, AND METAMORPHOSIS

The dynamics of the dyad are evidenced in yet another progression: movement, metaphor, and metamorphosis. The mobility of the Other destabilizes the self, compromises its project of possessive desire, even as it inscribes Proust's subversive genius. Whereas "realistic representations of the material world reinforce the stasis of the inanimate object," Proust's invests the inanimate with kinetic motion (Albertine's mole, the three steeples, the three trees, etc.). Whereas "realism" reinforces the subject-object divide, Proust explodes that binary, repeatedly spiritualizing the material, subjectivizing the objective. Whereas "realists" represent the fixed object, Proust imagines it in three critical and original ways: in motion, as something else, and in association with the self. Movement, metaphor, and metamorphosis inform the dynamics of the self-Other dyad, as evidenced in Marcel's encounter with the steeples of Martinville.

The implication of the self in the Other is variously manifested. In contradistinction to the hawthorns, which are figured within the context of nature, the steeples are evoked within the context of Marcel's development as a writer—and cannot be completely understood outside this context. As such, this moment comprises a second critical "date in the calendar" of his artistic "bildung." Immediately preceding his encounter with the steeples, Marcel falls prey to grave doubts concerning his calling to art. He confronts the possible death of this ideal self as if gazing into an inward abyss, and with a despair redolent of the "drame coucher":

> How often . . . in the course of my walks along the "Guermantes way," and with what an intensified melancholy did I reflect on my lack of qualification for a literary career, and that I must abandon all hope of ever becoming a famous author. The regret that I felt for this . . . made me suffer so acutely that . . . my mind of its own accord, by a sort of inhibition in the instant of pain, ceased entirely to think of verse-making, of fiction, of the poetic future on which my want of talent precluded me from counting. (SW 137)

He is beset by a "sense of my own impotence which I had felt whenever I sought a philosophic theme for some great literary work." He speaks of the "hope I had lost of succeeding one day in becoming an author and poet" (137). The symbiotic exchange of self and Other evidenced in the "privileged moment" of the steeples contrasts with the perpetual disconnect between self and Other that occurs just prior to it:

> Suddenly a roof, a gleam of sunlight reflected from a stone . . . appeared to be concealing . . . something which they invited me to approach and seize from them, but which, despite all my efforts, I never managed to discover . . . [which] had seemed to be to be teeming, ready to open, to yield up to me the secret treasure of which they were themselves no more than the outer covering. (137)

The disconnect between self and Other and the impotency of the creative impulse in this passage deeply informs the liberatory symbiosis of self and Other and the dramatic resurrection of the creative impulse that occurs in the "privileged moment" of the three steeples on the very next page. The deeper grammar of the steeples emerges only in the intertextuality of these two moments. The wish denied in the encounter with the "roof, the gleam of sunlight on stone," is fulfilled by the steeples, which not only surrender their "secret treasure," but by so doing, awaken the creative urge.

The imagined essence imprisoned within a "privileged" object (the steeples) is merely a projection of the artistic impulse imprisoned within Marcel. The steeples are midwife to the creative impulse. Unable to liberate the creative impulse within himself, Marcel turns to the external world to facilitate its release. The petites madeleines, the steeples, and the uneven paving stones are material allies in the self's quest for spirituality. The object helps the subject fulfill its wish: to compose the ideal self. The privileged object begets the privileged subject; the material is essential to the birth of the spiritual—or, to put it another way: the material is the womb of the spiritual, mediates between the spiritual and the eternal. The ideal is realized in the real. The fusion of the ideal and the real in the privileged moments contrasts with their disconnect throughout *Recherche*. In these moments, so critical to Marcel's "apprenticeship to signs," the impotence of the self is effaced by the potency of the Other's correspondence with the self.

The proximity of the self-in-the-Other to Marcel is always heralded by an inexplicable joy. As Marcel confides, "I experienced, suddenly, that special pleasure, which bore no resemblance to any other . . ." (138). The privileged moment, as Deleuze affirms, unfolds according to the "same procedure: First a prodigious joy" (11). The "privileged moment" begins with the agitation of the self by the Other and ends with the assimilation of the Other into the self—redoubling the initial joy, insofar as the original abstract happiness is now rooted in the concrete. Deleuze continues: "[T]hese are true signs which immediately give us an extraordinary joy, signs which are fulfilled, affirmative, and joyous" (Deleuze 12).

A MOVEABLE FEAST:
THE IMPLICATIONS OF THE MOBILE OTHER

This initial fixation of the self by the Other is disrupted by the fugitive mobility of the static object: as if Marcel has jumped the doe of a lost self. The pursuit is joined in earnest. The mobility of a static Other is realized through dramatic verbs and kinetic imagery. Upon the steeples the sun is "playing," its movement seeming to inspire their own, for the "movement of the carriage and the windings of the road seemed to keep them continually changing their position" (SW 138). Marcel detects the presence of something sublime, long sought after, which "lay behind that mobility." What he detects are the first stirrings of a creative urge, awakened by the steeples, whose external mobility mirrors the inward movement of this impulse. The mobility of the steeples, themselves the symbol of a resurrected spirituality, prefigures their reanimation of the creative impulse, which similarly begins to traverse at a bound vast inward spaces.

The fusion of the two-in-one, of the steeples with the creative urge, the immanence of the spiritual in the material, of the self-in-the-Other is evidenced by Marcel's assertion that "what lay buried within the steeples of Martinville must be something analogous to a charming phrase, since it was in the form of words which gave me pleasure that it had appeared to me," and as it had "framed itself in words in my head" (SW 139). What lies immured within the steeples is nothing more nor less than the creative impulse: the long-lost ideal self for which he has quested since the "drame coucher," and whose liberation holds the key to his salvation. The "outing" of this divine impulse by the steeples is concretized at last in words upon a page. The dry well into which Marcel has invested his fortunes begins at last, and of a sudden, to yield the black liquid of an idealized self. He borrows "a pencil and some paper from the Doctor, and compose[s] . . . the following little fragment":

> Alone, rising from the level of the plain, and seemingly lost in that expanse of open country, climbed to the sky the twin steeples of Martinville. Presently we saw three: springing into position confronting them by a daring volt, a third . . . the three steeples were . . . like three birds perched upon the plain. . . . Then the steeple of Viexvicq withdrew, took its proper distance [while the remaining pair] flung themselves so abruptly in our path that we barely had time to stop before being dashed against the porch of the church. (SW 139)

Though presented as the first fledgling composition of a novice writer, the passage is significant because it evidences, not a nascent, individualized genius, but the signature effects of the mature artist. For example, a "still life" is invested with mobility, as evidenced by the abundance of dramatic verbs associated with the movement of the steeples: "rising," "climbed," "springing." The static steeples are personified as kinetic subjects confronting and withdrawing from one another, flinging themselves to the ground before the narrator's carriage. They "waved" in farewell, "veered in the light," and go off "timidly seeking their way . . . stumbling . . . drawing close to one another, slipping one behind the other." Thus, after first depicting the effect of his pleasure, the narrator depicts its cause, first with kinetic verbs and then with imagery. Movement and metaphor unite to render an original evocation of the material. "Metaphor," as E. F. N. Jephcott observes in *Proust and Rilke* (1972), "has the function of animating the scene: the personification . . . gives movement and a kind of alertness to what would otherwise be static and inert. Even where metaphor is not directly involved, Proust uses verbs denoting movement rather than those denoting fixed postures" (148).

Proust's depiction of the "privileged" object, such as the three steeples, reflects not only the influences of Impressionism and Ruskin, but of his novel reinvention of these influences. What Jephcott observes of Rodin's influence on Rilke applies as well to Proust:

> The function of art is still to lure an elusive "something," which we have seen to be the quality of awareness during a privileged moment, into consciousness. . . . The desired quality of awareness is not now to be summoned by the incantory use of language, but by manipulating the surface. . . . "There is only a single surface, filled with a thousandfold movement." (Rilke, qtd. in Jephcott 105)

The creative impulse is repressed under a kinetic surface, whose mobility it engenders, in a transference of movement from the spiritual to the material—which reanimates the spiritual in return. The mobility of the surface is an effect of a repressed and immobilized creative impulse. Further, this surface animation is the second, telltale "sign" of the creative, following hard on the heels of the joy the object wafts to the narrator like an exotic perfume of the ideal self. The ideal self communicates to the self through the "privileged" object that imprisons it, and this sudden, fortuitous correspondence animates the creative self. The "privileged" object that brings the self in touch with itself awakens the creative impulse from its long dormancy. The displacement of its animation to the surface of the imprisoning object is the result of its own immobilization, is the means by which it signals its captivity to the only agent that can effect its liberation: the conscious mind. The surface ripples of the "privileged" object are the visible effects of an ideal self whose deep slumber has been fortuitously disturbed.

What we witness in the mobilization of the static Other is the creative impulse imprisoned within the unconscious mind frantically signaling the conscious mind in an effort to breach the barrier between them. The self-Other dyad of the "privileged moments" is merely an objectification of this psychological struggle between conscious and unconscious mind, whose governing aim is to bridge the divide between them—is yet another manifestation of the protean desire for the two-in-one, which is the deterministic desire par excellence of *Recherche*. The barriers that separate the self from a series of "privileged" Others signify nothing other than the formidable barrier separating the conscious and unconscious mind. The self-Other disconnect objectifies this psychological disjunction between the two minds of Marcel.

Moreover, the "privileged moments" reenact the inciting meta-drama of the "twilight psychology" insofar as they inscribe the two-in-one communion of the conscious and unconscious mind. Marcel's struggle to liberate the "essence" of a privileged object is in reality a struggle to liberate a fragment of the self, which reprises the self's struggle to "remember" a dream upon awaking, to literally re-member itself by recovering the self imprisoned in the dreamscape of the unconscious. The "privileged moments" resurrect the originary landscape of the unconscious, reprising this struggle of the self to breach the divide between its conscious and unconscious self. The numerous selves imprisoned within "privileged" objects are merely surrogates for the primal ideal self imprisoned within the unconscious, embodied in the creative impulse. The Herculean effort required to pierce the "sealed vessel" of the "privileged" object in order to apprehend the "essence" it sequesters is redolent of the self's epic struggle to breach the barrier of forgetfulness in order to remember what has been dreamed or experienced. The creative impulse immured within the steeples and the memories sequestered in the madeleine are alike imprisoned in the unconscious. The steeples and the madeleine are merely objectifications of the unconscious mind that imprisons memories and the creative impulse alike—which is why once the self breaches the unconscious mind, it liberates not only involuntary memories but the creative urge. The artistic impulse escapes through the breach hard on the heels of the involuntary memories, like thoroughbreds through a barn door that a fortuitous gust has thrown ajar.

The surface motion of the steeples signifies the impending end of the paralysis of the creative impulse. Their movement heralds the reanimation of the artistic urge, of which it is both an effect and a cause. No matter what "privileged" object is ficted, one of its essential characteristics is that "its surfaces are 'in motion' . . . the interchange between them, gives an impression of movement" (107), as if the given object "vibrates internally, rising and falling back into itself without a single stationary point" (108). Another characteristic of this movement is that "it must, though it be from infinite distances, though it be from the depths of the sky, it must return to [the object], the great circle must be closed, the circle of solitude in which an Art-Thing spends its days" (Rilke, qtd. in Jephcott 109). This "solitude" of the "thing" is emphatic, consists of "the total isolation from its surroundings produced by its closed movement," and comprises yet another distinguishing feature of the privileged moment.

Proust's depiction of the three steeples not only embodies these principles of movement and solitude ("alone, rising on the level of the plain, and seemingly lost in that expanse . . . alone, gilded by the light of the setting sun . . . abandoned in a solitary place") but goes one step farther, appropriating the three steeples as emblems of his own melancholy differentiation: of his sexual and artistic isolation, as an Other akin to the Other of the steeples. The feedback loop of the self-Other dyad closes around the sign of mutual isolation. Finally, this movement on the microcosmic level of the steeples (or the given surface of any privileged moment) mirrors the movement on the macrocosmic level of time: "Time implies movement, and movement is an essential element of *Time Lost*. The movements in the novel are however, like time, preserved in the structure, a structure composed of movements all parts of which are simultaneously visible" (Jephcott 285).

The flux and mobility with which an inanimate object (such as a steeple) is invested prefigures its movement in time, which is effected through metaphor: the third phase of the privileged moment's evocation.

Thus, movement through space (via verbs) foreshadows movement through time (via metaphor), as the present and past merge. An object's fixation in time (like its stasis in space) is shattered—and this too is one of the hallmarks of the many privileged moments in *Recherche*. In Jephcott's words, "[T]ime is not confined to the present moment; it shows its whole span at once, so that the sense of its passing disappears" (107). The eternal within the temporal is revealed; the temporal is revealed as a moment in a pattern of eternity—and this extension into the fourth dimension of time, coupled with its movement through space, is what characterizes the Proustian " privileged moment."

FIGURATION AND THE PROUSTIAN SUBLIME

Figuration completes the alliteration of the self-Other dyad, rendering the Other in terms of the self, which not only facilitates its assimilation into the self, but the liberation of the ideal self from within the self. Metaphors of the steeples proliferate in a progression that commences in the Other and culminates in the self: "like three birds perched upon the plain," "like three golden pivots," "three flowers painted upon the sky," and finally, like "three maidens in a legend abandoned in a solitary place over which night had begun to fall" (SW 139). The fact that the steeples are compared, not to real flowers, but to flowers "painted upon the sky" is significant inasmuch as it reinscribes the primacy of art over nature, of the abstract over the concrete, of the painted object over its objective correlative—the sky here serving as the easel. More importantly, while "birds" and "golden" and "flowers" are common tropes of the creative impulse, it is the image of the "three maidens in a legend abandoned in a solitary place over which night had begun to fall" that effaces the gap between self and Other insofar as it not only reinscribes the imprisonment of Geneviève de Brabant in her Merovingian tower, but Marcel's incarceration in his bedroom during the "drame coucher": "abandoned in a solitary place over which night had begun to fall." The three steeples isolated on the plain as night is falling become emblems of Marcel's profound sense of solitude, isolated in the enchanted wasteland of differentiation, lost in the expanse of his Otherness (as a male, as a homosexual, as a Jew, and as an artist)—effecting the two-in-one.

The steeples of Martinville are emblems of a differentiated self. This is the essence of their deep correspondence with the narrator. They kindle a sense of kinship even as they rekindle a creative impulse whose candle flame was guttering in doubts. The novel that is the culminating effect of the creative impulse reawakened here will itself be a free-standing monument to a differentiated self as provocative as the three spires on the darkling plain of Martinville: the holy triumvirate of Marcel's rebirth to art.

The three steeples are a topos of the ideal self, dramatically resurrected after its death on the first "black date in the calendar." All the dynamics of the self-Other dyad (of penetration, conversion, and assimilation, of movement, metaphor, and metamorphosis) are abundantly in play in the "privileged moment" of the steeples. They sustain the allegory of differentiation and invention, as figures of redemption that brighten the bleak landscape of damnation that is *Recherche*—a discontinuous fragment that fosters the continuity of the self across time and space.

Metaphor allows the narrator to relate the Other to the self by finding within it that which is common to the self (in this case, the isolation of the steeples). If the tea-soaked madeliene is a metaphor for the undifferentiated communion of a self with itself, than by contrast the steeples trope on the self's differentiation from its surroundings, even as they evoke, like the madeleine-infused tea, the artistic solution to this fundamental problem. Figuration is the dominant element of Proust's style—or, as Deleuze asserts, style is, for Proust, "essentially metaphor. But metaphor is essentially metamorphosis, and indicates how the two objects exchange their determinations, exchange even the names which designate them, in a new medium which confers the common quality upon them" (47). In these privileged moments, metaphor is the medium for the metamorphosis of the Other into the self, which enables the self to "envelop" the Other in the "necessary rings of a beautiful style" (PR 1008). The dynamics of the self-Other dyad are largely informed by the series of movement, metaphor, metamorphosis, operating in servitude to possessive desire, functioning as a strategy of self-possession—whose ultimate desire is to possess the ideal self (the artist).

The protean, liberatory role of metaphor at Martinville distinguishes this "privileged moment" from that of the madeleine and the uneven paving stones that begin and commence The Search. Whereas involuntary memory is the medium for reintegrating the self in those moments, it is metaphor that reunites the self at Martinville: that erases the hyphen of the self-Other dyad, precipitating a selfobject hybrid. Deleuze's reading is informative: "[T]his is why Proust carefully distinguishes the two cases of sensuous signs: reminiscences and discoveries—the 'resurrections of memory,' and the 'truths written with the help of figures'"(52)—the difference between remembrance and invention.

In yet another provocative departure from the critical tradition, Margaret Gray argues that the metaphors of the three steeples (birds, pivots, flowers, and maidens), far from connoting a coherent progression, signify instead a contradiction: "[E]ach image thus negates and replaces the preceding in a fractured, disjointed succession whose rupture of all progression has escaped critical attention" (122). Gray argues that this series of contradictory images, far from investing the steeples with mobility, "arrests and fixes the steeples in immobilized 'stills' that fracture the narrator's moving perspective":

> [T]he effect of the images is thus to fix the spectacle . . . fractur[ing] the experience he purports to describe. . . . [F]iguration here seems to work to hide, distance, and protect the world it claims to represent . . . would seem to act as a protective screen against interpretation's aggressions. (123)

Gray asserts that, far from converting the essence of the Other into a fragment of the self which can then be assimilated into the self, extending the domain of the self both spatially and temporally, metaphor actually functions to resist the aggressions of the interpreting self, actually betrays the purpose for which it was deployed—contradicting and mystifying the self it purportedly serves, exposing the text (even the "text" of Marcel's own writing) not as coherent and unified but as fragmented and self-contradicting: a text that deconstructs itself. However, the very series of images itself suggests an instability, a mobility, a tendency of the steeples to shift rapidly among these diverse images—a refusal of the very fixation allotted to them by Gray. Moreover, this series of images is evidence of a figuration that is not contradictory and fixating, but unstable and fecund—evinces not a tendency to fixate meaning in a single image, but to distribute it among many (sometimes contradictory) images.

Meaning as figured in this privileged moment is not static but kinetic, not simple but complex, not reductive but multiple. The steeples are like a bird, like a pivot, like a painting—but finally and most importantly, like individuals who are isolated from one another—as the sexes are isolated from one another, as the homosexual is isolated from society, as the Jew is isolated among his kind, and as the artist stands apart from society. In his perceptive analysis of optical imagery in *Recherche*, Roger Shattuck observes that "when the testimony of our senses reaches the mind, it becomes image. But . . . never one only: many images, in rapid and delayed and intermittent succession, and for the most part contradictory" (22). Each of the images captures a different essence of the steeples—the three maidens "abandoned to a solitude in which the night was falling" poignantly trope on the lonely isolation of Marcel in his bedroom, sundered from the maternal sublime. The contradiction between these images is not one that calcifies the meanings of the steeples, but sets those multiple meanings in motion between these diverse signifiers, frees them to fly from one post to the other in this signifying chain—like the carriage that is itself flying across the Martinville landscape. Shattuck continues: "[A] succession of contradictory images going under one name and 'passing' by convention as a single person or sentiment or social entity—this is probably the most striking aspect of the Proustian universe. . . . His vision is not of a unified, comprehensible, and motionless world . . ." (23–24).

The chain of Proustian signifiers is often multiple, contradictory—refusing to shut down meaning in a single signifier. From the steeples he frees multiple signifiers, like the ravens that burst from the steeple of St. Hilaire each dusk, whose flight signifies the freedom of the creative impulse loosed from its subjective prison. The bird, the painting, and the pivot each tropes on an essence of the steeples: if the bird signs the liberation of the creative self, "painting" reinforces the privileging of the abstract over the real, and "pivot" posits the steeples as a figurative fulcrum that leverages Marcel between the space/time, material/immaterial, objective/subjective continuum. Further, the fragmentary nature of these disconnected images recuperates the autonomy of the free-standing fragment throughout *Recherche*: Vermeer's "patch of yellow light," Vinteuil's "little phrase," Wagner's shepherd's solo in *Lohengrin*, Mme Verdurin's "little clan" all attest to the ubiquity of the discontinuous fragment. Finally, the seeming contradiction between the birds, the flowers, and the maidens vanishes amidst their common isolation: "perched on a plain," "above the low line of the fields," and "abandoned to a solitude"— images that are united in the common sediment of solitude, to which the steeples belong as well.

Far from concealing or contradicting the essence of the steeples, these images manifest and reinforce it: as signs of solitude whose proliferation in Marcel's imagination attest to the animation of the creative impulse, from which these signs arise and to which they return. Therefore, I must disagree with Gray's interpretation, provocative though it may be, that "figuration's excesses rupture their confines as description and begin to usurp the world described . . . throttling narrative momentum, which [has] run aground by the weight of figuration" (125). Figuration not only preserves the relations between signifiers, but by figuring the steeples as emblems of a differentiated self, enables that self to extend its domain spatially and temporally. Figuration sustains the ardent search of the self to find the lost and scattered fragments of itself, dispersed across the landscapes of space and time. Figuration, finally, helps the self recompose itself from these rediscovered fragments— each of which comprises a piece in the uncompleted puzzle of the self. Far from "throttling narrative momentum," figuration sustains it through the diverse topoi of Méséglise and Martinville, of Balbec, Hudimesnil, and Venice, through the vicissitudes of doubt and discovery, epiphany and mystification, suffering and salvation.

Far from "throttling" narrative momentum, figuration, if anything, quickens its aggressions—is the effect of a narrative it has helped accelerate—which quickens in the presence of metaphor by throwing off more metaphor like a torrent that slips the constraints of its banks. Far from immobilizing the steeples, these images reanimate them, propelling them through a chain of signifiers. While they do not contradict interpretation, they resist the essentialization of the steeples under any one sign while paradoxically reinforcing their association with the sign of isolation—and with the even broader sign of "Marcel." Far from resisting the aggressions of interpretation, these images reinforce its aggressive designs on the Other. Thus, the "interpretive, appropriative work of the mind" is not, as Gray asserts, "confounded" by its own figuration, by a "persistently impossible image," but indeed accomplishes its greatest work through figuration, by creating a work that is metaphorical in the literal as well as the figurative sense—in which virtually everything in the work is associative, is understood only through its associations: associations that, moreover, do not conceal meaning, but reveal it, do not "throttle" narrative momentum, but recuperate and redouble it, through the transformative associations they reveal to the self.

Far from signifying the collapse of the "assimilative enterprise" (127), figuration brings it to its spiritual climax. Interpretation, far from being "overtaken" by figuration, realizes its desires through figuration (128). In contradistinction to the opaque signs of the "roof, the gleam of sunlight on stone," the opacity of the sign at Martinville is converted into a transparent sign of the self, evidencing not the impotency, but the efficacy of the interpretative act. The "flattening" of reality into an abstract image, as evidenced by the conflation of the flowers, the steamer, and the butterfly at Balbec, and again by the figure of an Albertine "painted against the backdrop of the sea," far from "effacing the world" as Gray argues, merely reinforces the narrator's tendency to abstract it, to reconfigure it in a figurative image that transfigures our understanding of reality by contradicting the habitual disfigurements of the intellect. The essence of Proustian impressionism is an illusion that precedes intellectualization, which undoes impressionism's striking re-creation of the world. Far from "effacing" reality, the Proustian image recreates it—along impressionistic lines, by flattening three dimensions into two. In the final analysis, Proustian figuration is, like everything in the work, ambiguous: if on some occasions it reinforces the aggressions of interpretation, then on others it confounds them. However, even the association of the steeples with an image painted upon the horizon reinforces Marcel's preference for the abstract over the concrete, reinscribes his tendency to dematerialize three-dimensional objects into two-dimensional images, in what is essentially a celebration of art over "reality"—which reflects a preference for interpreted reality over reality itself.

The excesses of Proustian figuration are prompted by the desire to "display" the idealized self—evidence of a desire to apparel that self in figuration once it is fortuitously "outed" from the closet of its "privileged" object. To the extent it mirrors the ideal self, figuration satisfies the "ideal-hungry" and "mirror-hungry" desires of the self. The prolific flowering of the Proustian figure is a displacement of the narcissistic gaze, an objectification of the ideal self that satisfies the self's dual need to "read" and to "be read." The desire of the profane self to be the object of a collective gaze is thwarted in reality, displaced onto the plane of illusion where it apparels itself in figuration, crossdresses in the costume of the ideal self (the artist), vicariously satisfying the desire to become the fixated object of the collective gaze.

Imagery, figuration, metaphor is the effluence of a sublimated exhibitionism. Every effort to liberate the essence of an object is merely a displacement of the desire to free the self from itself, to liberate the creative and profane selves within the living self. When figuration expends itself in excess there follows a little death of the self, a lapsing back into the self, that renews the desire to display the self, which it fulfills by objectifying its profane and sacred selves in ink. In *Recherche*, this display is always an effect of a rediscovered self, upon whose chance discovery it is dependent. The self is thus impelled to search for itself, for the lost fragments of the self that resonate across the years. Metaphor is the vehicle by which the self reintegrates itself across time, in the process liberating the creative self that will narrate the self's long struggle to constitute and reconstitute itself. Only figuration can bring forth this ideal self from itself—as if the narrator is driven by a solitary mandate: "Go figure!"

The image of the "three maidens" elevates the steeples above the images of themselves (birds, pivots, painting) to an image of the self. Figuration, in the throes of its own excess, consummates the desire for the two-in-one. This desire is fulfilled at the moment the self comes to "know" the Other: a knowledge it gains through metaphor or involuntary memory. In this sense then, the creative process in Proust does constitute a working off of sublimated sexual desires—but to claim it is this and nothing more is to oversimplify the complex origins of the creative impulse.

I agree with Gray's assertion that Proustian figuration is, in the last analysis, postmodern insofar as he resists deploying metaphor for merely mimetic, or descriptive, purposes—as a medium for ficting objective reality, using it instead to explode the subject-object binary. Gray writes, "Proust's postmodern use of figuration . . . is coercive in its subtlety, imperceptibly entwined as it is within the very mimetic conventions it overturns" (132). In contradistinction to Gray, however, I disagree that Proustian figuration restores and replenishes the opacity of the privileged object, acting as "protective shields against the narrator's aggressive, 'sterilizing' interpretive efforts . . . that explicitly interrupt and explode the mind's domestication of experience . . . suggesting the baffling power of the sublime" (134). If the sublime is fugitive, it is so only that it may ultimately be possessed in the signs of art—signs that are not mere shields, but lances as well, and which sign the fugitive sublime as immortally as the heraldic shields of the Merovingian sublime. If, as Kant asserts, the sublime "was what could not be absorbed by the mind, which encountering the sublime, could only fall back upon itself" (Gray 134), then we must modify the Kantian sublime as that which formerly could only be apprehended by religion, but which now (since the liberation of art from religion), can only be apprehended in art, that is, through a religion of genius imparting immortal form to the sublime essences of the self apprehended through involuntary memory and figuration. The sublime is a fugitive of the self, until apprehended and objectified in art. Figuration does not reinforce the opacity of the sublime, but reveals it through a transparency that is also transformative. In converting the Other into the self, metaphor facilitates the assimilation of both into the artist. Marcel's ensuing "rapture and felicity" do not arise (as Gray asserts) "in the gaps between experience and interpretation," in the disjunction between object and subject, but in their immortalizing reintegration through art. It is his deep conflict, his persistent sorrow that arises in the gaps between subject and object; his profound ecstasy is born from the closing of this gap—a breach that was created in boyhood, if not at birth, by his separation from the maternal sublime. This wound remains raw until healed in the winding shroud of art, by the suturing of the wound between the material and the immaterial: a suturing effected by the rediscovery that the two are indeed one.

Recherche is an allegory of suffering that ends in salvation, of damnation that ends in redemption, of sickness that ends in health, of vice that ends in virtue, of disintegration that ends in reintegration, of differentiation that ends in association, and of imprisonment that ends in liberation—in which a self destabilized by sexual differentiation is restabilized by the associative chains of invention. The differentiation of self and Other ends in the "perpetual alliteration" of the self with its ideal self—an inward alliteration which is the principal effect of the self's external alliteration with the Other-as-self.

IMPLICATIONS OF THE RUSKINIAN SUBLIME

The image of the three maidens in a legend also reflects the influence of Ruskin, as well as the predominance of a pattern of representation whose recurring goal is to apprehend the eternal within the temporal. This is often the hidden essence of any given object whose existence not only inspires the narrator's absolute faith and diligent search, but which comprises as well the means of his salvation after the bitter disappointments of love, friendship, and society. His quest is nothing more (nor less) than an attempt to separate the false from the genuine avenues of salvation. In this, he is genuinely inspired by the career of Ruskin, who "seemed to have gained sure access to an eternal reality that . . . Proust saw in [him], and in imitation of [his life] and work, a way to [his] own salvation" (Jephcott 104). I will develop the implications for the creative impulse of Proust's liberatory critique of Ruskin in the final chapter. For now I want to concentrate on the aesthetic alliteration between Ruskin and Proust which preceded Proust's break from the master, and which engendered in his writing an idolatrous mimesis. To what extent is *Recherche* informed by Ruskin's aesthetic ideology?

Ruskin revealed to Proust the means of achieving through literature his own salvation, by revealing the immanence of the eternal in the temporal. Consequently, his work was for Proust prophetic. The centrality of the "privileged moment" in *Recherche* (of which the encounter with the steeples is typical) is Ruskinian. As Jephcott asserts, "[T]he privileged moment, realized by artistic creation, is described by Ruskin as a major formative experience in his life" (104–105). Proust evolves a novel in which the evocation of a series of privileged moments is inseparably yoked to the narrator's own salvation (the means to which is revealed to him in the final volume, through a series of "privileged moments") and for which he searches throughout, exploring the equally enchanting though ultimately fruitless avenues of friendship, love, and society before finding his true salvation through art. This plot unifies and dramatizes The Search in a manner that elevates it above *Jean Santeuil*, that resolves the critical flaws of its predecessor, which includes a similar series of privileged moments that are nevertheless disconnected from the plot, that are not a unifying means to a dramatic end, but posited as ends in themselves. Yet little of the "failed" *Santeuil* is wasted; the essence of its privileged moments is absorbed into the mature work, as is its basic vision of reality. After the critical revelations of Ruskin, Proust is able to associate art in general, and writing in particular, with spirituality and salvation, was "able to believe in the possibility of identifying work with spiritual and artistic progress. . . . It gave [him] not only a doctrine of salvation, but also a practical program," if not the plot for his masterpiece (Jephcott 106). Venice thus becomes the logical, if not inevitable destination of his spiritual pilgrimage toward artistic salvation: a role for which Proust has been preparing the reader since Combray, where it is foregrounded in Swann's discourse on the Venetian sublime, and on the singularity of its "ancient architecture," which prompts the narrator's Venetian pilgrimage, even as this interest in Venetian architecture leads Proust to Ruskin. As Deleuze asserts, "Swann is the great unconscious initiator, the point of departure for the series" (73). That Marcel's final epiphany foregrounds the stone steps of this citadel of high art is altogether fitting insofar as "steps" trope on the developmental process of the artistic bildung whose "steps" The Search recounts. The baptistery to which these steps lead is a symbol of the eternal redemption that awaits Marcel as a reward for his successful and faithful pilgrimage to art. The object that is the subject of each privileged moment comprises a "piece of a more intense reality isolated from the everyday world" and is capable of propagating itself through space and time (110, 111). The critical flaws of *Santeuil* are absorbed into the "perpetual alliteration" between the plot and the "privileged moments" of *Recherche*. It is evident from the nature of the self-Other dyad that Proust reaped rich dividends from his study of Ruskin, that he "found confirmation of [his] most intangible belief: that there exists beyond the empirical world a realm of eternity which is also a realm of memory and inwardness" (112). The spires of Martinville incarnate a self that is lost in a circle of solitude, even as they eternalize a self as continuous as the circle of seasons that rounds on itself.

The encounter with the steeples ends as it began: in the spiritual ecstasy of the self. The pleasure experienced at the conclusion of this encounter, however, is quite different from Marcel's initial pleasure: it is the pleasure of creation versus the awakening of the desire to create; it is the pleasure of artistic fulfillment as opposed to the pleasure of artistic yearning; it is the creative counterpart to the consummation of a physical desire as opposed to the desire itself. The pleasure of the desire to objectify the self is surpassed by the objectification of the self in writing, and his redoubled joy is nothing more nor less than this remainder, than this surfeit of pleasure. The fusion of the $1 + 1 = 1$ releases energy in the form of writing, throws the ideal self off in the light of creation. The long struggle to free the ideal self from within the profane self is suddenly, if temporarily, crowned with the liberation of that self: a release attended with joyous shouts. At this juncture language fails, lapses into nonverbal expression, having reached that realm of spirituality beyond language. Creation breeds a joy for which there are quite simply no words:

> I had finished writing it, I found such a sense of happiness, felt that it had so entirely relieved my mind of the obsession of the steeples, and of the mystery which they concealed, that, as though I myself were a hen and had just laid an egg, I began to sing at the top of my voice. (SW 140)

The expression of his voice in song reflects the discovery of his voice in writing. Having inscribed the ideal self once in ink, having objectified it in writing, he knows he can do it again—and indeed the pleasure experienced engenders the need for the experience of creation, for which reality provides no substitutes. Further, unlike possessive desire, the desire to create does not perish in the act of creation. The consummation of desire in creation instead of killing desire, renews it. The desire to create is a renewable resource—is a self-sustaining feedback loop—that sustains the ideal self. The idolatry of possessive desire yields to the religion of creative desire, by which it is absorbed. The two idolatrous and divided ways of love and society merge into the authentic path of art—as a sensual apostasy evolves into a spiritual pilgrimage where sins of the flesh and of the heart prepare the way for the soul's salvation.

Marcel's long pilgrimage to art, embodied in the pilgrimage to Venice, the citadel of art, and for which the pilgrimages to Balbec and the gardens of the Faubourg St. Germain are false surrogates, is in reality an objectification of an inward pilgrimage to the ideal self. This liberation of this imprisoned self is the Holy Grail of his quest. In *The Religion of Art in Proust*, Barbara J. Bucknall articulates the primacy of metaphor in this process:

> The literary expression of this escape, of this jailbreak from the prison house of matter, is provided by the metaphor which, by its nature, breaks through

all conceptual restrictions, binding the most disparate elements together. . . . Hence the importance of metaphors in the book the narrator plans to write. . . . A work of literature celebrating a sense of intellectual and emotional release through an experiential metaphor fittingly relies on metaphor to express that release ["a hen that had just laid an egg"]. (11)

Metaphor is a cause of the narrator's escape from temporality and an effect of it. The metaphors of *Recherche* are as ubiquitous as the equals signs in Einstein's revolutionizing equations: are the binding force in a literary calculus whose fictional universe foregrounds its laws, and particularly its laws of motion. Through his manipulation of fixed surfaces, Proust animates objects, in the process moving our souls in ways they have never been moved, coursing them in directions never traveled—though all trajectories converge in a deeper correspondence with the self.

The steeples of Martinville stimulate the premature birth of an exalted self. This self does not survive. It lapses back into the profane self. But its brief emergence facilitates the genuine birth of the creative self in the spiritual denouement of *Recherche*—even as a second birth is eased by the labors of the first. The spiritual birth canal has been primed by this false birth of the ideal self, which perishes in the blood of its own ink, which dies in the act of being born. But the lasting significance of Martinville is that the laboring self has succeeded in throwing itself off in creation, has completed the long pilgrimage from impulse to ink. The joy it experiences is plowed back into the self, like fertilizer into the earth, enfecundating the seed of the self immured there. The happiness it earns is reinvested in the business of the self—and that business has but one aim: the liberation of the creative impulse into the Sistene labor of creation.

The birth of the creative impulse is the result of a protean dialectic between self and Other: a dialectic that had devolved into a tragic isolation of opposites, overdetermined by differentiation. The spark of invention dwells in the synapse of the self-Other dyad, travels a two-way circuit that leads from the self to the Other and back to the self: in which the Other is figured with mobility, transfigured with imagery, and configured as an extension of the self. The sign first announces itself as a resonance within the self: a resonance that betrays and foreshadows its essence as a fragment of the self, and which is in reality a displacement of the creative impulse struggling to free itself. The fetus kicking at the walls of the womb. The surface movement of the "privileged" object is not an "echo from without, but a resonance from within" (64), akin to the skin of the pregnant womb in whose sudden movements one detects the life growing within.

First, the implications of the sign are developed, after which it is explicated, extracted, evacuated from the object, converted into a sign, not of the object, but of the self, to which it beckons like an imprisoned mate. As

Deleuze observes, "[I]mplication and explication, envelopment and development: such are the categories of the Search. First of all, meaning is implicated in the sign; it is like one thing wrapped within another. The captive, the captive soul signify that there is always an involution, an involvement of the diverse." Deleuze continues:

> [B]ut the metaphors of implication correspond further to the images of explication. For the sign develops, uncoils at the same time that it is interpreted . . . still half sheathed in the object . . . [its] meaning half depends on the subject. . . . What is essential in the Search is not memory and time, but the sign . . . what is essential is not to remember, but to learn. (89)

As evidenced by the meta-drama of Martinville, and elsewhere in The Search, the "sign" to which Marcel apprentices himself is the artistic sign—not absolutely, but as part of a problematic, yet generative dialectic between the signs of art and life, whose conflict intensifies the creative impulse, thereby facilitating its consummation in creation. If at times, Marcel appears to be "nowhere near a pen" (Gray 148) and the artistic bildung seems naught but a fiction of criticism, this is as it should be in a dialectic struggle between art and life, where as often as not the creative impulse is subsumed by the impulse to live, so deliciously embodied in the hedonistic vices of Paris in the Belle Epoch. Yet even Marcel's repeated apostasies from his pilgrimage to art, ("apprenticeship to signs") are an essential part of it insofar as the conflicts associated with them, and the psychological effects engendered by them (guilt and shame) reanimate the creative impulse, even as they supply the material for it.

The outcome of the narrator's encounter with the steeples recuperates the vitality of the interpreting intellect in the knowledge-making process. Interpretation develops the meaning of the sign as a chemical solution develops the image of a negative. Deleuze concludes: "[W]e are wrong to believe in facts, there are only signs. We are wrong to believe in truths; there are only interpretations" (90). Having been a critic himself, it is not surprising that Proust's narrative not only foregrounds the creative imagination and the involuntary memory, but critical interpretation itself as a means of making meaning. All are united under the sign and The Search. Deleuze continues:

> What unites . . . is the sign and the corresponding apprenticeship. . . . Everything is implicated, everything is complicated . . . everything exists in those obscure zones which we penetrate as into crypts, in order to decipher hieroglyphs and secret languages. The Egyptologist . . . is the man who undergoes an initiation—the apprentice. (91)

The apprenticeship, however, is not merely an apprenticeship to signs, but an apprenticeship to signs of the self that hide in plain sight. The Search is no mere search for knowledge, but a Search for those scattered fragments of an immortal self that longs to reconstitute itself immortally. *Recherche* could just as accurately be retitled, "In Search of Lost Selves"—for the dominant image it generates is of a self searching for its dismembered parts, its dominant pattern one of disintegration and reintegration, its dominant psychological model that of a personality splintered by childhood trauma into fragmentary personalities, which are therapeutically re-fused into a core personality through art. That which was whole dissociates into its determining fragments, until reconstituted in art.

At the root of this urge is a need to differentiate the self from the world through art. The self-Other dyad is governed by this tension between differentiation and undifferentiation: it produces the central conflict, the resolution of which drives the narrator's search. The self's search for a means to merge the self with the Other masks a deeper motive: which is to assert the self's dominion over the Other. The "merger-hungry" personality is in essence a parasitic personality: the parasitism of the self functioning in servitude to a creative impulse, which risks being subsumed by the Other in order to subsume the Other in itself. The ultimate outcome of the self-Other dyad is one of ingestion, replicating the moment of the petites madeleines, whose "essence" is literally consumed by the self, is in fact an essence of the self, that bloats itself on its self. Rank succinctly foregrounds the critical role of language in differentiating the creative self: the aim of language (and of art) is not merely to "identify with what it imitates but, more than that, to dominate it and make itself independent of it. This is, however, the formula for all creating, which fundamentally aims, not at a duplication, but at a substitution. By creating, man makes himself independent of that which exists" (240). Doubrovsky concurs: "You are never yourself, unless you create yourself in language" (31). Creation, which is a form of language expression, facilitates the self's dominion over the world through the word—or other signs of the symbolic.

The real significance of the privileged moment of the Martinville steeples is that it prefigures the narrator's rebirth through the signs of art in the novel's climax. Deleuze's observations are instructive:

> At the end of the Search, the interpreter understands what had escaped him in the case of the madeleine or even of the steeples: that the material meaning is nothing without an ideal essence which it incarnates. . . . Now the world of art is the ultimate world of signs, and these signs, as though dematerialized, find their meaning in an ideal essence. Henceforth, the world revealed by art reacts on all the others . . . it integrates them, colors them with an esthetic meaning and imbues what was opaque. . . . This is why all the signs converge upon art: all apprenticeships, by the most diverse paths, are already unconscious apprenticeships to art itself. (130)

Marcel's "apprenticeships" to love and high society are unconscious apprenticeships to art insofar as they not only enervate the impulse to create, but provide the raw material it reshapes into art. The signs of love and high society are clay in the potter's hands of the creative urge, as well as splinters under the fingernails of his soul, which only objectification in the realm of the symbolic can remove from his soul.

The encounter with the three steeples is typical of many "privileged moments" insofar as the self projects itself into the Other, rendering a material sign that is not static, distinct, and mimetic, but dynamic, alliterative, and transformative. By the time he pens *Recherche*, Proust "has departed from the direct transcription of experience" (Jephcott 268). Objective reality is a fiction, "not a duplication, but a substitution"—an imaginative surrogate whose symbiosis with the self reinscribes the lost symbiosis with the mother. As such, the material world is a surrogate for the mother, with whom the narrator's profane self desires to merge, even as his ideal self struggles to emerge from its dependency on the mother. Hence, the emotionalism of Marcel's relation to material things. Finally, and most significantly, only one thing can sever his emotional dependence on the mother and the material world: art. Only language (writing) makes possible the complete differentiation of the self from the mother/Other. This transcendent differentiation of an ideal self in artistic signs, which subsumes the sorrows of sexual differentiation, is the goal toward which the narrator struggles throughout. The inability to fully and finally differentiate the self from the Other is the reason for the cosmic delay of the narrator's birth to art. The birth of art is coincidental with the mother's death. The end of the son's dependency on the mother signifies the independence of the artist, who then becomes the mother of his own invention.

The privileged moments in *Recherche* undergo a quantitative reduction and a qualitative heightening relative to their counterparts in *Jean Santeuil*. There are fewer of them but, as Jephcott observes, they play a "decisive part . . . in Marcel's literary vocation":

> The incident involving the Martinville steeples . . . shows how these moments can lead to literary creation [though] it is not until the end of the novel that a series of privileged moments of involuntary memory reveals his vocation to him and at the same time provides him with the material for his novel. (268–69)

Jephcott notes the critical distinction as well as the significant similarity between the two types of privileged moments (those deriving from direct perception and those associated with involuntary memory): "The vocation is first revealed by moments of direct perception, but is only realized through involuntary memory." Jephcott continues:

> Proust's task is to show that there is a continuity between the two kinds of experience, that the reality revealed by the steeples is the same as that dis-

closed by the "madeleine," the napkin, etc. In *Time Regained* [PR 1000]he argues that the two experiences are the same because they both demand a creative effort. (269)

Jephcott's analysis underscores the importance of both "interpretation" and "conversion" to the self's meaning-making process. As Deleuze observes, these "sensuous signs of the imagination" (the steeples) take Marcel a critical step closer to the signs of art inasmuch as they activate the creative process, unlike the sensuous signs of memory (the madeleine), which form only a "'beginning of art,'"

> [only] "set us on the path of art." Our apprenticeship would never find its realization in art, if it did not pass through those signs which give us a foretaste of time regained, and prepare us for the fulfillment of esthetic Ideas. But they do nothing more than prepare us: a mere beginning. (53)

These privileged moments of the sensuous signs of memory and imagination herald the privileged moments of art, which finally liberate the creative impulse into a sustained creation: which sustains the ideal self for the rest of its life, and gains for it the guarantee of afterlife. Deleuze develops the implications of art for spirituality: "[I]t is only in art that the sign becomes immaterial, at the same time that its meaning becomes spiritual. . . . Art is the splendid final unity of an immaterial sign and a spiritual meaning" (84–85). Proust has reinvented Ruskin's vision of art as the locus of the spiritual sublime, situating that vision, not in an "ancient architecture" that bears the "stain of time," but in a cathedral of words whose architectonics reflect the implication of the eternal in the temporal, of the spiritual in the symbolic. The steeples of Martinville enact the rebirth of the ideal and the spiritual through the symbolic.

THE TREE OF [ANTI] KNOWLEDGE: HUDIMESNIL AND THE MYSTIFYING SIGN

The three trees of Hudimesnil comprise, paradoxically, a contradiction and a reinscription of the three steeples of Martinville. The same aesthetic principles of composition are in play, the same dynamics that governed the self-Other dyad at Martinville are in evidence, but the outcome is the precise opposite: the mystification of an interpreting self. The same fourfold process governs the representation of this second triad, commencing with the pleasure that is suddenly aroused in the narrator:

> We came down towards Hudimesnil; suddenly I was overwhelmed with that profound happiness which I had not often felt since Combray; happiness analogous to that which had been given me by . . . the steeples of Martinville. . . . That pleasure which I must create for myself, experienced only on rare occasions, but . . . in attaching myself to the reality of that pleasure alone, I could at length begin to lead a new life. (WBG 543, 544)

The narrator's observation is significant inasmuch as it reinforces the artistic nature of this pleasure ("which I must create for myself"). The pleasure is embedded in the act of creation. Marcel's failure to discover the correspondence between self and Other that is struggling to fight its way into his consciousness frustrates the creative impulse and produces the existential gloom with which this "privileged moment" concludes. Whereas the privileged moment of the three steeples ends in the transformative ecstasy of creation, this one ends only in the bitter disappointment of a lost opportunity to bridge the abyss between self and Other, to rediscover the self immured within the Other and give it artistic expression. The disappointment of Hudimesnil is redoubled by the realization that he was on the brink of discovering a similar alliteration between self and Other. His agony is quickened by this "so close, and yet so far" experience. Better to have never felt the immortal presence of this lost self, than to be teased by its resurrection. Instead of a transformative association, self and Other remain in their "sealed vessels." Marcel's desire "remained incomplete" because it is not consummated in cognition. The failure of Hudimesnil reinscribes the tragic and neurotic disconnect between the unconscious and conscious mind. He hears the divine prisoner calling to him, but cannot locate the captive. After approaching his consciousness, it lapses back into the perpetual gloom of oblivion that is the forgetfulness of the unconscious mind. Marcel draws close to one of his lost selves only to be sundered from it finally and forever, kindling an anxiety of separation as acute as that experienced toward the mother, and which similarly has about it the savor of death and oblivion.

Oblivion and resurrection comprise a recurring dialectic in The Search, and both are in play in the privileged moments, the outcomes of which hover between the death and the rebirth of the self: an immortal fragment of which lapses back into the abyss of nonbeing from which it will arise nevermore. The finality of this loss is what prompts Marcel's sorrow—in contradistinction to the ineffable happiness he experiences at Martinville. An allegory of liberation and immortality devolves into a recurring allegory of captivity and oblivion. In this "privileged moment" it is the self's perpetual isolation that is signified, as opposed to its "perpetual alliteration" with the Other as figured in the series of the petite madeleine, the steeples, the "little phrase" of the septet, and the final progression of "alliterations" at the Princess de Guermantes's reception. Moreover, this inability to bridge the abyss between a volitional intellect and the involuntary memory, between the conscious and the unconscious self, at Hudimesnil prefigures the intellect's impotency before the sign of the Sapphic sublime, incarnate in Albertine—and Marcel's subsequent descent into madness.

Martinville and Hudimesnil comprise a narrative couplet whose contrasting outcomes dramatize the dialectic between being and nothingness. Whereas Martinville heralds the victory of art over oblivion, Hudimesnil signifies the "black date" of the eternal calendar of oblivion into which the entire universe of *Recherche* will plunge by novel's end—with one notable exception: the immortal fragments of the self eternalized in art. Hudimesnil signifies the impotency of art and the intellect before oblivion, whose gravitational pull is akin to that of a "black hole" from which neither light nor matter escapes. To rescue a fragment of the self from oblivion, Marcel must overcome the gravitational tug of time—and the effort required is akin to that of rescuing a ray of light from a black hole. The defeat registered at Hudimesnil makes the victory achieved over oblivion at the Princess de Guermantes's reception the more remarkable—especially as it is achieved while the entire universe of *Recherche* is plunging into oblivion in what is tantamount to a Rembrandtian tableau of the Last Judgment in which the members of a civilization are being hurled into oblivion, largely as retribution for their vices: a mass damnation that contrasts with the solitary redemption to art of Marcel.

THE WILL VERSUS INVOLUNTARY MEMORY: IS MARCEL A CREDIBLE NARRATOR?

The implications of this defeat are registered at Hudimesnil in the words and imagery Proust deploys: "If you allow us to drop back into the hollow of this road from which we sought to raise ourselves up to you, a whole part of yourself which we were bringing to you will fall for ever into the abyss" (WBG 545). The imagery tropes on the failed efforts of the dead to rise from the grave—and on that fragment of the self that will "fall for ever into the abyss." If the steeples dramatize the Christ-like resurrection of a self that is eternal, the three trees evoke the specter of an oblivion that entombs previous selves in crypts comprised by the objects of Marcel's everyday world, whose proximity mocks his perpetual isolation from them. The potency of the creative impulse at Martinville is juxtaposed to the impotency of the intellect at Hudimesnil. The steeples, the trees, the cup of tea, or the uneven stone underfoot: all are caskets in which Marcel's various selves are entombed—and whether they are resurrected through art or remain forever interred in oblivion depends entirely on the ability of the conscious self to free them from their captivity in the unconscious: a fate governed by chance and dependent upon the will.

Whereas Hudimesnil dramatizes the disease of the will, which the narrator cites as the primary defect in his character and the deterministic cause of his neurosis, Martinville and the climactic series of epiphanies evince the triumph of the volition over oblivion. The narrative of *Recherche* unwrites its own most fundamental assertion: that the creative impulse is dependent on involuntary memory—is a function, not of the individual's will, but of chance. I would argue, however, that the development of the creative impulse owes as much to volition as to involuntary memory. If the "privileged moments" foreground the association of involuntary memory and the creative impulse, then the rest of Marcel's "apprenticeship to signs" evidences the conscious application of his volition over time, until it literally subsumes time. Marcel claims his neurosis is rooted in a defective will. Yet, if The Search evidences anything it is the self's ability to apply its will over time toward the realization of its primary goal: the liberation of the creative impulse.

As a novel rooted in fin-de-siècle ideologies, *Recherche* reflects the era's obsession with diseases of the will. As Michael Finn observes in his perceptive analysis, *Proust, The Body and Literary Form* (1999), "When Andre Gide's *Cahiers d'Andre Walter* appeared in 1891, Marcel Schwob interpreted the work as a symbolic representation of the nervous exhaustion that seemed to have affected a whole generation of fin-de-siècle youth" (37). If true, this would explain the focus and efficacy of Rank's "will psychology": a therapeutic method whose principal goal was the reactivation of a diseased will. Finn continues,

> *A la Recherche de temps perdu* may well have been seen, by its author, as a biography of a neurasthenic, the story of an individual who suffers from a disease of the will, but who succeeds in understanding his ailment, and overcomes it by discovering special sources of energy. (41)

As a "special source of energ(y)," creativity is more therapeutic in and of itself than involuntary memory in curing a diseased will. The era's literary, scientific, and historical focus on the will is significant insofar as it assigns much greater agency to the individual in realizing the creative impulse than Freud's collective and biologically deterministic theory of the Oedipus complex, even as it calls into question the credibility of Proust's narrator in attributing the origins of the creative urge to involuntary memory. The careers of Proust and Rank converge on these theories of the will and "willpower deficit," which explains their mutual idolatry of Schopenhauer (Finn 47), whose *The World as Will and Idea* (1888), endeavored to "explain the world by the notion of the will (or intuition), and to downplay the importance of the rational intelligence" (47). Rank's idolatry of Schopenhauer surfaces in his Daybooks: "The high point of this period, and perhaps its unconscious goal was my acquaintance with the philosophy of Schopenhauer. What I have him to thank for, I will express in another place. Here I will only note that I looked at the world with other eyes" (qtd. in Taft 14).

While the disease of the will in *Recherche* has received much critical attention, the efficacy of the will in actuating and realizing the creative impulse has been largely overlooked, if not overshadowed by the attention given to involuntary memory, not only by Proust, but by criticism. Yet, the glamorous determinism assigned to involuntary memory in the "privileged moments" of The Search has more to do with satisfying the aesthetic demands of art than in providing an explanation for its genesis. This fictional emphasis on involuntary memory sheds a false, if seductive light with respect to the origins of the creative urge, even as it calls into question the narrator's credibility. In contradistinction to the claims of the "privileged moments," and as evidenced by Marcel's long "apprenticeship to signs," the volitional self is equally responsible for the liberation and development of the creative impulse. As Rank observes, it is the will that distinguishes the "neurotic from the productive type":

> With the productive type the will dominates, and exercises a far-reaching control over (but not check upon) the instincts. . . . And here we reach the essential point of difference between the productive type who creates and the thwarted neurotic. . . . Both are distinguished from the average type, who accepts himself as he is, by their tendency to exercise their volition in reshaping themselves. There is, however, this difference: that the neurotic, in this voluntary remaking of his ego, does not get beyond the destructive preliminary work and is therefore unable to detach the whole creative process from his own person and transfer it to an ideological abstraction. The productive artist [is able] to shift the creative will-power from his own person to ideological representations of that person and thus to render it objective. . . . [A] real understanding of these neurotic illnesses could not, however, be satisfactorily obtained as long as we tried to account for them in the Freudian sense by thwarted sexuality. What was wanted *in addition* was a grasp of the general problem of fear and of the will-psychology going therewith which should allow for the exercise of the will. Only through the will-to-self-immortalization . . . can we understand the interdependence of production and suffering . . . production [is the expression] of the will-ego . . . [of this] internal dualism of impulse and will, and in the creative type it is the latter which eventually gains the upper hand. Instinct presses in the direction of experience . . . while will drives to creation, and thus to immortalization. (40–44, my emphasis)

Freudian and Rankian theories of the creative impulse are not mutually exclusive. As criticism of *Recherche* evinces, Freudian readings have usefully informed the text for almost a century. What was wanted, however, was something *in addition:* a theory that accounted for the influence of neurosis, the desire for immortality, the need to replace what is lost, and the role of the will in realizing the creative urge—which Rank theorizes as a manifestation of the "will to form."

The advent of the cork-lined room is compelling evidence of a will determined to achieve its ends—by creating a solitude that optimizes the influence of the will, as it bends its determined gaze into the dark universe of the self. Indeed, the absence of solitude undermines the liberatory efforts of Marcel's will at Hudimesnil, sealing the doom of the self he was trying to save: "But if my mind was thus to collect itself, to gather strength, I should have to be alone. What would I not have given to be able to escape as I used to do on those walks along the Guermantes way, when I detached myself from my parents. It seemed indeed that I ought to do so now" (544). The volitional self that is usurped in the company of others is at his command when alone. What is required for the realization of the creative impulse once it is awakened by involuntary memory is an act of pure volition: is time alone to labor for its release. Only the will can raise the lost self from the depths of the unconscious mind into the conscious memory. To accomplish this requires absolute solitude, heroic effort, and time: all of which are guaranteed in the cork-lined bedroom. Society is anathema to the will laboring in servitude to the creative impulse: hence, the deflation of friendship in *Recherche*, which thwarts the needs of the ideal self while satisfying those of the profane self, though initially it may satisfy the needs of the ideal self to objectify itself in an idealized Other-who-is-same. Hence, the primacy assigned to images of solitude, such as the three steeples, the three trees, the "little phrase," and the "patch of yellow light": to all free-standing fragments of differentiation, which are emblems of a differentiated self, as well as the fragments of that self they entomb. These isolated fragments of a differentiated self seek their corresponding signs in the material world—become lodged in objects privileged for their own differentiation (steeples, trees, a musical phrase, a fragment of paint).

THE "DOUBLE EXPOSITION" OF THE PROUSTIAN SIGN

If opposite outcomes underscore the disparity between these two "privileged moments," then imagery reinforces the "perpetual alliteration" between them. The most obvious of these is the triadic nature of the trees and steeples. Kinetic imagery is another common element. As with the steeples, Marcel is viewing the trees while on the move, though this movement is similarly displaced onto the trees, which he "could see coming towards me," "gesticulating," and then withdrawing, "waving their despairing arms" (544, 545)—as the steeples had waved in farewell. A series of metaphors enhances the "alliteration" between Martinville and Huidimesnil, adding to the three dimensions of space the fourth dimension of time that associates the three trees with a past self: an association that frees them from their prison of temporality into a pattern of eternity, "making a pattern at which I was now not looking for the first time." Through metaphor, the trees are defined in terms of the self: they are compared to "a ring of witches or of norns who would propound their oracles to me," to "phantoms of the past, dear companions of my childhood, vanished friends who recalled our common memories. Like ghosts they seemed to be appealing to me to take them with me, to bring them back to life" (545). Metaphor invests the trees, as it did the steeples, with the ability to move in space and time. Further, the imagery of "witches," "norns," "ghosts," and "phantoms" underscores the fatalistic determinism of time, prefiguring the triumph of oblivion over art, of death over transfiguration. Whereas Martinville is a topos of the self's immortality, Hudimesnil is by contrast a topos of the self's mortality. Whereas the steeples engender a metaphysical ecstasy, this allegory of death and nothingness plunges Marcel into a morbid crisis: "I felt as wretched as though I had just lost a friend, had died myself, had broken faith with the dead or had denied my God" (545). If the steeples signify the soul's resurrection, the trees of Hudimesnil are akin to a hangman's oak.

The skillful manipulation of these "privileged moments" evidences the artistic growth Proust experienced from *Jean Santeuil* to *A la Recherche*. As noted by Jephcott, the privileged moment now plays a much greater part in the novel: "[I]nstead of evoking the experience as a source of pleasure, Proust uses it as a structural element in his work . . . uses a technique of juxtaposition in which the symbolized privileged moment throws light on other experiences . . . which are used only in direct relation to Marcel's vocation" (269–70). Georges Piroue also observes "the widespread use of this technique of 'double exposition' in the novel: 'The majority of main episodes in his novel go by twos'" (qtd. in Jephcott 279). For Marcel, redemption lies in that metaphysical contact zone where the three dimensions of space make contact with the fourth dimension of time, "at the immediate level where our experience is intense, unified, and individual" (Jephcott 272). If the impulse to create was rooted in neurotic conflict, then the aesthetic principles governing the form of his creation arose from his perception of that space-time continuum in which the spatial is forever moving toward the eternal and the eternal tending toward the spatial. In "Marcel Proust and Architecture: Some Thoughts on the Cathedral-Novel," J. Theodore Johnson Jr. writes,

> The passage on the steeples of Martinville where what is involved, according to Cattaui, is this "esthetic enjoyment partly occasioned by the displacement of the architectonic shapes and volumes in space and time," is one of the numerous key passages in *Combray*. As the reader progresses through the novel, he becomes more and more aware of this phenomenon of the parallax—occurring in time as well as in space. It is from this parallax—what Proust calls the "psychology of space and the psychology of time"—that a large part of his aesthetic enjoyment is derived. (156)

The involuntary memories of the "privileged moments" are more responsible for the form assumed by the creative impulse, than for the awakening of it—although they are ficted as the origin of it in *Recherche*. The Ruskinian epiphany solved Proust's most perplexing problem: what form to give to his aesthetic genius. It provides the retrospective frame that commences and concludes the work, the through-line that sustains The Search, the most dramatic moments of it, and the vehicle for realizing the novel's central theme: redemption through art. If neurosis incites the creative urge, then involuntary memory gives final form to it: by giving form to Proust's "psychology of space and time."

This extraordinary nature invests each privileged moment with a "self-contained quality, cut off from the rest. It is Proust's purpose to show each of these worlds as 'isolated, enclosed, immobile, arrested, and lost'"—and therefore in mutual correspondence with his own sense of isolation (Jephcott 279). The isolated self isolates the isolated Other, evoking and then arresting its mobility in metaphor, before colonizing it as self. As Doubrovsky asserts, "[S]eeking his independent being, he exists only as a parasite." Confronted by the mystifying sign of the Sapphic sublime, the self's parasitism of the Other turns upon itself. Instead of explicating the Other-as-self, it explicates itself as Other: a liberatory strategy of self-possession devolves into a neurotic bind of dispossession. The inability to immobilize the Other leads to the fatal immobilization of the self by the Other. As Bersani observes,

> Without a reliably fixed, immobile image of the outer world, possession of others and of the self is impossible. Identities disintegrate into several unconnected pictures; attempts to picture or recognize the self in visible external scenes are frustrated by the elusive metamorphoses of these scenes [or characters]. (75)

The mobility of the Other (and of the Sapphic Other in particular) reinforces the discontinuity and instability of the self. Further, this mobility of the Other reprises the initial flux of the space-time continuum in the novel, in which the narrator's various bedrooms swirl about him, dematerializing the distinction between space and time, troping on the unstable boundaries of the conscious and unconscious mind, soon to be trespassed by involuntary memory. As Bersani observes, "The dizziness described at the beginning of 'Combray' is the physical symptom of a general instability of being which Marcel tries to cure in various ways"(75): by locating the eternal in the temporal, by constructing a self that is continuous in time, by converting the discontinuity of self and Other into a stable association, which converts the Other into a projection of the self.

Arresting the perpetual motion of the Other becomes synonymous with arresting the movement of time: both of which stabilize the self in time for all time. The mystifying sign of the Sapphic sublime reverses the parasitic projects of possessive and creative impulses. Love and art devolve into madness, as the cycle returns upon the self, completing the feedback loop of pathological narcissism by plowing the self back into itself—until creativity becomes the only means of escaping the fatal pathology of the self. The creative impulse that seeks to liberate itself through the Other, is thwarted and then decisively enervated by the self's neurotic fixation with itself, which is prompted by its failure to possess the fugitive Other. The self, when confounded by the enigma of Sapphic desire, falls prey to its own parasitic tendencies: its impotent intellect, enfeebled memory, and hyper-imagination precipitate a descent into neurotic madness that leads straight to the sanitarium, and whose catastrophic closure is averted only by a serendipitous redemption to art in The Search's eleventh hour.

MARCEL AND THE SAPPHIC SWAN: LEDA AND THE LOSS OF KNOWLEDGE

Throughout *Recherche*, writing enacts the fantasy of imprisonment and liberation. The incarceration of the Other through metaphor ("enclosed in the rings of a beautiful style") paradoxically liberates the creative self into a semi-stable, differentiated subjectivity. It is no mere coincidence that Marcel comes closest to possessing Albertine when she lies immobilized by sleep in a prison of domesticity under his own roof. As Doubrovsky asserts, "the fantasy will become explicit in what is well known as 'Albertine's sleep'" (42). The hymenoptera of the self seemingly takes possession of the deep tissue of the feminine Other through the fixated and fixating gaze, and through the deployment of images that reflect their mutual fixation: "For this I had no need to make any movement" (*La Prisonnière* 427). His leg dangles "like an oar which one allows to trail in the water, imparting to it now and again a gentle oscillation like the intermittent flap given to its wing by a bird asleep in the air." A state of self-contained repose is evoked by the imagery of self and Other, in which the destabilizing flux of the feminine has been immobilized by a knowing and possessive self. Bersani notes the significance of these immobilizing images: "[T]he whole passage has images taken from the calm aspects of nature . . . her breathing has the slow majestic movements of the sea waves" (80). As Proust writes, "[H]er sleep brought within my reach something as calm, as sensually delicious as those nights of full moon on the bay of Balbec, turned quiet as a lake over which the branches barely stir" (LP 426).

The scene establishes a series of continuities and discontinuities with the steeples and the trees. In contradistinction to the objects of those privileged moments, Albertine is immobilized by sleep. Whereas verbs and images of mobility dominate at Martinville and Hudimesnil, images of stasis prevail here, in what amounts to the narrative equivalent of a musical "rest stop." Doubrovsky adds a novel turn to the interpretation of this scene, perceiving it as a fantasy of necrophilia. The arousal of Marcel's erotic desire by the sleeping Albertine, culminating in masturbation or intercourse, is tantamount to a "lethiferous love" (43). Albertine is figured as "almost dead" in her own words, and as "indeed a dead woman" in the words of the narrator (LP 632). Thus, "to have pleasure/to write, is then ideally to masturbate upon a tomb" (Doubrovsky 43).

Further, Marcel's desire to possess the "dead" Albertine not only anticipates his desire to repossess her after she is truly dead, but reinscribes his desire to possess through writing the dead mother/grandmother, whom he feels he has slain as a sacrificial offering to his art—a point I will revisit in the next chapter. Doubrovsky develops the necrophilial implications of the sleeping Albertine seduction: "[T]o have pleasure . . . is to possess your dead mother. Here the Oedipal complex is resolved by way of a detour through the 'tomb'" (42).

As with the steeples of Martinville, the Other also becomes a projection of the self. In this instance, however, it is not a projection of his isolation that Marcel finds in the Other, but of his own jealousy. The symbiosis of self and Other, however, is similarly effected through metaphor: in this case through the image of the "motionless swan," which becomes, retrospectively, a trope for Sapphic love: "Then I beheld no longer a leg, but the bold neck of a swan, like that which in a frenzied sketch seeks the lips of a Leda . . ." (LF 753). Objectivity gives way to subjectivity, as the Other is reduced to a screen for the images Marcel's jealousy projects upon it—even as the objects of his Combray bedroom were divested of their own identity when they became mere surfaces for the projections of the magic lantern, which tropes on the colonizing projections of the idealizing and the jealousizing mind. Albertine's identity is co-opted by Marcel's jealous imagination, as the innocent, sleeping woman morphs into an image of bisexual beastiality: Leda's swan. The stasis of the Albertine that confronts Marcel's senses contrasts with the kinetic creature that enervates his imagination, in what comprises a painful recuperation of her elusive mobility—as if she refuses to remain a "still life" in either realm: reality or imagination, material or immaterial, asleep or awake. She is animated with a kinetic multiplicity that mystifies any attempt to fixate her under a stable sign. Even in the vegetal paralysis of sleep, she rises from her body to haunt Marcel's imagination with images of infidelity.

The aggressions of Marcel's imagination, aimed at stabilizing the Other, destabilize the self. Whereas metaphor was the vehicle for possessing the Other at Martinville by redefining it in terms of the self, in this instance its aggressions return upon the self, opening it up to possession by the Other. Figuration, formerly a vehicle for the self's assertion of independence, now becomes the means for the collapse of the self into the Other, into an undifferentiated state of neurotic dominion by the Other that signifies not only the loss of identity, but of sanity. Figuration, formerly a sign of art, is now a sign of madness.

The innate flux of the feminine subverts the certainty of the senses, the acuity of the intellect, and the clarity of the memory, leaving Marcel virtually impotent in his epistemic quest for knowledge. The enigma of the Sapphic sublime reduces the virile aggressions of Marcel's intellect to a state of impotency. If the Albertine volumes depict anything, it is the intellectual emasculation of Marcel by the sign of Saphhic desire—as just retribution for sins committed against the mother.

Memory fails, reason clouds, and the senses deceive—through two volumes that subvert the narrative mastery of the ontological enterprise achieved in the privileged moments of the madeleine and Martinville. Albertine is one vast optical illusion, for which her mobile mole is a metonym. As Marcel observes, "[O]ur vision is a deceiving sense" (WBG 422), as a consequence of which Albertine "underwent . . . eclipses of perspective" (WBG 632). The flux of the feminine manifests the subversive assumptions of Elstir's impressionism: "Now the effort made by Elstir to reproduce things not as he knew them but according to optical illusions of which our first sight of them is composed" had led Elstir to paint "what were almost mirages" (WBG 631). Marcel's first impressions of Albertine are consequently false impressions—and inevitably so:

> The questing, anxious, exacting way that we have of looking at the person we love . . . all these make our observation, in the beloved's presence, too tremulous to be able to carry away a clear impression of her . . . the beloved model does not stay still; and our mental photographs of her are always blurred. (WBG 375)

The project of possession is thwarted by the Sapphic feminine not only at the intellectual level, but at level of the senses—by a reality that confounds his efforts to make sense of it. How to possess what cannot even be accurately perceived? The desire to possess is thwarted at the most immediate level of reality: the senses—like an army slaughtered rising from its trenches. The self's desire to possess through fixation is undone by the Other's refusal to be fixated—and this fundamental discontinuity between self and Other redoubles Marcel's morbid sorrows.

The possessive project of the self is further compromised by its own mediation of the self-Other dyad. In other words, the self comes between itself and the Other—so that the Other is always and forever at one remove from the self. In seeking to possess the Other, the self encounters only itself. The greatest defense the Other has against the self, is the self. In its efforts to possess the Other, the self is its own worst enemy. The autonomy of the Other is guaranteed by the self's projections of itself. Consequently, the only correspondence the self can enjoy with the Other is as a possession of the Other. The desire to possess gives way, of necessity, to a desire to be possessed.

Perception of the Other is destabilized not only by the multiple, shifting nature of the object, but by the self-reflexive vision of the subject. The beloved in Proust is a signified that forever slips the noose of signification, that habitually subverts the desire to know (which masks the desire to possess). The Sapphic sublime in particular resists the effort to "enclose it in the rings of a beautiful style" in contradistinction to the privileged moments of the madeleine and the steeples, which are "released from the chronological order of time" (PR 997).

If the flux of the feminine confounds, the flux of the Sapphic feminine doubly mystifies. To the shadows of the feminine, it adds the shadows of a secret society whose codes are not only unknown to Marcel, but can never be known, whose pleasures have not only never been experienced, but cannot even be imagined. And herein lies the secret to its mystification: Marcel cannot possess what he cannot imagine. Imagination is the locus by which Marcel first gains possession of the essence of any "privileged" object, whether it is Berma's acting or the Norman gothic ideal incarnate in Balbec church. Marcel's sorrows are the byproduct of a simple fact: he desires what he cannot imagine. Now his possessive desire must pursue its object without his weapon-of-choice: imagination. Sans the certainty of his senses, sans intellect, and sans imagination he pursues the Sapphic siren, the pathological self vanishing into the allegorical terrain of Odysseus, Narcissus, and Actaeon, whose wayward desires it reinscribes. The predatory self is turned into a stag by the siren it hunts—wastes away in the fixating pool of its neurotic narcissism. He futilely pursues the fugitive object, paralyzed by a triple impotency: of sense, intellect, and imagination. Moreover, the Sapphic feminine resists all "alliteration" with the self, unlike the petite madeleine, the steeples, the trees, or the "little phrase" of the septet.

The Sapphic sublime not only floats outside the realm of his senses, his reason, and his memory, but beyond the grasp of his imagination (that durable epistemological machine)—in essence, beyond the realm of all ontology. Marcel not only lacks the knowledge, but every means of acquiring it—is left writhing in the chains of his own epistemological impotency, calling into question the identity of the real captive in *La Prisonnière*. Of all the fugitive Others in *Recherche*, the Sapphic sublime is the most impenetrable: "an illusion created by the momentary flutter of signifiers, whether they be words or images" (Doubrovsky 69).

Albertine is always and already a fugitive in the making. Like Actaeon, Marcel takes up the futile pursuit of a prey that forever eludes his "questing, anxious, exacting" desire. He is incapable of imagining either the knowledge he seeks or the near-mortal wound she will inflict: reducing him in the end to naught but a blind beast, sans senses, reason, memory, and imagination, imprisoned in his own impotent desire, able to do naught but rattle the cage of his impotency while roaring his captivity to the world—until that remote moment when he is liberated from his sorrows by an indifference that sadly leaves him indifferent to life, until given second life by art.

Marcel's false first impressions of Albertine give way to corrected second impressions. Like a photographer, he adjusts his lens to achieve a clearer image of Albertine. However, he is prevented form taking the definitive picture because she is never a "still life," but a human counterpart to the steeples of Martinville and the trees of Hudimesnil—invested with a velocity that confounds perception and, therefore, possession. She is an object who resists "perpetual alliteration" with the self by virtue of her perpetual motion: an object "which I isolate today as though I were cutting sections, at different heights in a jet of water, rainbow flashing, but seemingly without flow or motion" (SW 66). Knowledge is always and forever a metonym for reality, never a metaphor for it—a fragment of a whole, comprised of moments metonymically isolated from time. As the narrator comments, "[M]y dreams of travel and love were only moments . . . were only drops in a single, undeviating outrush of all the forces of my life" (SW 66).

Albertine is written in a code Marcel can never break. When his possessive desire is confronted by an Other that refuses to be defined in terms of the self, it has no choice but to turn its aggressions upon itself. The self's expansive project of possession implodes, turning into an inward aggression in which the self collapses into itself, is emptied of itself, is defined wholly in terms of its jealous fixation with the Other. Marcel's sorrows are the byproduct of a mystifying femininity that refuses enclosure. As Marcel confides, "[A]fter this first transformation Albertine was . . . to change for me many times. . . . Thus, it can only be after one has recognized the optical illusions of one's first impression that one can arrive at an exact knowledge of the Other" (WBG 650). Yet Proust goes on to problematize the possibility of ever gaining an "exact knowledge of the Other," in a narrative that calls into question the efficacy not only of the senses, but of the reason and the memory as epistemological modes. Though his readjustment of the lens may bring Albertine into sharper focus, this is well short of an "exact knowledge" of her, which is always mediated by his own subjectivity. He is no more able to arrest the object of his desire than he is capable of arresting a current by gazing at it—and thus, is never able to snap the definitive picture of Albertine. At best, all he can do is take a series of widely displaced, often contradictory, images in motion—a realization that wrings from the narrator the following memorable observation: "Oh girls, oh recurrent ray in the swirl wherein we throb with emotion upon seeing you reappear while barely recognizing you in the dizzy velocity of light" (WBG 423).

Albertine's ability to escape containment, even while asleep, prefigures her impending escape from her Parisian prison. Her essence is forever fugitive. The moment that would signify the fulfillment of possessive desire instead underscores its futility, as the virile aggressions of the self lapse into self-reflexive impotence. As the narrator admits, "[E]ven when you hold them in your hands, these people are fugitives. To understand the emotion that they arouse . . . we must take into account that they are not immobile, but in motion, and add to their person a sign corresponding to what in physics is the sign that indicates velocity" (LP 441). Albertine's stasis in sleep is a seductive illusion, coded with erotic connotations, masking a fugitive velocity accelerated by Marcel's jealous imagination in its impotent quest to possess the secrets of Sapphic desire.

The velocity of the Sapphic Other contrasts with the paralysis of the self. Desire is not only desire for a fugitive beloved, but desire because it is for a fugitive beloved. As Marcel observes, "we perceive that our love is a function of our sorrow, that our love perhaps is our sorrow" (LP 442). Mystification is the food desire feeds upon. What it requires and pursues is a feminine Other who can, like Hamlet, "plumb one yard below his mind." The Sapphic sign incites Marcel's madness because it lies beyond perception, beyond reason, beyond imagination, and beyond language. Sans the sorrows of her mystification, Albertine would cease to be desirable: "[D]issociated from our emotion whatever it may be, they are only themselves, that is to say almost nothing, and, so long desired, are soon forsaken by the very man who was so afraid of their forsaking him" (LP 443). Sans the self, the Other is merely itself, and therefore incapable of inspiring desire.

Love is always and already love for a fugitive. The terrible irony of Proustian desire is that the possession so ardently desired comprises the death of desire—leaving desire to dwell in a state of perpetual nonfulfillment, if it is to exist at all: a condition whose only remedy is its own demise. Possessive desire is a malaise of the self whose development is catalyzed by a diseased imagination, which fattens on its own speculations like a parasite lodged in the intestines of its host, and whose only cure in the short term is the brief relief of the beloved's company or carnal embraces, even as indifference is the only remedy in the long term. Between these two polarities of desire and indifference, of carnal possession and proof of infidelity, lies a horrific terrain of uncertainty, suspicion, and suffering: uncertainties that are invincible, suspicions that are insistent, and sufferings that are incurable. *Recherche* consistently subverts the romantic tradition insofar as the beloved's company is never pleasurable in itself, is merely an antidote to suffering—as evidenced in Marcel's attitude toward Albertine's company: "I can never repeat it enough; it was first and foremost a sedative" (LP 431).

This distinctly unromantic, deterministic, pathological, and postmodern view of love incites in the reader a paradoxical sense of identification and revulsion. The dark regions of the self-in-love that *Recherche* explores are far removed from the ego's ideal conception of itself. The self as monstrosity, as objectified in the monstrosity of vice that is Charlus, in the monstrosity of jealousy that is Swann, and in the more egregious monstrosity of jealousy that is Marcel. All are monstrosities of neurotic narcissism—are monuments to a self desiring to totalize the world with itself. This self not only dwells in its own darkness, but revels in it: from the "first black date of the calendar" to the sanitarium and the brothel of Jupien some seven volumes later, when alas it is absorbed into the redemptive light of its own re-creation.

Albertine is the sign that confounds interpretation and that precipitates the inward turn toward darkness. She is a metonym for the flux and mystification of the feminine, anticipating postmodern assumptions about "knowledge" that call into question its certainty, or even its possibility. The impotence of the intellect before the feminine, and the Sapphic feminine in particular, calls into question deeply held assumptions about the knowledge-making process, revealing that it is not a question of epistemology, but of ontology; not a matter of how we come to know (whether through involuntary memory, the senses, the imagination, the intellect, or social discourse), but a matter of the impossibility of ever knowing. As Deleuze asserts, "[J]ealousy is the very delerium of signs":

> [J]ealousy is no longer simply the explication of possible worlds enveloped in the beloved . . . but the discovery of the unknowable world which represents the beloved's own viewpoint, and which develops within the beloved's own homosexuality. . . . [T]he logic of jealousy comes down to this: to sequester, to immure the beloved. . . . To sequester is to empty the beloved of all the possible worlds she contains, to decipher and to explicate these worlds . . . there is an astonishing relation between the sequestration born of jealousy, the passion to see, and the action of profaning: sequestration, voyeurism, and profanation—the Proustian trinity . . . thus, seeing Albertine sleep. To see is thus to reduce the beloved to the contiguous, non-communicating aspects which constitute her. (124–25)

Unlike the signs of the madeleine and the steeples (of the memory and imagination), which signify the spiritually transformative possibilities of knowledge, the signs of Albertine (which are the signs of Sapphic desire and the jealousy it inspires) signify the impossibility of knowledge. Whereas the earlier privileged moments evidence the mastery of Marcel's epistemological, if pathological enterprise, the signs of Sapphic desire signify its impotency, even as they attest to the dialectical nature of Proustian narration, insofar as they evidence his tendency toward "double exposition." The epistemological implications of the petite madeleine and the three steeples are powerfully contradicted by the mystifying signs of Sapphic desire, in which the certainty of the senses and the potency of the imagination are subverted by the impotency of the intellect.

The signs of Sapphic desire are even more inscrutable than the trees of Hudimesnil. The mystifying opacity of these signs refuses the transparency that, by giving back an image of the self, transforms it. Instead, Marcel remains imprisoned in the Elba of his own sexual differentiation.

Margaret Gray's provocative reading reinforces Deleuze's interpretation on this key point. Albertine confronts Marcel with an ontological enigma that subverts his narrative mastery. The aggressive potency of the involuntary memory and the figuring imagination as epistemological engines is neutralized by the indecipherable hieroglyphs of the Sapphic feminine, by the "inscrutable 'algebra' that is Albertine, a mask of abstraction he is unable to decipher" (86). Albertine becomes the object par excellence that can never be apprehended by the intellect. Indeed, the intellect becomes an impediment to knowledge of the feminine, and particularly of the Sapphic feminine: "[H]is own observing awareness—intervenes as an inescapable 'aura' preventing direct contact with the observed" (Gray 85). As Proust's narrator confides,

> [W]hen I saw an external object, my awareness that I was seeing it remained between myself and it, surrounding it with a thin spiritual border that prevented me from ever touching its substance directly; it would somehow evaporate before I could make contact with it, in the way that an incandescent body brought into proximity with something wet never actually touches its moisture, since it is always preceded by a zone of evaporation. (SW 63)

Albertine, like the feminine in general, is this "something wet": always emerging from the sea, striding with the sea at her back, figured as a bird of the sea, in the wetness of her profane desire for women, in the moisture of her kisses that reincarnate the incestuous maternal sublime, in her abstract incarnation as Leda and the swan—ever embodied in a feminine wetness that Marcel's intellect can never precipitate into the dry truths it would possess, the better to possess her. Moss offers a useful interpretation:

> In Albertine, Marcel attaches himself to an enigma, compounded of sea and sky . . . and yet tantalizingly human, an enigma impossible of solution . . . it is impossible to tell where Marcel's version of her ends and his own begins. . . . With Albertine, he plunges into a sea that has no discernible depth. . . . [W]hat he joins is not an ordinary group of girls but a tangle of ambiguous goddesses, slipping in and out of each other's identities—the mobile consciousness of the sea and sky which nevertheless exude the strong flavor of vegetation. (33)

Desire prompts Marcel's search for profane knowledges, which in this phase of his "apprenticeship to signs" devolves into a search for knowledge of the Sapphic sublime, but which exacts a terrible price, as it did for Adam and Eve. He is plunged into the fatal "labyrinth of Albertine's personality—his suspicions of her lesbian tendencies," which force him to "explore the labyrinth of himself" (Moss 52). Deprived of all human faculty (senses, reason, memory, and imagination), the self is fixated by the hymenoptera of the feminine Other whose mystification turns his aggressions back upon the self. Moss elaborates: Albertine "absorbs all of Marcel, his will [is] drained by obsession. For Marcel, all social life becomes meaningless. In both cases [Swann and Marcel], impossibility is the great propulsion to love. Odette is domesticated, Albertine imprisoned. Under Surveillance, they do not give up their secrets" (53).

To the enigma of Sapphic desire, Albertine adds the menace of a discursive mimicry (in her discourse on the "ices") that further mystifies Marcel's desire, even in the act of arousing it.[1] However, the fall is for Marcel, as it was for Adam and Eve, a fortunate fall: not into humanity, but into creativity. Art is the trapdoor that enables the self to escape from itself, that brings the conscious and unconscious self into liberatory communion. The sorrows of Sapphic desire not only provide the impetus to write, but the material for writing. By dying, however, Albertine gives Marcel something even greater: the freedom to write—although there is, of course, a lag between her physical death and her real death in his psyche, at the merciless hand of indifference.

The algebra of Albertine is given a sordid twist that ties Marcel's heart in a double knot when her "algebra lessons" with Morel are coded with erotic overtones. As Gray concludes, "[W]e can no longer ascribe the old algebraic attributes of purity . . . but now attach to algebra a highly charged atmosphere of sexual mystery. . . . Algebra becomes a metaphor for enigmatic sexuality" (86). Moreover, the inscrutability of Albertine's algebraic fragments, such as the "tip of her nose . . . epitomizing the permanent personality of a woman, this algebraic excerpt" (qtd. in Gray 87), exerts a deterministic influence over Marcel inasmuch as it prevents him "from disposing of a single one of his evenings." The inscrutability of Albertine's algebra underscores the impotency of Marcel's intellect, calling into question his narrative mastery. As Gray asserts, "[I]n his fruitless efforts to interpret an enigmatic Albertine, the narrator refers to . . . 'the approximate equation of that unknown which Albertine's thought was for me'" (87).

Marcel seeks a definitive knowledge, but gains only approximate truths—if he gains anything at all. Again, he suffers from the violent disconnect between his desire for an absolute knowledge and the reality of partial truths, unknowable facts, or indecipherable fragments. He yearns for composite truths, but must settle for contradictory fragments. His frustration is palpable, limitless, a form of divine madness—divine because it leads to art. The narrative devolves into "an increasingly tormented account of the narrator's bewilderment over Albertine's past and sexual inclinations" (Gray 88). To understand this "algebra of desire" Marcel is reduced to formulating equations in his imagination (Beckett 55). As Gray observes, "[T]he narratives of *La Prisonnière* and *La Fugitive* may even be read as the narrator's extended attempt to write an algebraic equation himself, to write the equation that will yield the solution to Albertine's sexual mystery, the equation that will derive the unknown" (87). He is confounded by the riddle of $1 + 1 = 0$—by the algebraic nonsense of $X + Y = 2Y$.

Indeed, Marcel's epistemological impotency with respect to Albertine calls into question the potency of the narrative mastery he claims to have found through involuntary memory and a figurative imagination. Gray develops the implications: "Marcel's failure in the position of possessing subject throws into question not only his own 'authority,' but as well the claims of a critical tradition that has repeated his 'authoritative' assertions, thereby endorsing the shaky hierarchy of a subject/object distinction" (96). Marcel's inability to "write" Albertine "marks the point of failure of representation's confident tautologies. . . . [W]hat is in question is the possibility of mimetic closure—whether a text can close around that which it claims to represent, to 'control'" (96). Marcel's efforts to posthumously determine Albertine's sexual inclinations never yields the definitive truths for which he searches. However, as Gray affirms, his intellectual impotency goes deeper than this: "Marcel's bewilderment is not only induced by his failure to discover whether Albertine has a lesbian past and inclinations; it is provoked, as well, by his failure to imagine—to grasp, possess—the lesbian possibility"(99). The image of Leda and the swan only underscores the frustratingly fragmentary nature of his knowledge: "Gomorrah's only history is speculation deriving from its association with Sodom. For the narrator, female homosexuality is not only unknown, it is 'too unknown'—undecidable, absolutely 'Other'" (99). As the narrator confides, "[T]his love of woman for woman was something too unfamiliar; nothing enabled me to form a certain, an accurate idea of its pleasures, its quality" (LP 649). In the final analysis, lesbians "inhabit a space beyond appropriation by the imagination"—beyond possession by the intellect (Gray 99). Moreover, Marcel's mystification with respect to Albertine's lesbianism is, as Gray observes, doubled in Charlus's pained bewilderment of Morel's fascination with Sapphic desire (100).

Even the "facts" that Marcel acquires regarding Albertine's lesbianism are problematized, inasmuch as they are mediated by Aime whose character and motives are called into question by the narrator. His search for truth devolves into an act of interpretation—leaving Marcel where he started: no nearer a definitive assessment regarding Albertine's sexuality, in a narrative that is forever lapsing back into its own postmodern ambiguity, problematizing its own claims to knowledge, forever refusing ontological closure. The intellectual autopsy Marcel performs on Albertine's past produces no definitive answers, is unable to satisfactorily resolve the mystery. Gray's assessment is instructive: "[T]he resolution of Albertine's mystery occurs in the context of an even greater mystery, that of Gomorrah; the certainty of Albertine's lesbianism pales before the far greater uncertainty—the 'unknowability'—of lesbianism itself" (101).

Marcel's knowing subject fractures against the mystifying opacity of the Sapphic sign: a fracturing that stimulates the creative impulse, by which the fragmented self is reconstituted. Further, Albertine's inscrutability is a metonym for the inscrutability of *Recherche*, and an allegory of the habitual inscrutability of the homosexual whose vice hides in plain sight. Marcel's efforts to penetrate the inscrutable sign of the feminine bisexual are as futile as the biographer's efforts to definitively possess the artist by penetrating the fictional traces that are his or her work.

Does this loss of narrative mastery before the Sapphic sign call into question the narrator's credibility throughout *Recherche*? As Gray asserts, the impotency of the interpreting intellect before the Sapphic sign problematizes our "belief in the hero's narrative mastery," even as it " implies excessive confidence in the male hero's role as detective and narrator, in his capacity to elaborate a coherent history" (98). I would argue that the absence of narrative mastery with respect to the Sapphic sign can only be fully comprehended in the context of the narrative mastery evidenced elsewhere. With respect to the worldly signs, the sensuous signs, and the signs of art, the narrative evidences Marcel's interpretive mastery. The potency of the interpreting self that demystifies the sign of the madeleine, the steeples, and the uneven paving stones is juxtaposed by the impotency of the interpreting self before the mystifying signs of Hudimesnil and Sapphic desire. Further, the erosion of narrative mastery before the sign of the Sapphic sublime underscores its dramatic recuperation before the signs of involuntary memory at the novel's climax. Consequently, the myth of narrative mastery implies its opposite, and can only be fully appreciated within the context of a narrative strategy whose dominant aesthetic is the "double exposition" of any sign—including the sign of narrative mastery, which is explicated as both myth and reality.

And yet, Marcel's futile search for profane knowledge yields something of far greater benefit to him: the impulse to create. The futility of his heartbreak is "recuperated as a necessary step in Marcel's apprentissage'" to art (Gray 101). As the narrator himself avers, "[W]hen a woman we adore betrays us . . . our grief over the desertion will then prove to be strange lands which we would otherwise never have known and the discovery of which, however painful to the man, becomes priceless to the artist" (PR 1016). Only suffering, as Marcel observes, provides, "the kind of lessons a man of letters needs in serving his apprenticeship":

> For the objective value of the arts is meagre . . . a woman for whom we have a great longing causes us suffering. . . . [T]he writer may embark upon a long work without apprehension. Let the intelligence but begin its task and there will come along the way sorrows in plenty which will undertake to complete it. As for happiness, it has hardly more than one useful quality, to make unhappiness possible. (PR 1020)

Prolonged study of the arts is as impotent as sorrow is potent in awakening the creative impulse—and this The Search repeatedly dramatizes. The real significance of the Sapphic sign is not that it subverts Marcel's narrative mastery in contradistinction to the signs of involuntary memory and the imagination, but that it, like those experiences, comprises a critical step in Marcel's apprenticeship to art. The most significant byproduct of Albertine's Sapphic caresses is not the emasculation of Marcel's intellect, but the reactivation of the creative impulse by the suffering this mystification produces.

This is why the writer "may embark . . . without apprehension," for whether the intellect succeeds or fails in apprehending the truth is of no consequence. Even where it fails, suffering will intercede to prompt the transformation of experience into art. The "truths" about Albertine's Sapphic history may have placated the lover's curiosity, but the "refusal of intelligibility" is what stimulates the artist. As Rank observes in his Daybooks, "[T]he most beautiful in an artist's life is that which he cannot work out" (qtd. in Taft 42). The frustration of interpretation is food for invention—when associated with the signs of love, and with the signs of Sapphic desire in particular. The sign of the Sapphic sublime synthesize the signs of art (the steeples) and the signs of mystification (the trees): the mystification that refuses knowledge at Hudimesnil is fused with the invention that derives from knowledge at Martinville, yielding a mystifying sign that produces, not knowledge, but art.

NOTE

1. For a fuller explication of the implications of Albertine's discourse on the ices, see my article, "Desire on Ice: The Menace of Albertine's Mimicry in *La Prisonnière*," *College Literature* (forthcoming).

chapter four

Three Moments of Desire:
The Ideal, the Real, and the Remembered

> We are not provided with wisdom, we must discover it for ourselves, after a journey through the wilderness which no one can take for us, an effort which no one can spare us, for our wisdom is the point of view from which we come at last to regard the world.
> —WBG

PROUST'S MODE OF NARRATION in *Recherche* consists in part of a threefold dialectical progression in which the romantic enchantments of the imagination are repeatedly contradicted by experience, only to be recuperated by a retrospective perspective that synthesizes the enchantment of the ideal with the empiricism of the real, revealing a lived reality that is nonetheless spiritual for its materiality. This "series" of the ideal, the real, and the remembered comprises three distinct yet interrelated moments in the narrative. As Walter Kasell observes in his penetrating analysis, *Marcel Proust and the Strategy of Reading* (1980), "[T]he constellation of different moments in a development describes a dialectic of nonexclusive alternatives, and forms an essential part of the novel's strategy" (9). Like the series of profanation, transposition, and transfiguration and the series of penetration, conversion, and assimilation, the progression of the ideal, the real, and the remembered constitutes a strategy of self-possession. For the true object of the desire to make the ideal real is not a "Norman gothic" Balbec church or a Normandy coastline that is the quintessence of a tempestuous Turner seascape, but the ideal self-as-writer. This is why the final synthesis of the ideal and the real through involuntary memory leads inevitably to writing. The remystification of reality through the climactic "privileged moments" turns creative desire into reality. As Kasell concludes, "[T]he directions which appear to structure the work are not univalent but dialectical, encompassing opposing tendencies . . ." (13). The series of the ideal, the real, and the remembered is a dialectical "search engine": one that powers the narrative through the antithetical vicissitudes of the ideal and the real, until it arrives at that "wisdom" that is the "point of view from which we come at last to regard the world."

Indeed, the work's "wisdom" is inseparable from this point of view, which is comprised in reality of three points of view. As Kasell asserts, "[N]o perspective is fully outside this dialectic":

> The novel arises from between these several directions. . . . Its special quality lies in the troubled nature of their difference and in the text's ability to form itself from these oppositions. . . . From between each group of diverging tendencies there arises new ground, capable of dynamically preserving the image of possibilities that is denied in more explicit form. (17)

Many (if not all) of the "privileged" objects in The Search are portrayed from these three perspectives, are sequentially triangulated from the perspective of the imagination, the senses, and the memory—or according to the Lacanian hermeneutic, from the perspectives of the imaginary, the real, and the symbolic. An object, a person, or place is experienced first from the idealizing perspective of the imagination, subsequently from the demystifying and disillusioning perspective of the senses, and finally from the retrospective, recuperative, and transformative perspective of the symbolic: that is, through memories recovered from the unconscious and given symbolic representation in language. These comprise, according to Lacan, the three realms of human reality (Ehrman 101). Moreover, if the first perspective is romantic in its idealism and the second modern in its realism, then the third is already and presciently postmodern in its reliance on the symbolic for the making of meaning and knowledge. Consequently, the entire sweep of the romantic, the modern, and the postmodern movements is absorbed in Proust's narrative, which modulates from one to the other mode of epistemology throughout *Recherche*.

Insofar as Proust is constructing a novel largely from the material of his unconscious mind, that is from his involuntary memory, it might be useful to interpret the whole work as a dream, similarly comprised of the material of the unconscious mind and consequently subject to the processes of distortion, displacement, and condensation, which have their counterparts in Proust's narrative mode throughout *Recherche* in the distortions of the ideal, the displacement of the ideal by the real, and the metaphoric condensation of both by the remembered. The aim of this analysis, however, is not only to explicate the series of the ideal, the real, and the remembered, but to demonstrate that both Marcel's neurosis and his spiritual redemption are deeply informed by it. Finally, I want to situate this explication within the context of Marcel's encounters with Berma, Balbec, and Venice.

The ideal, the real, and the remembered are the heat, water, and wind that drive the vast spiraling engine of *Recherche*'s narrative. Further, these three "views" do not function independently of one another, but as part of a dialectical progression. Reality is antithetical to desire. Moreover, at virtually every stage of The Search, "Marcel will reenact this drama of disappointment" (Kasell 84). More importantly, "the repetition of this drama suggests that perhaps the entire narrative of *Recherche* . . . is organized by a structure of recuperation" in which "the loss of a mystified moment is recouped through an imaginative act of reinvestment and retelling of the loss" (92).

Each of these three perspectives constitutes a separate moment of desire and privileges a different aspect of time. The idealizing imagination is future-oriented; the demystifying second moment of narration foregrounds the immediacy of the present; while the final retrospective view is oriented toward the past: is the wisdom-producing "vision" of involuntary hindsight. Taken together, these three views of a particular person, place, or thing (of Berma, Balbec, or Venice) elaborate a view of experience that is multiple, dialectic, and developmental. If the first view evokes the idealism of youth and the second the disillusionment of maturity, then the last gestures toward the redemptive wisdom of old age. Proustian experience is therefore Picasso-like in its wisdom insofar as we are presented with three overlapping temporal perspectives of the same model.

"Search engine" is an apt description, for the novel is nothing if not a search for a self that is continuous in time, for a reality that corresponds to Marcel's idealizing imagination—and when the two prove antithetical, for a means of reconciling the figurative and the literal, of reconciling the ecstasy of the ideal with the nausea of the real—and the flight of the spiritual with the weight of the material. This desire is realized through "an act of synthesis which turns this history into the work of art" (Kasell 102). Until this transformative third moment of the narrative, "the imagination and desire are stifled by the specificity and weight of the material object" (66). The errors of figuration are repeated and repeatedly compounded by the errors of literality, until both are corrected in the vision of involuntary memory, concretized in art. As Kasell asserts:

> Everywhere in the novel, Marcel is committing the "error of literality," yielding to the temptation to seize his illusion, yet he is everywhere discovering his error and "correcting" himself. Each revelation seems only to justify another attempt, leading him into the recommission of his error. (96)

—until the cycle of error is broken by the retrospective revelations of involuntary memory or by Socratic dialogue with an idealized Other.

THE DISEASE OF THE IDEAL:
THE FIRST MOMENT OF DESIRE

> The specificity of Proust's novel would instead be grounded in the play between a prospective and a retrospective movement.
> —Paul de Man

The first moment in the narrative progression is determined by Marcel's idealizing imagination. In this section I will develop the psychological and aesthetic implications of Marcel's "ideal-hungry" personality. In *Recherche*, a particular person or place first actuates the imagination, then the senses, and finally the memory. Any given object, whether it is a woman, a work of art, a cathedral, or an exotic destination is viewed successively from these three perspectives. Places, like people, are amalgamations of fantasy, reality, and memory—of the future, the present, and the past. They are, as Joseph Wood Krutch observes, "monstrous creatures straddling between the distant past and the present" (x). There is moreover a continuous tension and an ongoing dialectic between the imagined object, the encountered object, and the remembered object; between the illusory nature of desire, the disillusionment of experience, and the recuperative power of remembrance. These three perspectives are like three lenses through which Proust's narrator perceives experience.

Marcel first takes possession of any desired object in his idealizing imagination—which is in reality a means of possessing his ideal self. Further, this self has been sacrificed to his profane desire for the mother, necessitating its recuperation through a series of "privileged" objects. As evidenced in the "drame coucher," the frustration of Marcel's profane desire in the real world prompts the inward turn, away from the material toward the spiritual. Marcel's "ideal hungry" personality is an effect of a pathological self. As Kohut observes:

> Ideal-hungry personalities are forever in search of others whom they can admire for their prestige, power, beauty, intelligence, or moral stature. They can experience themselves as worthwhile only so long as they can relate to selfobjects to whom they can look up.... In most cases, however, the inner void cannot forever be filled by these means. The ideal hungry feels the persistence of the structural void and, as a consequence of this awareness, he begins to look for—and, of course, he inevitably finds—some realistic defect in his God. The search for new idealizable self-objects is then continued, always in the hope that the next great figure to whom the ideal-hungry attaches himself will not disappoint. (379)

Marcel similarly attaches himself to a series of ideal "selfobjects" (the mother/grandmother, Bergotte, Vinteuil, Elstir, Saint Loup, Charlus, and the Duchess de Guermantes), of which Berma is a useful example. His implication in the "ideal-hungry" pattern is reinforced by the fact that he similarly discovers "defects in his God," even as Proust's idolatry of Ruskin evolves into a critique that foregrounds the "defect" of Ruskin's idolatrous style.

The pathological projections of Marcel's idealizing imagination have their figurative and literal counterpart in the magic lantern, whose fanciful images of the Merovingian sublime dematerialize the walls of Marcel's bedroom prison. The desire for "perpetual alliteration" with the mother that is denied in the "drame coucher" is displaced onto the "privileged" objects of The Search—where its drama of disappointment is endlessly renewed. In its futile quest for "perpetual alliteration" with an ideal Other the pathological self of The Search reenacts the Sisyphean myth—of disappointment endlessly reiterated.

Marcel's desire is doomed by the non-alliteration between the ideal and the real, by the absence of an "objective correlative" to his pathological desire. His idealizing imagination is like an arrow that overshoots its target: reality. Marcel's romantic assumption that the ideal and the real correspond comprises yet another displacement of the desire for the two-in-one, which originally crystalizes around the mother-son dyad. The antithetical tensions between the ideal and the real are harmonized in their synthesis by involuntary memory, producing a spiritualized materiality that shimmers with poetic empiricism: like a butterfly wet with emergence from a temporal chrysalis.

Reality is a reincarnation of the wish-denying mother. That which denies his wish in the Combray bedroom, denies his wish in the world at large. Reality is a garden from which his dreams are banned—flinging him back into the gardens of his own invention, which will become a garden dedicated to invention—and through which he will finally take possession of the Edens of experience. Even the "two ways" (Guermantes and Méséglise) are landscapes of exile that symbolize Marcel's long apostasies into love and society, and away from art: seductive sojourns in the gardens of profane desire and the aristocratic sublime that delay his entrance into the true garden of creativity. His youthful sojourns along the two ways provide a foretaste of his exilic career, even as it prefigures the exilic career of Swann. Despite critical differences, the two protagonists are one in many respects: not only Other by virtue of their Jewishness (and in Proust's case, by virtue of his homosexuality), but exiles from their true nature when in love. As Kristeva notes, "[B]oth Swann and the narrator are familiar with exile. . . . The narrator is exiled because of his love and his race . . . he is both homosexual and Jewish" (25). Aunt Leonie's garden and the last garden of the Princess de Guermantes (Mme Verdurin) are tropes for the Garden of Eden and Heaven insofar as they reinscribe respectively the myths of original sin and eternal salvation.

Among the first of these "paradises" to seize his imagination (and be seized in return by it) are the Norman gothic church of Balbec and the citadel of art and profane desire, Venice:

> I need only to make them reappear, pronounce the names: Balbec, Venice, Florence, within whose syllables had gradually accumulated all the longing inspired in me by the places for which they stood. Even in spring, to come in a book upon the name of Balbec sufficed to awaken in me the desire for storms at sea and for the Norman gothic; even on a stormy day, the name of Florence or of Venice would awaken the desire for sunshine, for lilies, for the Palace of the Doges. . . . (SW 296)

Fueled by his imagination and the false assumption of "perpetual alliteration" between the spiritual and the material, the figurative and the literal, Marcel plots his pilgrimage to the real. Under the spell of an idealizing imagination, he commits the sin of idolatry, whose effects will be no less traumatic than his original sin of profanation: and similarly, no less protean with respect to the quickening of his creative impulse. The conflict between idolatry and reality thwarts his desire, even as it enervates his desire to write. The Search is not only a search for an original form, an original style, but for originals—whose originality becomes a surrogate for his own as yet undiscovered originality. Marcel's fetishization of the authentic (whether in art or the aristocracy, be it for a peasant girl who is the authentic embodiment of the pastoral or a Normandy coastline that is the genuine incarnation of a tempestuous, Turneresque seascape) is an objectification of his inward search for an authentic art. The ideal Other authenticates the ideal self-as-artist—and his desire to possess the "authentic" Other is a displacement of his desire to possess the authentic self: an intermediate, external solution to an inward problem. Marcel surrounds himself with originals, whether artworks (Corot's paintings, Sand's novels, Mme de Sévigné's memoirs), artists (Bergotte, Elstir, Morel), or "originals" of the Merovingian sublime (Charlus, Saint Loup, the Duchess de Guermantes) in hopes that some of their originality will "rub off," will spark his own latent genius. He keeps the company of genius (if only Odette's genius for fashion) until he is able to transform himself into one.

Marcel's rich association with every variety of genius is a form of wish fulfillment—as are the series of pilgrimages he undertakes: to Balbec, Venice, the Faubourg St. Germaine. He quests after "originals" in order to inspire his own originality, deceived by his romantic faith in an "objective correlative": "[T]hese visions of Florence, Venice, Pisa . . . I never ceased to believe that they corresponded to a reality independent of myself . . . a Christian in the primitive age of Faith, on the eve of entry into Paradise" (SW 299). He attaches himself to Elstir and Bergotte, who are impressionism and literary genius personified. He attaches himself to Saint Loup, who is feudal nobility incarnate. He yearns for Venice, a "fantasized topos of cultural and sexual fulfillment" (Collier 3). And he goes to see Berma perform, assuming he will find Phedre incarnate. He even uses Albertine to sate his desire for an authentic Venice, draping her in a Fortuny gown, compounding his pleasure by creating a hybrid of erotic and artistic pleasure. Collier develops the implications of Albertine's makeover in the image of the Venetian sublime:

> [The dress is a] deliberate reference to an Oriental and cultural as well as an erotic Venice. In *La Prisonnière*, Marcel dresses Albertine in gowns which recall Venetian buildings, Italian libraries and Arabic script. Proust multiplies references to the phoenix, a motif of the dresses, linking it with the thematics of resurrection. (Collier 6–7)

Albertine in her Italian gown is transposed into a sign of the Venetian sublime, into an ideal Other under the sign of an eroticized art—yet another variation of the two-in-one. The seeds of Marcel/Proust's idolatry of Venice are sown by Ruskin's *The Stones of Venice*:

> Our pilgrim's passion for stones . . . led us to hear such admirable prayers beside the waters. To the colours of the heavens of Venice, of the mosaics of St. Mark's, will be added new colours, more prestigious even because they are the very shades of a marvelous imagination, the colours of Ruskin, which in his prose, like an enchanted vessel, sail round the world. (CSB 521–22)

—even as the seeds of Marcel's idolatry of a "Norman gothic" Balbec church are sown by Swann.

As with Balbec and Venice, Berma likewise first occupies center stage in Marcel's idealizing imagination. No aspect of genius is excepted from his "ideal-hungry" search for originals. As Marcel observes, "[T]he motive force for my exaltation was a longing for aesthetic enjoyments" (SW299), in hopes that the aesthetic Other will arouse the aesthetic self. This is the true motive of his search for the literary, musical, painterly, and theatrical ideals, as personified in Bergotte, Vinteuil, Elstir, and Berma.

Yet the ideal can only exist in the abstract—does not survive its first contact with reality: like a star that disappears at dawn, or frescoes that fade upon contact with light. As Marcel confides, "My lot was the cruel anxiety of the seeker after truth. No doubt, so long as I had not heard Berma speak, I still felt some pleasure" (WBG 342). He goes to the theatre in a quixotic quest for that "divine Beauty, whom Berma's acting was to reveal to me [and which] night and day, upon an altar perpetually illumined, sat enthroned in the sanctuary of my mind" (WBG 340). As long as he remains outside the theatre, gazing at playbills, the ideal actress lives. It is only when he enters this theatrical garden of art that his dream is shattered by the reality he encounters there.

In the future, he will deliberately delay testing his ideal against the real, if not actually going out of his way to avoid it altogether (as with the peasant girl), knowing the pleasure-giving dream will perish upon contact with the flesh and blood girl, upon hearing her voice, encountering her defects—as he does here with Berma. As long as he stands outside the "Elysian Garden of

Woman" (SW 324), the objects of his amorous desires will be "invested with the charm of the unknown" (WBG 477), with "the magical appeal of imagination" (WBG 556).

The primacy of the ideal applies not only to artists and exotic destinations, but to Woman as well—and to Albertine in particular. She is invested with the projections of his idealizing imagination from the moment he first sees the group of girls proceeding along the beach, like a "classical frieze or fresco representing a procession" which he "had believed it possible for me, the spectator, to take my place . . . among the godlike hierophants" (WBG 600). Further, Marcel's predilection for the amorous ideal dates from earliest boyhood, reinforcing its connection with the maternal sublime:

> When I desired to be in love, I carried in my mind not only an ideal form of beauty . . . but also the moral phantom—ever ready to be incarnate—of the woman who was going to fall in love with me, to take up her cues in the amorous comedy which I had written out in my mind from my earliest boyhood. (WBG 588)

The signifiers "moral phantom," "incarnate," "cues," and "written out in my mind" are significant insofar as they reiterate his faith in an objective correlative that corresponds to his romantic imagination, in which reality is nothing more than an actress responding to the cues of his imagination. Unable to find an "objective correlative" for his ideals, he takes matters into his own hands, literally and figuratively, and shapes a creative correlative—selecting only those elements of reality that are compatible with his poetic imagination.

Marcel bemoans the absence of any "objective correlative" to his idealizing imagination:

> Had my parents allowed me, when I read a book, to pay a visit to the country it described, I should have felt that I was making enormous strides towards the ultimate conquest of truth . . . perpetually struggling to . . . break out into the world, with a perpetual discouragement as we hear endlessly, all around us, that unvarying sound which is no echo from without, but the resonance of a vibration from within. We try to discover in things . . . the spiritual glamour which we ourselves have cast upon them. (SW 65–66)

If some "originals" such as Vinteuil's "little phrase" effect the merger of the spiritual and the material, of the self and the Other, then others, such as Balbec church, Berma, or the man (Bergotte) from whom the genius of literature originates, reiterate the tragic disconnect between the real and the ideal—even as these antithetical juxtapositions further evidence Proust's tendency toward the "double exposition" in any given sign. The "spiritual glamour" he imagines reality to possess has no reality beyond his imagination. The material and the spiritual are as disconnected as the "two ways." Divorced of this "spiritual glamour," the particular "privileged" object ceases to be desirable.

Desire is rooted in Marcel's imagination—and wilts when it is uprooted by reality from his imagination. As the narrator observes, "[H]ow dreary a monotony must pervade those lives who . . . drive their carriages straight to the doors of friends whom they have got to know without having first dreamed of knowing them . . ." (WBG 657)—as he has long dreamed of knowing the Duchess de Guermantes, of watching Berma perform, of gazing upon the Norman gothic features of Balbec church, of exploring the canals of Venice where Ruskinian reflections of stone float like water lilies upon the Vivonne. Desire's manifold destinations lose their charm unless they have been first approached through the landscape of imagination.

This persistent disconnect between the ideal and the real is offset by their "perpetual alliteration" in nature: evidenced by Marcel's response to the hawthorns, seascapes, seasonal lighting effects, the Vivonne et al. In these sublime natural effects the spiritual and the material are alliterated: the beautiful becomes a source of the spiritual in these natural gardens of the ideal, whose hawthorns and water lilies objectify the idealized creations of Marcel's imagination, as evidenced by the transports of joy they inspire.

THE DRAMA OF DISAPPOINTMENT: MARCEL COMES TO HIS SENSES

The second moment in the narrative's dialectical progression is the "drama of disappointment" that is produced by the real's contradiction of the ideal. The material sign does violence to the spiritual sign when the two finally meet. The figurative, instead of corresponding to the literal, is violently incommensurate with it. As Kasell avers, this moment "postulates the impossible identity of two levels of reality whereby the fictional (figural) essence would be seized through its expression in empirical (literal) reality" (67). While overlooking the third and most significant perspective in the series of the ideal, the real, and the remembered, Collier aptly articulates the predominance of the first two: "During this adventure, there is a constant process of projection and displacement of potentially enlightening structures. Society, love, literature and even the city of Venice are invested with emotional and heuristic value, only to be drained of their plenitude, to be rejected as hollow, meaningless experience or unassimilable, grotesque motifs" (1). These wish-denying signs are the locus of a violence that proliferates throughout the novel, and that is compounded by the narrator's romanticizing desire. Violence in Proust is thus transposed from the realm of deeds to the realm of desire, and the disillusioning shocks it receives from a reality perpetually indisposed to fulfill it.

The "literal" in *Recherche* functions as an antithetical correction to the ideal. This antithetical disparity, moreover, reprises the conflict between art and life, which as Rank observes is one of the primary sources of the creative impulse: "[A] certain measure of conflict is, of course, necessary to creative work, and this conflict is, in fact, one of the fields in which an artist displays his greatness, or psychologically speaking, the strength of his creative willpower" (58). These tensions between art and life, which produce the dualism within the artist, are moreover "the profoundest source of the artistic impulse to create," which arises from a struggle that "forces him equally in the direction of a complete surrender to life and a complete giving of himself in production" (60). This conflict (and the futile effort to resolve it) results in Marcel's incessant vacillation between the realms of the real (life) and the ideal (art)—which result in his long delay to writing.

For Marcel, the comforting illusions of the ideal are shattered by the disillusioning shock of the real, which reprises the initial disconnect between his profane desire and its fulfillment in the "drame coucher." This "reality-shock" drives him deeper into the realm of the symbolic. Marcel foreshadows the disenchantment in store for him with respect to Balbec and Venice when he observes that "their names . . . by increasing the arbitrary delights of the imagination, aggravated the disenchantment that was in store for me when I set out upon my travels" (SW 296). The very sound of these signs stimulates fantasies of a materialized sublime whose correspondence to the dematerialized sign, alas, is fugitive.

Standing at long last before the church of Balbec, Marcel's disenchantment is palpable. The ordinary facade in no way corresponds to the Norman gothic edifice of his imagination:

> It was something less, perhaps, also. . . . My mind, which had exalted the Virgin of the Porch far above the reproductions that I had before my eyes . . . ideal, endowed with universal value, was astonished to see the statue which it had carved a thousand times over, reduced now to its apparent form . . . to a little old woman in stone whose height I could measure. (WBG 501)

Proust's representation subverts the binary of reality and illusion: the imaginary church is posited as the original, of which the real church is but an unsatisfactory "reproduction." Time and again, the dimensions of reality are reduced relative to those of his imagination with respect to a given object. His dreams undergo a traumatic amputation, as it were, by a reality that cannot support their romantic giganticism. He tries in vain to squeeze the inflated balloon of his ideals into the matchbox of the real: the ideal "pops" from the pressure of the real—is itself reduced to a fragment of itself.

Undaunted by the disappointment of the Virgin of the Porch, Marcel repairs to the steeple, only to discover that "it stood out against a background of houses with the roofs of which no upstanding mast was blended" (WBG 500). In contradistinction to the romantic edifice of his dreams, the real church is disconnected from the sea: a disjunction that tropes on the disconnect between the real and the ideal.

This "drama of disappointment" is repeated with Berma, which in actuality, precedes it. Marcel confides: "Alas, that first matinee was to prove a bitter disappointment. . . . In vain might I strain toward Berma's eyes, ears, mind, so as not to let one morsel escape me of the reasons which she would furnish me for admiring her. I did not succeed in gathering a single one" (WBG 344). As with the Virgin of the Porch, the idealized Berma is vandalized by reality. Marcel instinctively fears the defacement of the ideal by the real, as Collier affirms:

> Approach toward attainment of the desired object in reality provokes withdrawal: he falls ill at the moment of leaving for Venice [as he does when departing for Balbec] . . . and these withdrawal symptoms are related to actual disappointments, as the real Balbec and the real Phedre, which spoil his type of imaginary perfection in travel and art. (21)

Collier notes the associative chain that conjoins Balbec and Venice: "[H]e begins to suspect that his disappointment in Balbec will necessarily be repeated when he goes to Venice" (25). Here Kristeva raises an interesting question: Do the narrator's repeated disappointments mask a "desire to be disappointed" that is masochistic and (by implication) artistic in nature (26)? Is disappointment instinctively sought, if not indeed created, by an overromanticizing imagination as a precondition for artistic productivity?

These dramas of disappointment, as well as the fear and the withdrawal they engender, may also explain the procrastination of Marcel's desire to write. The inability of the real to fulfill the ideal with respect to Balbec and Berma engender a fear that perhaps his ideal self-as-writer is destined for a similar fate, bound to perish in the abyss between the ideal and the real: cursed with a desire to write, but sans the genius for writing. At this stage of his career, Marcel has the impulse to be a writer, but lacks the means of realizing that impulse. Fear of failing in reality prompts his deferment of that reality. With respect to writing, Marcel postpones the contact of the ideal with the real—as he does with Venice. Consequently, the ideal of writing persists as pure desire throughout most of The Search, wary of the lessons of Balbec and Berma, which it is in no hurry of seeing repeated—the more so, since his ideal self is defined almost exclusively in terms of the desire to write. To safeguard that self he must protect it from a reality that implies its destruction. This he does by the long deferral to writing, by preserving the creative impulse in vitro, as it were: as pure desire.

This only partially explains Marcel's "delay" to writing, however, which is as critical to understanding Marcel's character (and just as problematic) as Hamlet's delay to action. Reality everywhere signifies the impending death of the ideal, and with respect to the desire to write it signifies the death of the ideal self. Reality reinforces the mortality of the self. The death of the ideal self in the "drame coucher" is reenacted at Balbec and elsewhere, as evidenced by the serial destruction of the ideal by the real throughout *Recherche*.

Marcel's delay to writing signifies a fear of mortality in another regard. If reality reinforces his fear of mortality because it signifies the possible death of writing, then by ironic contrast, the realization of the creative impulse similarly reinforces his fear of mortality because of the exhaustive output associated with it. Marcel notes the morbid effects of creativity upon Bergotte: observing that the "powers of the writer were no longer equal to the inconsiderate demands of the work" (PR 1119), which must be "endured . . . like an exhaustive task . . . overcome like an obstacle" (PR 1112). Hence, opposite outcomes (the failure or realization of the creative impulse) have similar effects: a renewed fear of mortality. With respect to the signs of art, the real signifies mortality no matter whether it leads to the death or rebirth of the ideal. Marcel is trapped between the Scylla of the ideal and the Charybdis of the real, both of which signify his mortality. If the ideal becomes real, he dies to art. If the ideal dies without becoming real, his soul perishes forever: to be followed in time by his body. The realization of the ideal signifies the death of his mortal self; the death of the ideal in the real signifies the death of his immortal self.

For Marcel, the object desired but unpossessed is more appealing than the object possessed but no longer desired because it no longer inhabits his imagination. In its migration from the imagination to the senses, from the spiritual to the material world, a "privileged" object loses something precious: desire. The iridescent sheen of the self vanishes when the Other is possessed, when it devolves into pure object. It's charm is reduced by half; what it lacks is the self. In speaking of this disparity between the real and the imagined, the narrator asks, "How could I be expected to believe in a common origin uniting two names [Villeparisis and Guermantes] which had entered my consciousness, one through the low and shameful gate of experience, the other by the golden gate of the imagination?" (WBG 529). Instead of testing the ideal against the real, he withdraws from the real, sensing the incompatibility of the two. He prefers to preserve the ideal in a state of pure desire: for which the cork-lined bedroom is the objectified topos of this ideal self: the final defensive posture against the real—a utopian bunker of art, where the ideal is realized and the real idealized: sans sights, sounds, and smells.

His ideal of Venice survives its first contact with the real city, but only because he is with his mother. Upon her departure, the city loses its charm: the real is evacuated of the ideal:

> The town that I saw before me had ceased to be Venice. Its personality, its name seemed to me to by lying fictions . . . I saw the palaces reduced to their constituent parts, lifeless heaps of marble with nothing to choose between them. . . . This Venice without attraction for myself in which I was going to be left alone . . . (*La Fugitive* 837)

Like a Florentine fresco whose stone cannot preserve the precious pigment, the pseudo presence of Venice devolves into an absence in the absence of the mother. All of the icons of this cathedral of art in which he once believed, including the Arch of the Rialto, are transformed by the song "solo mio," which "reduced them to dust and ashes and completed the ruin of Venice" (LF 839).

When his mother is present, it is not Venice Marcel perceives, but the architecture of his own desire. Instead of disappointing, the Aladdinish city has merely disappeared—under the projections of his profane desires for the mother. If Albertine is draped in the Venetian sublime, similarly Venice is draped in his desire for the mother. As Collier asserts, "[T]he cultural image of Venice itself is distorted by the gravity of his desire. . . . In fact, the figure of desire so saturates the Venetian topos that even when comparing Venetian buildings to exhibitions of Dutch paintings Marcel sees the [windows] filled with girls" (24). The real is subsumed by the ideal: the citadel of profane desire is superimposed by Marcel's profane desire for the mother. The surfaces of its "ancient architecture" are dematerialized by the projections of his desire. Amidst the architecture of Marcel's desire, Venetian architecture all but disappears.

Though dire and disappointing as this second moment of the narrative may be, it is nevertheless more "wholesome" than the captivating visions of an idealizing imagination. As Proust asserts, "And yet, whatever the inevitable disappointments that it must bring in its train, this movement towards what we have only half seen . . . is the only one that is wholesome for our senses, that whets the appetite . . ." (WBG 656). The repression of desire by the real, instead of extinguishing it, enervates it. The Search for the two-in-one is renewed. The ideal is mobilized by the contradictions of the real, as if finding new life in the antithetical tension between the figurative and the literal.

THE RE-MYSTIFICATION OF THE REAL: THE RECUPERATION OF THE IDEAL

> Art is the most real of all things, the sternest school in life and truly the Last Judgment.
>
> —PR

Fortunately, The Search does not culminate in this second moment of the narrative, in the nausea and nihilism of an existential materialism. The demystification of the real results in its "re-mysticiation" by the ideal. Kasell observes this process at work in Marcel's "re-mystification" of the Duchess de Guermantes: "[I]f his first reaction is disappointment and demystification, this imaginative perception enacts a 're-mystification.'" The rapport found lacking between the image and the perceived figure is "retroactively restored, so that the original vision—and Marcel's expectations—may be verified"

(91). Thus, the disappointments of the real are not absolute. "The story of that loss becomes," as Kasell asserts, "a refutation of that loss . . . a story built around a repeated movement of loss and recovery" (92). The recuperative frame that commences and concludes *Recherche* is metonynically reinscribed in Marcel's intermittent recuperations of the ideal throughout The Search. His retrospective "remystification" of Balbec and Berma is a metonym for the metaphoric "remystification" of experience by involuntary memory.

This persistence of the ideal, even when contradicted by the real, sustains The Search and results in the transformative revelations of involuntary memory, and the ultimate alliteration between the ideal and the real: when the impulse to write becomes writing. The antithetical oppositions of the ideal and the real are synthesized in the involuntarily remembered, as a precondition for the redemptive assimilation of all three into the symbolic. As Kasell observes, "[A] new space is created by this juxtaposition of incompatible elements," a "middle distance" is discovered between them "within which the activity of fiction can take place." This tension between the ideal and the real "maintains the ground of fiction by preserving the tension in which it can exist" (5). Kasell continues:

> [T]his intermediary position often expresses Marcel's desire to have things both ways, that is, to possess his ideal in real form . . . to actualize an imaginary reality, not in order to indicate a moral quality, but to describe the serious conviction that one can cross the fictional distance. (9)

The poetic wisdom of "the point of view from which we come at last to regard the world" corrects the "error of literality" committed in the narrative's second moment. Involuntary memory concretizes the two-in-one, yielding a spiritualized materiality that fully and finally realizes the desires of the "ideal-hungry" and "merger-hungry" personality, as objectified in the "rings of a beautiful style."

It is retrospectively that Marcel comes into greater wisdom regarding Berma's acting. The dialectic progression of the third moment is sustained in each case, not by involuntary memory, but by Platonic dialogue with a Socratic elder (Elstir and Bergotte)—and retrospectively by a review in *Le Figaro*. Marcel's appreciation of Berma's genius is adjusted retrospectively: "[T]his new idea of 'the purest and most exalted manifestation of dramatic art' . . . sped to join the imperfect pleasure which I had felt in the theatre, added to it a little of what was lacking, and their combination formed something so exalting that I cried within myself: 'what a great artist'" (WBG 368). Berma's artistry enjoys a "posthumous" fame, as it were, in the narrator's mind. Whatever "wisdom" he discovers does not come from direct observation of the Other. Rather, it is the product of two disparate moments in time which through their fortuitous association yield his wisdom. If the "wisdom" of the ideal is contradicted by the "wisdom" of the real, then similarly the error of this "wisdom" is exposed by the association of the second moment with a retrospective third moment, which not only corrects the "wisdom" of the second moment, but fuses it with the "wisdom" of the first, producing a third wisdom as exalted as it is eternal, in which the weight of the literal is infused with the "spiritual glamour" of the ideal.

As evidenced by the progression of the ideal, the real, and the remembered, Proustian "wisdom" is inherently dialectic, associative, metaphoric. As his narrator asserts, "[L]et us then declare whether, in the communal life that is led by our ideas in the enclosure of our minds, there is a single one of those that makes us most happy which has not first sought, a very parasite, and won from an alien but neighboring idea the greater part of the strength that it originally lacked" (WBG 369). Marcel's "idea" of Berma is influenced by the "communal life" it enjoys, by the ideas of Bergotte, which retroactively inform his idea of Berma—a process that is replicated in the "communal life" led by his idea of Balbec, similarly informed retrospectively by the ideas of Elstir. The "wisdom" of *Recherche* is produced dialectically through the temporal juxtaposition of ideas. The false wisdom produced by the dialectic association of the figurative and the literal is corrected and superseded by the retrospective wisdom of the third moment, privileging Platonic dialogue and involuntary memory. Meaning precipitates out of this associative chain of temporality.

It is only ex post facto that a real sense of Berma's artistry emerges. Delueze elaborates: "[T]he mechanism of objective disappointment and of subjective compensation is specially analyzed in the examination of the theatre":

> [T]hose signs we had not been able to relish or to interpret so long as we linked them to Berma's person—perhaps their meaning was to be sought elsewhere: in associations which were neither in Phedre nor in Berma. Thus Bergotte teaches the hero that a certain gesture of Berma's evokes that of an archaic statuette the actress could never have seen but which Racine himself had certainly never thought of either. (34)

The "sign" of Berma's artistry is further explicated retrospectively—is revealed to be a sign that deeply informs the plot of *Recherche*, and the two great loves of Marcel's life, in particular. It is not until years later during his grief over Albertine, that Marcel comes to his deepest understanding regarding Berma's artistry (as evidenced in her performance of Phedre) and its meaning for his own experience. Marcel discovers in Phedre's relation to Hippolyte and Thesee a transposition of the critical turning points in his loves for Gilberte and Albertine:

> I opened the newspaper; it announced a performance by Berma. Then I remembered the two different attitudes in which I had listened to Phedre, and it was now in a third attitude that I thought of the declaration scene. It seemed to me that what I had so often repeated to myself, and had heard

recited in the theatre, was the statement of the laws of which I must make experience in my life. . . . But did not the plot of *Phedre* combine these two cases. . . . [T]hen, like myself when I decided to give my letter back to Francoise, she decides that the refusal must come from him, decides to stake everything upon his answer . . . and there is nothing, not even the harshness with which, as I had been told, Swann had treated Odette, or I myself had treated Albertine, a harshness which substituted for the original love, a new love composed of pity, emotion, of the need of effusion . . . that is not to be found also in this scene. . . . So it is that jealousy, which in love is equivalent to the loss of all happiness, outweighs any loss of reputation. . . . Thus at least it was that . . . this scene appeared to me, a sort of prophecy of the amorous episodes of my own life. (LF 705)

Marcel's "wisdom" regarding Berma's genius is indeed the "point of view from which [he] comes at last to view" her art. Retrospectively, he discovers in the play "the laws of which I must make experience in my life." He discovers a direct correspondence between the "plot of *Phedre*" and his own amorous experience. This play, when he first views it as a boy, already contains the kernel of his amorous experience, exerts a prophetic, deterministic influence over his amorous destiny—an influence of which he remains unaware until an ad in the newspaper triggers involuntary memories foregrounding the deep association between art and love, here fully explicated for the first time. The "wisdom" that his experience has been deeply informed by art helps convert the long-standing impulse to write into writing. The "perpetual alliteration" Marcel discovers between art and desire helps fulfill his desire to write, helps heal the pathology of possessive desire by absorbing it into artistic desire. In this third moment of the narrative, Marcel awakens to the artistic determinism that has been shaping his destiny throughout—in love, society, and art, furnishing the themes that will liberate into the real the ideal-of-all-ideals: the impulse to create. This recuperative moment evidences that the whole of *Recherche* is deeply inflected in its metonymic fragments.

This retrospective restoration of Berma's artistry foreshadows the resurrection of Marcel's romantic ideal of Balbec church as well. This time, it is the artist, Elstir, whose ideas retrospectively influence Marcel's, recuperating the lost ideal of "Norman gothic" architecture. As Marcel notes, "[W]hen I confessed to him the disappointment that I had felt upon seeing the porch at Balbec: 'What . . . Why, it's the finest illustrated Bible that the people have ever had'" (WBG 632). With a few swift strokes, the brush of Elstir's tongue accomplishes the restoration, which is enacted dialectically: not only through dialogue with another, but through the synthesis of the ideal and the real. Once again, the ideal is reborn from the ash heap of the real. The alliteration between art and experience, between *Phedre* and Albertine, is reinscribed in the correspondence Marcel discovers retrospectively between Balbec church and Albertine:

> I should not have known Albertine had I not read in an archaeological treatise a description of the church at Balbec, had not Swann, by telling me that this church was almost Persian, directed my taste to Byzantine Norman.... To be sure, in that Balbec so long desired I had not found the Persian church of my dreams, nor the eternal mists. Even the famous train at one twenty-two had not corresponded to my mental picture of it. But in compensation for what our imagination leaves us wanting ... life does give us something which we were very far from imagining. Who would have told me at Combray, when I lay waiting for my mother's good night kiss with so heavy a heart, that those anxieties would be healed, and would break out again one day, not for my mother, but for a girl who would at first be no more, against the horizon of the sea, than a flower.... Well, this Albertine so necessary, of love for whom my soul was now almost entirely composed, if Swann had not spoken to me of Balbec, I should never have known her. (LF 734)

Like Swann at the end of *Swann's Way*, Marcel awakens to the associative, deterministic nature of experience, discovering that both the "sufferings through which he had passed" and the "pleasures ... which were already being brought to birth" are "linked by a sort of concatenation of necessity" (292). As with *Phedra*, Balbec church retrospectively appears to him "as a sort of prophesy of the amorous episodes of my own life." A deep alliteration is discovered between the material and the spiritual, between the architecture he loves and the architecture of desire. This is the essence of the alliterative wisdom that inheres in the third moment of the narrative. That which is differentiated in time is revealed to be part of an associative pattern. The particular "wisdom" that is the true destination of The Search is joyous for the very reason it heals the deepest wound in Marcel's soul: the wound of differentiation. The tragic and traumatic differentiation of the ideal self is assimilated into a transcendent alliteration: of the ideal and the real; of the past, present, and future—an alliteration perpetually enshrined on the level of the symbolic, concretized in ink on paper, under the immortal sign of art. The "spiritual glamour" of the ideal that faded in the glare of the real is restored to the real by the reemergence of the real in time—when it is draped in the Fortuny gown of the ideal.

The "concatenation of necessity" discovered in this alliteration between art and love is not merely prophetic, but fatalistic—privileging a darker wisdom, informed by matricidal guilt:

> [I]f Swann had not spoken to me of Balbec, I should have never known her. Her life would perhaps have been longer ... and also it seemed to me that, by my entirely selfish affection, I had allowed Albertine to die just as I had murdered my grandmother. (LF 734)

The determinism of *Phedre* is eclipsed by the fatalism of Balbec church—reinscribing the "curse" of the "little phrase." The narrator's retrospective wisdom further implicates him in original sins, become mortal sins: an awareness that gives the dagger of guilt a cruel twist. Marcel's "wisdom" invests art (the "little phrase," *Phedre*, architecture/sculpture) with a fatal determinism, which is perhaps the primary distinction between the artistry of *Recherche* and the fatal flaws of *Jean Santeuil*. Further, the atavistic determinism associated with these works of art contrasts with the redemptive determinism associated with Venice, whose architecture in general, and whose Baptistery of St. Mark's in particular, prefigure the cathedral in words erected to consecrate art's dual capacity to damn and redeem. As *Recherche* abundantly evinces, art is an ambivalent terrain of damnation and redemption, of vice and virtue.

The recuperation of the two-in-one (of the art/life, ideal/real, mother/son, Other/self dyads) attests to the "amphibious" nature of involuntary memory, doubly sheathed in the selfobject: "[E]very impression has two parts, one of them incorporated in the object, the other prolonged within ourselves" (PR 1010). Knowledge and spirituality do not come before, are not a function of reason and faith, are not "a priori," but come after, are a function of memory and chance, are "a posteriori." As Marcel affirms, "[Albertine] alone could give me that happiness. The idea of her uniqueness was no longer a metaphysical a priori based upon what was individual in Albertine . . . but an a posteriori created by the contingent and indissoluble overlapping of my memories" (LF 772). The "a posteriori" wisdom of love, however, is melancholy insofar as its wisdom, instead of healing the wound of differentiation, deepens it—either through guilt or indifference. As Deleuze observes, "So it is with Gilberte, so it is with Albertine: in love, the truth always comes too late. Love's time is a lost time because the sign develops only to the degree that the self which corresponded to its meaning disappears" (86). Nevertheless, the retrospective explication of the signs of love, by deepening the wound of differentiation, not only prefigure the liberatory explications of involuntary memory that reveal the continuity of the self in time, but herald the self's redemption through art.

Proust subverts the intellect as an organ for constructing knowledges insofar as knowledge in *Recherche* "always comes after," as an effect of chance or as a gift bestowed dialogically by an Other (hence, the Platonic roots of The Search). Deleuze continues, "[T]here is a certain Platonism in Proust . . . and the disjunct use of the faculties in their involuntary exercise has . . . its model in Plato's education of a sensibility open to the violence of signs" (96). Proust reinvents the dialectic knowledge-making model of Plato, however, retaining its oppositional aspects as an essential ingredient of the educative process, but positing the knowledge gained as something that comes after, not before—that is the byproduct of a retrospective gaze determined by chance or Platonic discourse, not the inevitable result of an "Idea that is always 'before'":

always presupposed, even when it is discovered only afterwards ... so that the disjunct use of the faculties is merely a "prelude" to the dialectic which unites them in a single Logos ... as Proust says, summarizing his whole critique of the dialectic, the Intelligence always comes "before." (97)

The intellect's inability to demystify the literal signs of love reveals a double impotency: it not only fails to uncover the truth, but constructs falsehoods. Proust's subversion of Plato's dialectical model is evidenced "in the meanders and rings of an anti-Logos style that ... makes the requisite detours in order to gather up the ultimate fragments ... each one of which refers to a different whole, to no whole at all, or to no other whole than that of style" (Deleuze 103).

DEATH (AND TRANSFIGURATION) IN VENICE: THE THIRD MOMENT OF DESIRE

Venice is a topos of death and resurrection—not necessarily in that order. On the one hand, it is the scene of Albertine's resurrection and figurative death, as effected respectively by the telegram Marcel believes he receives from her and by the advent of his indifference toward her, which signifies her genuine death to him. On the other hand, Venice also prefigures Marcel's redemption to art: a resurrection that is realized retrospectively when a slip on a paving stone leads not only to the rebirth of Venice but to the birth of Marcel's artistic self: both enacted through the medium of involuntary memory. In Venice, the past, the present, and the future converge. Albertine floats in on the gondola of the past, even as Marcel explores the pleasures of the city by gondola with his mother. Ruskinian impressions of light and water blend with the ghosts of the Venetian past: images of stone floating on water stained with time. The floating city is at once a topos of eroticism and art, which renews Marcel's amorous sorrows and heralds his artistic resurrection—even as it reinscribes the recuperative taste of the petites madeleines floating in tea.

The Venetian sublime determines the story's future as well, as images of Marcel's impending resurrection proliferate amongst the ruins of his desire for Albertine and the resurrection of Combray. The juxtaposition (and transposition) of stone and water in Venice sustains this symbiosis of death and transfiguration, as embodied in the paving stone and the madeleine. Venice represents the logical destination of Marcel/Proust's idolatry of Ruskin: signified by the mimetic transposition of light, water, and stone—where the floating reflections of Venetian architecture are figured in terms of stone, and where the stones are dematerialized into light. The Ruskinesque mastery Marcel displays announces that the moment of rupture between master and pupil is at hand. Venice signifies Proust's assimilation, and the impending eclipse of Ruskin, even as it prefigures Marcel's transfiguration into an artist.

Only the presence of the mother, and the web of profane desire, yet prevents his liberation to art. Perhaps more effectively than any critic, Peter Collier has fathomed the significance of the Venetian sublime for *Recherche*: "[T]hese mini-resurrections of memories of Albertine lead straight away into the apparent resurrection of Albertine herself in the celebrated telegram. . . . He himself now yearns for a kind of resurrection, a survival beyond the body" (29). Albertine's ephemeral resurrection through writing prefigures Marcel's own redemption and eternalization through art. Ironically, if this telegram momentarily resurrects Albertine from the grave, it also announces her actual death in Marcel's heart: "[T]he telegram . . . makes Marcel at last realize that the prospect of living with her leaves him indifferent; only at this moment does she become effectively dead for him" (Collier 121).

It is ex post facto that the significance of Venice is revealed to him as well. This retrospective epiphany occurs when "Marcel stumbles on a paving stone one morning in Paris, and this sensory experience brings back the forgotten experience of walking on the uneven flagstones of the Baptistery of St. Mark's Basilica in Venice":

> From this moment, Marcel's shattered self is reconstituted like a mosaic. In fact, he had long fantasized a journey to Venice as the ultimate cultural experience, but, like other dream figures . . . Venice was a source of disappointment as much as of experience when it was finally attained in *La Fugitive*. (1)

The theme of death and resurrection now shifts from the Other to the self, from Albertine to Marcel. Though the resurrection of the Baptistery is figured as an effect of chance, it is (of all the topoi in The Search) the most logical and aesthetically satisfying choice as the medium of Marcel's redemption. Marcel enters the Baptistery while engaging in the two most spiritual pastimes of his life, reading and writing: in this instance, about Ruskin—the patron saint of his own art. The presence of both the mother and the muse of his art comprises a double objectification of the ideal—even as it gestures toward the impending liberation of the ideal self into the real, through writing. The harmonic convergence of this holy trio (Marcel, mother, and Ruskin) in the Baptistery of St. Mark's tropes on the impending fusion of the two-in-one through involuntary memory and art, consecrated in a work of art that the artist himself will compare to a cathedral. Collier writes,

> The hero finally works on Ruskin and art in the presence of his mother in the Baptistery of St. Mark's, in a scene of great import, since the return of this scene via involuntary memory . . . will provide him with the revelation of the meaning of his life and the means of its salvation through art. Venice, after being a chimerical erotic and cultural ideal . . . becomes in *La Fugitive* a latent figure of Marcel's memory and creativity. (4)

Proust's imagery reinforces the retrospective determinism, as figures of resurrection proliferate and combine. The mother's presence resonates in the image of the Virgin Mary. She prays for her son, "as if she were presiding over his redemption as a man and his rebirth as an artist" (Collier 9). Love, having degenerated from the sacred to the profane, from the spiritual to the erotic, from the familial to the incestuous and the illicit, is once again purified, recuperated in the figures of a sanctified Albertine (Magdalene) and a purified mother, whose "newly purified love is due partly to her charitable, maternal sacrifice, draping him in her shawl amid the cold, baptismal dampness"(Collier 127)—a trope for the moistness of the maternal kiss. Thus, the Baptistery is not only a site for the regeneration of the past, for the spiritual and artistic redemption of Marcel, but for the recuperation of love, and for the eternalization of the mother in particular. Not only religious iconography (such as the Baptistery and the tomb of Dandolo), but mythical bird images and modern cultural artifacts (such as the phoenix and the Fortuny dresses) combine to herald Macel's impending redemption. Collier elaborates:

> Proust multiplies references to the phoenix, a motif on the dresses, linking it with the thematics of resurrection, no doubt inspired by the presence in the Venetian architecture of a similar motif, that of a peacock. Proust appears to have invented his own Fortuny dresses with phoenix or peacock motifs, and evokes disturbing movements of the birds on the folds of the dresses in order to suggest a link between sexuality and death. . . . Proust's whole text suggests that the bodily has to be transcended, has to be translated into form, in order that the spiritual be reborn. The intertwined birds everywhere present in St. Mark's Basilica reveal the same message of desire transcended and resurrection prefigured. (7)

The ideal must perish in the real before it can be reborn to the real in time through art. As Collier asserts, "[T]he death of the substance of the original material is required, so that its aesthetic structure will survive in more enduring form" (8)—a structure that is temporal in essence. The discovery of the real in time resurrects the ideal, effacing the difference between the ideal and the real.

The regeneration of Marcel's own spirituality is announced by the resurrection of Combray that occurs in Venice: the first gestative stirrings of a lost past. Upon arriving in the fabled city of desire, "the whole of Combray is regenerated in Proust's description of Venice" (Collier 9): as if the floating city was itself a flavored tea in which the past magically takes shape once his senses are dipped into it. The stones and waters of Venice are invested with a regenerative force, with the power to resurrect not only his past, but his spirituality. As Collier observes, "Proust's exploration of Venice and Venetian artifacts opens out into a universally valid aesthetic, regenerating all our experience through the structures of memory, perception and art"(10).

Of all the images that trope on Marcel's impending redemption through art, it is the image of the mosaic (and particularly the mosaics of St. Mark's) that resonates with the greatest significance, insofar as its fragments suggest a composite whose timeless artistry tropes on the involuntary memory itself. For Proust, "real artistry lies in the art-form of memory, seen as mosaic" (Collier 128):

> It is only when he resurrects this primal Venetian scene by the accident of tripping over the paving stone which recalls the mosaic pavement of St. Mark's that the revelation will be codified. Nonetheless, the Baptistery scene captures a complex psychological relationship with the world in a formal, artistic patterning as of a mosaic. The figure of the mosaic itself is the major formal model of . . . resurrection—the missing piece of the puzzle of Marcel's experience . . . the floor and walls of St. Mark's are themselves one vast mosaic constructing a resurrectional message . . . rebuilt into the jigsaw of memory, the mosaic of literature. (131)

The mosaics also complete the loop back to Ruskin, who "had announced the enormous importance of the artistic and religious creativity of the mosaics of St. Mark's" (131)—which embody, as it were, Ruskin's aesthetic ideal, in which art enshrines the religious sublime. Proust parts company with Ruskin in the Baptistery, charting his own creative course by liberating the artistic impulse from servitude to religious idolatry. He appropriates the mosaics of St. Mark's not as symbols of religious redemption but of the redemptive power of art. For the first time, Proust emerges from the shadow of Ruskin into the light of his own artistry—which is why the Baptistery, of all topoi in The Search, is the ideal site of artistic redemption. As Collier notes, "[I]n the Baptistery at last the act of memory is assimilated into the practice of artistic transposition" (132)

In the climactic volumes of *Recherche,* the darkness of the narrator's annihilation of society and of his own atavistic descent into vice and suffering is only exceeded by the spiritual glow of his reintegration and redemption through art. Collier continues:

> The pulverisation of a structure, followed by a reconstruction meticulous enough to count as a resurrection, is also an image of Proust's *A la Recherche du temps perdu.* Enormous mental and social constructions . . . are elaborated in the course of *Recherche,* only to crumble to dust. Meanwhile, the novel keeps hinting at some miraculous resuscitation of the lost experience. But Proust's transcendental recuperation of his experience at the end . . . is both a total rearrangement of the fragments of that experience, and an artistic preservation of their fragmentary integrity. Proust's reconstruction is both creation and salvation through the medium of an aesthetic reworking of superficially non-aesthetic experience. (11)

In the dialectic "search engine" of the ideal, the real, and the remembered, the moment of desire and the moment of its death are both recuperated in a third moment that realizes the desire to transcend death in art. The correspondence between the conscious and unconscious mind that characterizes the final redemptive perspective of *Recherche* is evidenced by the absorption of involuntary memory into the symbolic realm of art. This transformation of the remembered into the symbolic and the mythical in the third and final phase of the dialectical process of knowledge making is a vital precondition for artistic production as well. Not until Proust is able to envision his experience in terms of the mythical, the symbolic, and the metaphoric is he able to convert it into art; not until he is able to conceive of it in the symbolic terms of an exile from Eden, of a heroic search, of a Medieval cathedral, of a paradise lost, of the Magdalenic redemption of a sinner, of a Sisyphean labor, or of a descent into the decadence of Sodom and Gomorrah does it cease being mere experience and become art.

THE "LIE" OF THE MADELEINE: THE "PRIVILEGED MOMENTS" RECONSIDERED

In the final retrospective view, the past is not merely recuperated but constructed anew, as involuntary memory gives rise to fiction. Margaret Gray posits a critical question: "[W]e have been working with memory and fiction. Just what is the relation between the two . . . ?" (90). Gray argues that "memory is fiction," seemingly putting the lie to the privileged moment of the madeleine (as well as all the other privileged moments in *Recherche*). I tend to agree.

In contradistinction to the critical tradition, whose assumptions privilege the primacy of involuntary memory with respect to the origins of the creative impulse, I believe the "privileged moment" can be more usefully interpreted as an effective literary device that solves Proust's most intractable aesthetic problem: what form to give the themes that interest him. The problems of unity, form, plot, and dramatic emphasis are all solved by Proust's novel treatment of the "privileged moment," which constitutes a variation on a theme by Ruskin. The aesthetic focus of the novel assumes dramatic and coherent form when art becomes the locus of a governing, if not fatalistic determinism through a series of dramatic disappointments and revelations that overcome the discontinuities in the narrator's "apprenticeship to signs." The "privileged moments" do not inform the origins of the creative impulse (as ficted in *Recherche*), as much as they meet aesthetic imperatives: for form, drama, unity. They are less a cause of the creative urge than an effect of it: the solution to an aesthetic problem that perplexed Proust in *Jean Santeuil* and which distinguishes that critically flawed failure from the enduring work of art that is *Recherche*.

In assessing the "privileged moments," I therefore find it necessary to "read against the grain" of the narrative, whose narrator in this critical regard is unreliable. Whereas the "drame coucher" narrows the narrative space between "Marcel" and Proust, the "privileged moments" widen that gap: are more deeply informed by the aesthetic needs of the artist than by the psychological needs of the man—which evidence a creative impulse deeply informed by the neurotic pathology of the self. To more fully appreciate the correspondence between the "privileged moments" and the origins of the creative impulse, criticism must "reread" them. As ficted in the "privileged moments," the origins of the creative urge are rooted in the alliteration between chance and involuntary memory. This depiction leads astray the critic in search of the manifold and complex origins of the creative impulse. What is not explicitly dramatized in The Search is the alliteration between the "privileged moments" and the pathology of Marcel's self. Only by reestablishing this correspondence can we more fully appreciate the extent to which the creative urge is informed by the "privileged moments."

It is by virtue of their ability to heal the long-standing wound of differentiation, that the "privileged moments" of *Recherche* inform the creative impulse—not as some mechanism of pure chance. They satisfy the deepest need of the pathologically differentiated self, by fulfilling the need for the two-in-one, by uniting the ideal and the real self through writing. This implicit alliteration between involuntary memory and self-pathology supersedes the overt alliteration between involuntary memory and chance, when it comes to assessing the correspondence between the "privileged moments" and the origins of the creative impulse. As depicted in the "privileged moments," the correspondence between memory and fiction is the work's greatest fiction.

What is posited as the cause of art (the transcendence of time through its serendipitous recuperation) is in reality an effect of art, whose primary impetus is the need to transcend neurotic conflict—which also becomes its most beneficent effect. I am not denying the authenticity of involuntary memory, as figured in *Recherche*, I am simply calling into question the primacy assigned to chance and involuntary memory with respect to the origins of the creative impulse. In the final analysis, *Recherche* is much more the result of voluntary will than involuntary memory, operating in the service of psychic needs that foreground survival of the self in the here and now through the objectification of neurotic conflicts. As Gray asserts, "[W]e have seen that the behavior of fiction seems to be the behavior of memory; both unfold according to the principles of creation and revision" (91). Gray's definition of narrative underscores the fictional nature of the "privileged moments": narrative is "the ordering of meaning in time [preceded] by the activity of making sense: literally producing it, creating it, writing it, such that memory's 'history' is constantly being ficted and reficted"(91). Of the many fictions that inhere in *Recherche*, perhaps the most significant is the fiction of its genesis from involuntary memory.

The narrator himself belies the fictive nature of the "privileged moments": "[T]he images chosen by the memory are as arbitrary, as narrow, as elusive as those which the imagination had formed and reality had destroyed" (III 149, Gray 92). As Gray concludes, "[I]f indeed memory is necessarily ficted, the status of autobiography as genre, long in question, becomes increasingly problematic . . ." (92). What Proust's narrative suggests is that "perhaps memory itself only takes shape as fiction" (93)—a tendency implied by the climax of *Recherche*, which ends with memory on the eve of becoming art. Doubrovsky is succinct on this issue: "[N]othing is less innocent than memory. If it tells the truth, it's always with a lie" (1).

Recherche is as much a monument to invention as it is to involuntary memory, to "craftsmanship" as it is to revelation, to continuous labor as it to spiritual epiphany, and to neurotic conflict prolonged over decades as it is to the random discoveries of a remembered moment. Indeed, Proust's narrator observes that memory tends toward fiction when he drops the guise of his own fictional existence, when he admits that Swann is pure fiction, self-reflexively exploding the myth of his own fiction, exposing memory itself as myth:

> And yet, my dear Charles ____, whom I used to know when I was still so young and you were nearing your grave, it is because he whom you must have regarded as a little fool has made you the hero of one of his volumes that people are beginning to speak of you again and that your name will perhaps live . . . it is because they know that there are some traces of you in the character of Swann. (LP 518)

Nowhere does the narrative of *Recherche* so explicitly unwrite itself, opening from fiction into memory, from fictional involuntary memory into autobiography. What has been portrayed throughout as the byproduct of involuntary memory is here revealed for what it really is: memory transposed into fiction. That is, not pure involuntary memory at all, but an amalgamation of voluntary memory, involuntary memory, and imagination. Only Proust can reveal where one ceases and the other begins.

The revelations of the madeleine are neither a complete fiction nor an absolute verity—are simultaneously, paradoxically, fact and fiction—expressing a truth amplified to suit the needs of art. As Patrick Brady asserts, "[S]uch cases remind us forcibly of the degree of pure invention involved in a narrative of this type—not merely invention by the implied author (let alone Proust the man) but invention of an invented entity, namely, the fictional narrator. It is invention of the third degree" (18). Leo Bersani concurs: "[T]o the extent that characters and situations illustrate the resources of the narrator's metaphorical imagination, we feel that Marcel is inventing the world he describes. He seems to be not only remembering impressions, but also creating novelistic drama in order to provoke his own impressions" (239):

The narrator himself presents his work both as a faithful report on his past and as an exercise of pure invention. He speaks of his book as one "in which there is not one fact that is not imaginary, nor any real person concealed under a false name, where everything has been invented by me to meet the needs of my story," but he is also obviously encouraging us to believe that he is remembering a past which involuntary memory has recently allowed him to relive.... (PR 976, Bersani 247)

The narrator calls into question his own assertions regarding the alliteration between involuntary memory and the creative impulse, observing that his invention has as much to do with "craftsmanship": an act of pure volition. Using Wagner again as his prototype, he asserts that "in him, however great the melancholy of the poet, it is consoled, surpassed . . . by the delight of the craftsman" (LP 491). If we grant that the poet's melancholy is rooted in experience, then Proust's assertion deflates experience (and by implication involuntary memory, which is rooted in experience) as the determining source of art, attributing a greater role to the creative imagination, to pure invention, to a "Vulcan-like craftsmanship" allied to "industrious toil." The significance of this assertion is that it brings art down from the inaccessible, supernatural realms of the gods, where like Wagner's music it reigned "more real than life," grounding it instead in the delights of craftsmanship fueled by a love of labor.

Perhaps the most we can assert is that the narrative is a compendium of the imagination, the senses, and the memory (the ideal, the real, and the remembered), each of which alliterates with the original wound of differentiation, each of which is the object of the self's search, pursued as the hoped-for cure to its pathology—and each of which enjoys its moment in the narrative: of pure desire, of desire's disappointment, and of desire's fulfillment—played out across the entire space-time continuum of *Recherche*. Involuntary memory does not come before writing, as ficted in The Search, but comes after: is not a cause, but an effect of the desire to write. Deleuze develops the significance of this fictive memory:

> [T]o remember is to create, not to create memory, but to create the spiritual equivalent of the still too material memory, to create the viewpoint valid for all associations, the style valid for all images. It is style . . . which substitutes for the individual in the world the viewpoint toward a world, and which transforms reminiscence into a realized creation. (99)

The first creation of this viewpoint is the style needed to express it. The revelations of involuntary memory produce the aesthetic form required for their content. The original impulse to create, however, has other, darker sources—are as deeply rooted in neurotic conflict as in involuntary memory. As Jephcott concludes, "Proust recognizes . . . that the privileged moment can only be incorporated into the narrative if it is made part of a deliberately constructed framework" (209). As Bersani succinctly asserts, "[T]he memories belong to the character Marcel, but the novel is Proust's invention" (188).

THE UNCHAINED SIGN: (DE)COMPOSING THE UNITY OF ULTERIORITY

Deleuze raises a fundamental question: "[W]hat constitutes the unity of a work. . . . What constitutes the unity of art, if there is such a thing?" And posits an answer as provocative as it is postmodern: "We have given up seeking a unity which would unify the parts, a whole which would totalize the fragments" (144). The unity of *Recherche* itself was imposed retrospectively, did not come before, but after, was not antecedent but a posteriori: "[T]o claim that Proust had the notion . . . of the antecedent unity of the Search . . . as animating the whole from the start, is to read him badly, applying the ready-made criteria of organic totality which are precisely the ones he rejects, and missing the new conception of unity he was in the process of creating" (103). The unity of the work can only be comprehended in terms of its contradictions, its disjunctions, and its disruptions. The "associative chain" in *Recherche* is not continuous, but fragmented, contradictory, and recursive. The immaterial, as Deleuze writes, is emptied of its idealized contents by the material:

> [N]ot only are we present at this "dynamiting" of the containers by their contents, but at the explosion of the contents themselves which, unfolded, explicated, do not form a unique figure, but heterogeneous, fragmented truths still more in conflict among themselves than in agreement. Even when the past is given back to us in essence, the pairing of the present moment and the past is more like a struggle than an agreement, and what is given us is neither a totality nor an eternity, but a "bit of time in a pure state," that is, a fragment. (109)

Deleuze's interpretation subverts traditional readings of *Recherche*, which have argued that the work is, if anything, unified to a fault—and deliberately so: the embodiment of an aesthetic ideal that privileges the work of art as a self-contained, unified whole. Deleuze's reading not only calls these assumptions into question, not only invites a critical reassessment of *Recherche* in this light, but is able to locate even within this canonized work of high modernism, postmodern sensibilities—arising from its disjunctive, self-contradicting, fragmentary narrative. The unities that are achieved through struggle of opposites are unstable, generative, protean:

> [I]t is doubtless this which accounts for that extraordinary energy of unmatched parts in the Search [and which] testify separately to a whole

from which each part is torn, different from every other, in a kind of dialogue between universes. . . . [B]y setting fragments into fragments, Proust finds the means of making us contemplate them all, but without reference to a unity from which they might derive. . . . Even the final revelation of time regained will not unify them nor make them converge. . . . (110)

There is in *Recherche* a determinism of the metonymic fragment. Proust constructs his characters from the dismembered parts of humanity only to dismember them again into fragments. The Other ends as it began—as a fragment. The fragment is both the origin and the destination of the Other—its composite only an unstable phase between generation and degeneration, composition and decomposition, integration and disintegration. The dominant process seems to be one not of composition, but of decomposition, not of assimilating the part into the whole, but of liberating it from the whole—as if the whole is forever deconstructing itself into its constituent parts. Characters are composed of human fragments and decompose into them.

In Vermeer's *View of Delft,* it is not the whole painting that is privileged, but a mere fragment: a "patch of yellow light." Similarly, in Vinteuil's sonata it is not the entire work, but the fragment of the "little phrase" that inscribes its immortal, deterministic beauty. This "patch" and this "phrase" are the metonymic "piombi" in which the artistic sublime is immured. The meaning of human experience is not to be found on the cosmic, but on the microcosmic level. The cosmic inheres in the microcomsic: the eternal, in the immortal fragment. The meaning of human experience is not discovered in the eternal grandeur of the hereafter, but in the divine littleness of the here and now, in those sublime moments when spirituality is materialized.

Recherche is not so much a unified work of art as a collection of immortalized and immortalizing fragments. To celebrate the unity of *Recherche* obscures the primacy of the fragmentary in it: protean, immortal, and forever disruptive—forever wafting through its cathedral-like form, a vagabond incense of incompleteness, forever calling our attention to its "fragments without totality, vessels without communication, partitioned scenes" (Deleuze 133). Each immortal fragment is a metonym for the self that refuses to be assimilated into the collective whole: that dissociated, immortal, and immortalizing fragment of society we call the artist.

Proust beheld in these fragments an image of the creative self: isolated, immortal, protean. Deleuze offers a lucid view:

> The essential point is that the parts of the Search remain partitioned, fragmented, without anything lacking: eternally partial parts . . . swept on by time without forming a whole or presupposing one, without lacking anything in this quartering, and denouncing in advance every organic unity we might seek to introduce into it. When Proust compares his work to a cathe-

dral, or to a gown, it is not to identify himself with a Logos as a splendid totality, but on the contrary to emphasize his right to incompletion, to seams and patches. (143)

—even patches of yellow light. When Proust compares his work to a cathedral he is imposing an organic unity that is not absolute but relative. Likewise, the dialectic hermeneutic I have applied to Proust's narrative in this chapter is not driven by a desire to essentialize, totalize, or absolutely systematize it, but by a desire to explicate some of the dynamic tensions inherent to it. In the final analysis, the narrative subsumes any hermeneutic laws it obeys by virtue of its contradictions, disjunctions, synapses, inconsistencies, paradoxes, protean fragments, and irreducible totalities. Deleuze continues, "[A]ny associative chain is broken [including the dialectical chain of associations I have elaborated in this chapter] and gives way to a Viewpoint superior to the subject":

> But these viewpoints upon the world, veritable Essences, do not in turn form a unity or a totality: one might say rather that a universe corresponds to each, not communicating with the others, affirming an irreducible difference as profound as that of the astronomic worlds. . . . [E]ssence appears alongside these chains, incarnated in a closed fragment, adjacent to what it overwhelms, contiguous to what it reveals. Even the Church, a viewpoint superior to the landscape, has the effect of partitioning this landscape and rises up itself . . . like the ultimate partitioned fragment adjacent to the series which is defined by it. Which is to say that the Essences, like the Laws, have no power to unify or to totalize. (144–45)

The only unity extant in *Recherche* is one that paradoxically acknowledges the discontinuity of its fragments. Deleuze continues: "[B]ut there is, there must be a unity which is the unity of this very multiplicity, a whole which is the whole of just these fragments . . . the 'effect' of the multiplicity and of its disconnected parts" and that establishes "among their solitudes a spontaneous 'correspondence'" (144–45).

The unity of *Recherche* is an "a posteriori"—a retrospective effect of creativity which is indebted to the great works of the nineteenth century, to the literature of Balzac and the music of Wagner, whose unity is the result of "retrieving some exquisite scrap from a drawer of his writing-table, to make it appear as a theme, retrospectively necessary" (490). Proust continues:

> [A]nd perceiving all of a sudden that he had written a tetralogy, [he] must have felt something of the same exhilaration as Balzac, when . . . he suddenly decided, as he shed a retrospective illumination upon them, that they would be better brought together in a cycle in which the same characters would reappear, and added to his work . . . the brush of a stroke, the last and most sublime. A unity that was ulterior . . . perhaps indeed all the more real

> for being ulterior . . . when it is discovered to exist among fragments which need only to be joined together. A unity that has been unaware of itself, therefore vital and not logical. (*LP* 491)

In contradistinction to the deliberate, contrived artifice of a unity that is imposed on a work of art before it is composed, Proust privileges an organic, a posteriori, "involuntary" unity that arises from the "finished" work—and which indeed comprises its finishing touch. Proust's involuntary unity is also an anti-logos, the result not of the intellect but of a fortuitous discovery that "comes after": unifying without totalizing. The "unity" of *Recherche* evidences a dialectic between its free-standing fragments and its symphonic, cathedral-like structure: a "unity" that is deeply informed by the music of Wagner, as the narrator observes:

> Then there is diversity within the work itself, by the sole means that it has of being effectively diverse, to wit combining diverse individualities . . . allot[ting] to each denomination a different reality . . . at once complicated and simplified, that . . . inscribes itself in the vast sonorous mass. Whence the completeness of a music that is indeed filled with so many different musics, each of which is a person. (490)

Proust elaborates his nineteenth-century conception of "unity," which allows for, indeed insists upon, its opposite: incompleteness:

> I thought how markedly . . . these works participate in that quality of being . . . always incomplete, which is the peculiarity of all great works of the nineteenth century, with which the greatest writers of that century have stamped their books, but watching themselves at work as though they were at once *author and critic*, have derived from this self-contemplation a novel beauty, exterior and superior to the work itself, imposing upon it retrospectively a unity, a greatness which it does not possess. (490)

The fictional unity of *Recherche* (its self-contained narrative) continually opens upon itself into criticism—in a work in which the artist is continually commenting upon his art. As Fernand Gregh observes, "He was . . . one of those minds that are to be counted among the most original today, an 'artist-critic,' one of those intellectual systems that flourish at times when there is a welter of culture and in which the critical faculty is the equal of the creative" (qtd. in Hodson 32). I will revisit the implications of this fluctuation between art and analysis of art in the final chapter. The closed circle of the narrative opens instead into a self-reflexive spiral, in which the creative and the analytical inform one another. The "unity" of the work is constantly disrupted by its postmodern self-reflexivity and its free-standing fragments. Proust continues: "[A] unity . . . that has not banned variety, chilled execution. It emerges . . . like a fragment composed separately, born of an inspiration, not required by the artificial development of a theme, which comes in to form an integral part of the rest" (LP 491). "Unity" in *Recherche* is a protean paradox: "[T]his very special unity which appears afterward, which assures the exchange of viewpoints as it does the communication of essences, and which appears according to the laws of essence, itself a fragment alongside others" (Deleuze 149). It is a unity that enables contiguity between parts without "suppressing their difference or distance" (149). The imagery that Proust deploys throughout *Recherche* brilliantly figures the dynamic tension between partiality and totality. Paul de Man explicates this relationship of part to whole as evidenced in one of the work's dominant figures:

> [T]he miraculous interference of water and light in the refracted rainbow of the color spectrum makes its appearance throughout the novel, infallibly associated with the thematics of metaphor as totalization. It is the perfect analogon for the future of complementarity, the differences that make up the parts absorbed in the unity of the whole as the colors of the spectrum are absorbed in the original white light. (126)

Doubrovsky similarly departs from an earlier critical tradition emphasizing the work's unity. In contradistinction to the interpretations of Deleuze and de Man, however, which reconcile the tensions between the text's continuities and discontinuities through the tropes of "transversals" and "complementarity," Doubrovsky's reading eschews such reconciliation in favor of an interpretation that reads the violence of repressed desire as always and already disrupting the "conscious narration." In Doubrovsky's view, the continuities of the narrative constructed by the conscious mind are forever being disrupted by the repressed desires of the unconscious mind. As Carol Mastrangelo Bové observes, "[F]or Doubrovsky the stages of fantasy—that is, unconscious discourse itself—constitute the primary source of change in Proust's novel":

> Doubrovsky demonstrates the way in which the madeleine scene may be understood as the most significant instance of a disruptive unconscious creating a gap in conscious narration. . . . For both analysts [Sartre and Doubovsky] the psyche, like the text in which it exists, has a mode of being that is discontinuous. (Preface xiii)

Yet, the very recursivity of desire's disruptions itself constitutes a pattern that is continuous, that reinforces the continuities of other recursive elements in the text—is itself absorbed into a larger pattern of recursivity that undermines the autonomous agency that Doubrovsky assigns to discontinuity.

Proust's own comments inform the paradoxical nature of "unity" in *Recherche*, as evidenced by comments to Celeste Albaret (his live-in servant for the last eight years of his life): "You know, Celeste, I want my work to be a sort of cathedral in literature. That is why it is never finished. Even when the construction is completed there is always some decoration to add, or a stained-glass window or a capitol or another chapel to be opened up, with a little statue in the corner" (Albaret 240). Proust's valorization of the incomplete masterpiece may be the result of his negotiations with time, his way of turning an inevitable defect of his work into a virtue. Lacking the necessary time to give his masterpiece the "finish" it merited, to eliminate the redundancies and contradictions, to give the Venice chapter the elaboration it warranted, he makes a virtue of incompleteness, finding solace in a turn that anticipates the postmodern resistance to closure, creating a masterwork which, like the great cathedrals he admired, is a work-in-progress: not finished and static, but forever in motion, in the process of becoming, of tending toward the ideal work of art. A more apt symbol for the novel's vast, circular, well-organized, and nearly self-contained atmospheric unity might be that of the tropical storm system or the spiral nebula. As Kristeva observes in *Time and Sense*, her pioneering work on Proustian criticism:

> The cyclical end of *In Search of Lost Time* offers us a taste of childhood regained. We believe we are still at the beginning, but the closed spiral of *Time Regained* has been set into motion. This magnetized spiral sets off in search of a depth that is certainly childlike. At the same time, it relies on the magic of metamorphosing circles to condense the narrator's foreseen destiny. (3)

Shattuck similarly favors the trope of a spiral, as opposed to a circle, to describe the novel's "unity": "Achieving its deepest insights and formal beauties by returning to and surpassing itself, *A la recherche* must be seen as reflexive in shape, a narrative which turns back upon itself and rises out of itself in a spiral" (132). The novel approximates closure, gestures toward a self-contained unity, without ever realizing it—leaving the final finishing touches undone, embracing its own incompleteness as the final expression of its genius. A figurative Duomo without its capstone. A work-in-progress—that privileges perpetual progression toward an ideal work of art as opposed to the solidified actualization of it. A work that eschews the stasis of absolute fulfillment for the perpetual motion of its desire.

chapter five

Recherche and the Rankian Gaze

To eavesdrop in the text upon the narration of its genesis, where could we better attempt the experiment than in this *Recherche*, where a man relates the birth of his vocation as a writer?
—Doubrovsky

THE FUNDAMENTAL CLAIM that *Recherche* is a bildungsroman of the artist (novel of development) has recently come under critical attack in a growing body of postmodern scholarship, and particularly in the works of Doubrovsky, Gray, and Kasell. Yet even postmodern criticism is divided on this point, as evidenced for example by Deleuze's interpretation, which posits Marcel's career as an "apprenticeship to signs," the most significant of which are the signs of art. Doubrovsky, Gray, and Kasell, in contradistinction to Deleuze, argue that the end of *Recherche*, far from depicting Marcel's transformation into a writer leaves him "nowhere near a pen." They go even farther, arguing that his own assertions in the climactic passages of the Princess de Guermantes's soiree comprise a complete renunciation of literature. They further assert that Marcel's final metamorphosis into a writer is unwarranted given his long delay, his repeated deferral of writing in the previous six volumes, as well as the erosion of his narrative mastery in the Albertine volumes. On this critical point, postmodern scholarship argues that this disjunction between the novel's ending and its previous volumes comprises an irreconcilable contradiction. Marcel's career, with its persistent deferral of writing and its final renunciation of literature, simply does not provide enough justification for the final redemptive transformation into an artist, which seems more convenient than credible: an expedient device that meets the demands of art, as opposed to the logical outcome of a developmental process in play throughout The Search. To the postmodern gaze, the climactic artistic turn seems contrived, not inevitable. In the end, the novel deconstructs itself: the transformation of Marcel into an artist simply does not jibe with the career of Marcel the narrator.

Provocative as it may be, this postmodern interrogation of *Recherche* invites closer scrutiny of Marcel's alleged "apprenticeship to signs." I want to revisit his "apprenticeship" from a Rankian psycho-critical perspective, for I believe such an analysis calls into question not only the recent claims of postmodern criticism, but the assumptions of the Freudian psycho-critical tradition. As a closer look at the career of Proust's narrator evidences, Marcel's final transformation into an artist is deeply informed by his "apprenticeship to signs." Further, the artistic bildung can be usefully "read" from a Rankian psycho-critical perspective inasmuch as it evidences the critical phases in Rank's developmental paradigm for the artiste manqué.

For Rank, as for Proust's narrator, that bildung begins with a simple, but critical "self-nomination" to art. This is followed by a period of "self-training," often involving apprenticeship to a recognized master and the mimetic elaboration of an aesthetic ideology, followed by the overthrow of this influence under the prompting of the artist's own genius, which invents this aesthetic anew or formulates an entirely new one. If the career is particularly productive, the artist will struggle against the totalizing effects of art. Further, the creative impulse is informed throughout the artist's career by impulses that go far beyond the Freudian presumption of sublimated sexuality. Though these may include a "will to form," a desire to immortalize the self, an ideology of sacrifice, and prolonged conflict between the individual and the collective, the most significant determinant of the creative urge for the purposes of this study are "morbid crises of a neurotic nature."

Postmodern criticism is correct in asserting that the narrating "I" has no identity throughout much of *Recherche*, which is nothing if not a search for an artistic identity. The narrator's search is compelled by two needs (or desires): the need to escape the sorrows of sexual differentiation (from the maternal and from the feminine), the "incurable wound from which, in the end, emerges the Book" (Doubrovsky 33)—and the need to assert the creative self, which devolves into a search for the means to liberate that self from within the self, through the external stimuli of other artworks, of nature, of the social sublime, and of love. The quest to spiritualize all these with the self is part of a broader quest to spiritualize the self in a work of art. Consequently, there is no disconnect between the novel's final transfiguration and the preceding search. Marcel's quest is to discover, assert, and eternalize his identity as an artist. Again, Doubrovsky's observations are instructive: "In and through his book, he will offer himself identity and eternity" (82).

Also critical to the development of the creative urge is the desire to replace what has been irretrievably lost: a loved one, one's youth, a homeland. *Recherche* is pervaded by a deep sense of loss. Celeste Albaret even traces Proust's sudden desire for certain dishes to a sense of nostalgia:

I think now that those sudden fancies occurred at times when he was seeking times he'd lost—lost in the sense that a paradise is lost. And every fancy always corresponded to a particular shop or caterer, dating from his youth. . . . And all this was of course connected to his mother. . . . Perhaps, if he struggled so against time in order to finish as soon as possible, it was because he sensed the approaching end of many of the things he loved, which were already no more than shadowy memories. (76, 80)

The will to form, the need to escape neurotic suffering, to eternalize the self, to replace what has been lost—all inform the creative impulse, as much if not more than a sublimated sexual urge. Further, one can find in *Recherche* (as in *A Portrait of the Artist*) evidence of each of these origins of the artistic impulse, which I would like to revisit in greater detail, beginning with the will to form.

THE WILL TO FORM: SELF-NOMINATION AND SELF-TRAINING

Marcel's "apprenticeship" to art illustrates Rankian theory from its earliest phases, as evidenced by his "self-nomination" to art. As Rank asserts, "[T]he religion of genius and the cult of the personality thus begin, in the creative individual, with himself; he, so to say, appoints himself as an artist" (27). This self-nomination, however, is only possible if the society in which the individual lives "has an ideology of genius, recognizes it, and values it" (27). This cult of genius is evidenced in Marcel's immediate society by the veneration given to works of art by his grandmother and mother, who surround the boy with photos of masterpieces by Corot, Titian, and Turner, who read to him from the pastoral novels of George Sand, who quote to him from Mme de Sévigné and Saint Simon (the great chronicler of the Court of Louis XIV), who inculcate in him a love of cathedrals as art, and who place in his room a magic lantern that projects upon his bedroom walls artistic images of a feudal sublime. Marcel's youthful soul is immersed in this cult of genius, like a film in the solution that develops its images. Albaret's memoirs establish a correspondence between the narrator and author in this regard: "[H]e had been storing up material for years, first as a child, even more as a young man. It was as if he had a presentiment that all this would be material for his work" (150).

The narrator's close identification with this cult of genius is evidenced in a variety of ways: he identifies closely with the works of art with which mother and grandmother surround him to the point of wanting to visit the originals to receive their divine inspiration, to enervate the development of his own latent genius. He spends hours debating the merits of the French theatre with his playfellows—drama occupying the highest position in his youthful hierarchy: soon to be complemented by literature, painting, and music. As the narrator states, "[A]ll my conversations with my playfellows bore upon actors, whose art . . . was the first of all its numberless forms in which art itself allowed me to anticipate its enjoyment" (SW 57). He similarly spends his time alone reading the works of the French masters, and of one in particular (Bergotte). The image of the youth reading in the garden under a tree alliterates with the Garden of Eden and the Tree of Knowledge, setting in motion the fatal correspondence between knowledge and damnation.

More significantly, we find Marcel has already decided upon a literary career, as evidenced not only by his many statements to this effect, but by those passages that dramatize his early efforts in this direction: the literary passage on the three steeples (later published in *Le Figaro*); the notes he pens to mother and grandmother in which he recognizes traces of Bergotte's genius; and the prose poem he presents to Norpois for evaluation. Proust's narrator is a card-carrying member of the cult of genius, as evidenced not only by his literal and figurative association with genius, with art and with artists, but by his desire-of-all-desires: to be an artist. Marcel's active pursuit of art and artists is merely a displacement of the desire to become one. As Rank observes, this "self labeling" of the individual as an artist comprises the first stage of the search, the first efforts of the creative individual to differentiate the self from the collective. Rank elaborates:

> [T]he individual raises himself from out of the community by his inclusion in the genius type . . . the individual, as it were, abstracts himself in the style demanded by the genius-ideology and so concentrates the essence of his being, the reproductive urge, in the genius-concept. He says, more or less, that he needs only to create, not beget . . . this creativity begins with the individual himself—that is, with the self-making of the personality into the artist, which we have described previously as his appointment to the genius type. The creative personality is thus the first work of the productive individual. (28)

Marcel's association with genius, in the abstract and in the flesh, evidences this "self-labeling" and "self-training" phase of the artist's career. The ideal essence of his being is crystallized in the genius concept—and this concept totalizes his childhood world, is personified in Swann, Bergotte and Vinteuil, is concretized in the magic lantern, *Francois le champi,* and the memoirs of Mme de Sévigné, extends to Francoise's genius for cooking, Odette's genius for fashion, Cottard's genius for healing, and Norpois's genius for diplomacy. The genius concept (and its accretion of the ideal self) is Marcel's sole consolation for the sorrows of sexual differentiation from the mother and the female Other. The negative differentiation of the sexual self is consoled, if not mitigated, by the positive differentiation of the artistic self, whose development is ironically facilitated by the sorrows of sexual differentiation.

The choice of an artistic career produces additional conflicts between the individual's personal ideology of genius and the society's collective ideology of achievement, as embodied in parental aspirations for the child to become a lawyer or an ambassador that are dramatically at odds with his own creative ambitions. As Proust's narrator confides,

> [M]y father had always meant me to become a diplomat, and I could not endure the thought . . . I should have preferred to return to the literary career that I had planned for myself, and had been abandoned, years before, in my wanderings along the Guermantes way. But my father had steadily opposed my devoting myself to literature, which he regarded as vastly inferior to diplomacy, refusing even to dignify it with the title of career. . . . (SW 337)

The significance of this passage warrants further comment. It not only verifies the narrator's "self-nomination" to art; but evidences the conflict between the individual and the collective, here manifested in the tensions between son and father over his choice of a "career." Even more significantly, it informs the deeper psychological grammar of the Guermantes way, and by implication of "the two ways," insofar as the Guermantes way is posited as the place where Marcel for years abandons his literary calling. The "Guermantes way" is a terrain of self-betrayal, a topos of exile from the ideal self, a terra firma of the profane self. It signifies Marcel's long apostasy from the "signs" of art in pursuit of the "worldly signs" of society, incarnated in the seductive salons of the Faubourg St. Germain. He abandons the pursuit of his own genius in search of the genius of the Merovingian sublime, whose false glamour supplants the "spiritual glamour" of his own authentic genius—prompting yet another conflict that fuels the creative impulse, insofar as it brings Marcel's genius into conflict with his profane self. For years, the sacred within is sacrificed to the profane without: which ultimately brings the self back to its senses by liberating it from them, when the material is finally transcended by the spiritual self. Hence, even the digressions of the profane self prove useful to the development of the ideal self, concretized in the genius concept. The apostasy of the Guermantes way is replicated in the digressions of the Méséglise way, signified by the "signs" of love: the other great diversion of Marcel's life that delays his redemption through art.

The climactic "privileged moments" of involuntary memory associate the topos of apostasy and the topos of redemption (the Guermantes courtyard and St. Mark's Baptistery), bringing into "perpetual alliteration" the material and the spiritual. As Jean-Pierre Richard observes, the Marcel of the Baptistery "is very much a Christ-like, baptized, and redeemed figure" (qtd. in Collier 117). Collier concurs: "In the Baptistery at last the act of memory is assimilated to the practice of artistic transposition. This is why it is this moment rather than any other which has to be resuscitated at the Guermantes" (132). It is of all moments in *Recherche* the one that signifies the end of Marcel's long digression through society and love. It signifies the death of the profane and the ephemeral self, as well as the birth of the ideal and immortal self. It signifies the end of his apostasy from art and the beginning of his rebirth to eternity through art: a calling "that I had planned for myself, and had been abandoned, years before, in my wanderings along the Guermantes way." An apostasy to art which commences along the Guermantes way culminates in the Guermantes courtyard.

After the individual's self-appointment to art, conflicts immediately arise: not only between the individual and the collective, which tries to coerce him/her into a renunciation of this self-nomination, but within the individual himself, who struggles to provide proof of his or her talent through some recognizable achievement. This achievement, as evidenced in the career of Marcel, may be delayed for years, if not decades. Moreover, in the absence of recognized achievement, the artist often falls prey to his darkest doubts and her deepest despair: doubts and despairs that further fuel the creative impulse, unless that impulse is destroyed by the self-destructive impulses generated by these doubts and despairs. Proust's narrator provides many examples of this struggle against doubt and despair: The scene with Norpois is instructive:

> Paralysed by what M. de Norpois had just said to me with regard to the fragment I had submitted to him, and remembering at the same time the difficulties I had experienced when I attempted to write an essay or merely to devote myself to serious thought, I felt conscious once again of my intellectual nullity and that I was not born for a literary life. . . . I felt myself to be struck speechless, overwhelmed, and my mind . . . was entirely contained . . . in the straightened mediocrity in which M. de Norpois had of a sudden enclosed and sealed it. (WBG 364)

Only achievement can eliminate this species of despair, and only productivity or escapist behavior can mitigate against it. As Rank affirms, "[T]his leads straight to the realization that the productive personality, if it has once accomplished this self-appointment by the aid of his community's ideology of the artist, must justify this self-assertion under compulsion by its work and by ever higher achievement" (27). Marcel wrestles not only with the disapproval of his father and the disappointment of his mother when the lapse of years produce no visible evidence of his genius, but with his own acute sense of guilt and shame for being the "author" of their pain and disappointment. These tensions with the family and struggles with the self are repeatedly and incisively drawn by Proust.

THE BOOK, THE GARDEN, AND THE TREE

Those passages in which the narrator speaks of his own writing (the steeples, the notes to his mother and grandmother, the prose-poem delivered to Norpois) are evidence that his self-nomination to art has been followed by a period of self-training as a writer. However, this comprises only one half of his self-education as an artist. The self-training process is complemented by Marcel's close identification with a particular genre (the novel) and later with a particular novelist (Bergotte). The narrator's identification with the novel emerges in those scenes where he analyzes the pleasure he derives from reading: a scene that occurs in a garden, under a tree, and which resonates with biblical images of Eden and the Tree of Knowledge:

> The novelist's happy discovery was to think of substituting for those opaque sections, impenetrable by the human spirit, their equivalent in immaterial sections, things that is which the spirit can assimilate unto itself. After which it matters not that the action, the feelings of this new order of creatures appear to us in the guise of truth, since we have made them our own, since it is in ourselves that they are happening.... (SW 64)

This passage is worth noting because it not only privileges a genre (the novel), but because it enunciates an aesthetic that foregrounds the material world as a source of spirituality for the self. The events, characters, and settings Marcel encounters in the abstract realms of a novel seem more alive to him than their counterparts in reality for a simple reason: they engage his imagination, awaken in the "mental pictures of those joys or misfortunes," as opposed to their counterparts in the material world which are "perceptible only through our senses" (SW 64). The novel and the self mutually inform one another, constitute one of the first variations of the two-in-one. The imagination is the locus for this merger of the material and the spiritual. Consequently, when Marcel reads he is reading himself, becomes, as he avers in the opening passages, "the immediate subject of my book: a church, a quartet, the rivalry between Francois I and Charles V" (SW 3). Reading thus becomes the first vehicle for the symbiosis of self and Other, the yearning and need for which fuels the search engine of *Recherche*.

Reading mitigates the pathological effects of the self's differentiation from the Other. Reality reinscribes the role of a wish-denying mother, thwarting the wish for the two-in-one as exclusively as a private club bars Jews or homosexuals. Reading, by contrast, fulfills this wish. Reading initiates the self-object series, as a "privileged" Other which prefigures the progression of "privileged" objects that incite the self's possessive desire: Bergotte's style, Berma's theatrical genius, the steeples of Martinville, the trees of Hudimesnil, the Norman gothic ideal concretized in Balbec church, Albertine's illicit past, the quintessence of Merovingian nobility that is the Guermantes clan, the Venetian sublime et al. Reading is the first means by which Marcel's pathologically differentiated self gains possession of a "privileged" Other. This reading-in-the-garden metafiction establishes the centrality of the most dominant law of the Proustian universe, as well as its deep correspondence with Rankian theory: "[T]he psychology of the self is to be found in the Other" (*Beyond Psychology* 290).

Marcel's conversion of the text into a function of his imagination facilitates the assimilation of the text by the ideal-hungry and merger-hungry self. Insofar as it actuates Marcel's imagination, the text becomes a "sign" of the ideal self. The imagination becomes the "equals" sign between the pathologized self and its ideal Other-as-text. Reading invites the participation of the self, involves the self in the Other, and by so doing involves the self more deeply in itself than any other aspect of the material world. As such, it mitigates against the alienating and pathological effects of asthma and sexual differentiation which problematize the self's alliteration with the Other and the mother respectively. Reading is a surrogate for the material world denied the self by asthma: consequently, the act of reading is masculinized by the aggressions of the possessive self, enervated by their displacement from the material world. Reading re-masculinizes the self, as an object of possessive desire. And this meta-drama of desire is reenacted in every "privileged moment," if not in every encounter between the self and a "privileged" Other, with results that vary from fulfillment to frustration and failure. But whether fulfilled or frustrated by the Other, the effect is always beneficial to the creative impulse, which is aroused equally by the sublime effects of the longed-for two-in-one or the cruel heartbreak of the self's alienation from the Other. In the garden, the text becomes an alter ego of the idealized self, whose crystallization on paper Marcel simultaneously envies and vicariously enjoys inasmuch as it objectifies his own deepest desire: to liberate the ideal self in ink upon a page. The text is a "sign" of the ideal self, whose traces Marcel mimics until he is able to "sign" his own ideal self in reality, translating it out of his soul, as if taking dictation from a divinity within.

Herein lies the deeper psychological significance of Proust's passion for pastiche, mimicry, and translation, as evidenced by his mimicry of other genius in writing, his "stand-up" mimicry of friends (Montesquiou) in society, and his word-for-word translations of Ruskin. Mimesis of the ideal Other-as-self is an intermediate surrogate for the authentic expression of the ideal self-as-genius. As Finn observes, "[A]rtistic individuality begins with imitation, and [these] oral and literary pastiches served quite literally as the trampoline for Marcel Proust's launching as a writer" (98). In *Recherche*, mimesis finally yields the stage and the page to genius. Until the moment of its composition, the page has been a surrogate for the mimetic stage, as evidenced by the works of Proust's pre-*Recherche* career. In mimesis, the self vanishes into the Other. Only "original expression" as Finn observes, can objectify the ideal self. Without this, "he does not exist." Hence, The Search may be viewed as a long apostasy of the "profane" self from its ideal self (not only in love and society, but in pastiche and translation). The ideal self-as-writer is profaned as well in pastiches and translations wherein its identity is lost in the literary Other. The Search is in reality a quest for the recuperation and liberation of this ideal self-as-artist.

The written word is the medium of the self's colonization by the Other (pastiche, translation) until it discovers the word and thereby not only recovers its ideal self, but comes into possession of the Other-as-self as well. The word as a sign-of-the-self supplants the word as a sign of the self-in-the-Other: and this is the difference between Marcel's damnation and redemption, between his apostasy and apostolic rebirth. As Finn succinctly observes,

> [T]he image of being drawn out, like a crab somehow vacuumed from its hiding place and absorbed into the void through a transparent tube of words connected to the Other, illustrates the most fundamental level of fear in the Proustian individual, a fear of being drained of individuality through language. (81)

The "signs" of Proustian pastiche and translation are embedded with deeper psychological implications. They inform as well the "merger-hungry" desire of the pathological self. This is evidenced by "Proust's impulse to fuse with the figures of admired writers like Flaubert, Baudelaire, Nerval, even Balzac" (82)—an impulse objectified in *Recherche*, as evidenced by Marcel's desire to possess the secrets to Bergotte's style, to literally follow in the footsteps of the master (Ruskin) to Venice, as he followed in the "footsteps" of his style on paper. Mimesis of the literary Other reveals the "nervous absenteeism" of the self. The self's tendency to "perform the Other" reflects its inability to enact its ideal self—and this drama is deferred until it can get "beyond performing the Other" (Finn 38). The self is reduced to a surface reflection of the Other. The salons of the Faubourg St. Germaine are the locus of an exotic, aristocratic Other who "performs" the self, that converts the self into a shallow reflection of the Other, denying it access to the spiritual depths of the ideal self—whose recuperation implies the renunciation of the Other and the profane self implicated in it. The Search narrates the profane career of a self "prevented by a sort of laziness or frivolity from descending spontaneously into the deeper parts of the self where the true life of the spirit begins ... they live in the surface in a perpetual forgetfulness of themselves, in a sort of passivity which makes them the plaything of every pleasure ..." (ASB 212). The deeper psychology of *Recherche* informs Rank's view of human experience "as potentially a process of continuous rebirth in which more inclusive selves may emerge, however painfully, from preceding levels of incomplete development" (Taft 123).

Recherche is largely the saga of a struggle between a profane and a spiritual self, of a long defeat converted to triumph at the eleventh hour of its agony. The "text" of the garden reading scene is significant insofar as it brings the profane self into contact with a deeper, ideal self. And the tension between the desires of these two selves, which are antithetically oriented toward life and art, provide the drama of profanation and redemption that is *Recherche*.

Reading becomes a second domain of the self, a surrogate garden of immateriality for the material and maternal gardens from which the self has been banished for its original sin of profanation. Revisiting Marcel's career in light of recent postmodern criticism, we find that the text not only reveals the narrator training himself for a literary career throughout The Search, but shows the "hero" is already a "narrator," has already become a "writer" not merely through the act of self-nomination, but through his own self-training, and the various acts of writing he describes. This evident and persistent self-training not only contradicts the narrator's assertions regarding his deferment of a literary career, but calls into question the arbitrary division by some postmodern critics of the "Monsieur, qui dit je" ("the man who says 'I'") into a "hero" and a "narrator." This division of the fictional self posits a false opposition between a "hero" who acts and a "narrator" who writes (though not until the end). This false dichotomy reductively posits the "hero" of The Search as nothing more than a man of action prior to his unlikely transfiguration into a man of letters, into an artist, triggered by a misstep on a paving stone at the Princess de Guermantes. Doubrovsky's comments on this point are indicative of the postmodern critique:

> [T]hat the subject is "split open" by his own discourse, that an absolute cleavage separates for him the order of Being and the order of Logos is neither Freud's discovery, nor Lacan's but Proust's; his whole book consists in the setting in place of the . . . unbridgeable distance that divides "I" as referent from "I" as reference, subject of existence ("hero") from subject of discourse ("Narrator"). It's a question here not of temporal disjunction, but of an ontological break. (89)

This false dichotomy between "narrator" and "hero" disregards the wealth of evidence showing the "hero's" self-training to art throughout *A la Recherche*: a self-training that commences with *Francois le champi*, is continued by close identification with a recognized master (Bergotte), that involves not only reading and literary analysis, but practice (as evidenced by the pastiches of Mme de Sévigné he composes for his mother and grandmother), and that involves as well the formulation of an individualized aesthetic ideology, informed not only by his study of literature, but his study of drama, music, painting, and architecture (as personified in Berma, Vinteuil, Elstir, and a Ruskinian Venice). In contradistinction to the claims of postmodern criticism, which posit an irreconcilable break between a "hero" who becomes a "narrator," I see the "hero" as already, if not always, a "narrator" in the authentic sense of that word: insofar as he already writes and is always and already training himself to be a "narrator," "writer," or "artist" from the earliest pages of *A la Recherche*. Marcel's fictional "apprenticeship" is no fiction, but an authentic allegory of an apprenticeship to art.

Early in his career, the narrator discovers the novel as a vehicle for actualizing the ideal self. The Search recounts a journey that begins with the discovery of the ideal self within a novel and ends with the liberation of the ideal self into a novel—which signifies an abiding alliteration between the careers of the "hero" and the "narrator." It is no coincidence that the end of the journey reiterates the beginning. Whereas Marcel's apostasy from art begins along the Guermantes way and ends in the Guermantes courtyard, than similarly, his rebirth to an ideal self-as-artist begins with the novel in the garden and the novel in the bedroom and ends with the novel in the library of the Guermantes (the very same *Francois le champi*) and the novel he has just written. The "two ways" that lead Marcel into the profane pleasures of love and society devolve into detours, until he literally stumbles on the true path to fulfillment. The "two ways," whose disassociation signifies the alienation of the profane and the ideal self, contrast with the two-in-one fulfillment of the path to art

Reading comprises a significant first step in Marcel's apprenticeship to art insofar as it models for him the process of abstracting from experience that which is essential to art. As Paul de Man asserts in "Reading (Proust)," "[T]he moment that marks the passage from 'life' to writing corresponds to an act of reading that separates from the undifferentiated mass of facts and events, the distinctive elements susceptible of entering into the composition of the text" (117). Reading a text is a form of self-training that teaches Marcel how to "read" the "text" of experience, and how to "select" from its undifferentiated mass those fragments whose immortality alone informs the ideal self—and are therefore worthy of eternalization in a work of art. Reading conditions Marcel's eye for the immortal fragments of reality, where the material and the spiritual commune. The deeper grammar of the text, as de Man reveals, derives not just from what is read, but from the power of the text to immortalize as well the tissue of the reader's life while he or she is reading: impressions of light and sound, as well as thoughts, concerns, anxieties not associated with the text—indeed, the entire material world that envelops the text while it is being read. Thus, the text is an analogue for the madeleine and the steeples insofar as it preserves fragments of the self while it is being read: fragments of the immortal self that will be reread years hence when the reader encounters the same text in the "library" of the prince (which is in reality a "library" of lost selves, sequestered within a single text like so many dust-ridden pages).

The book is a double preservative: immortalizing not only its contents, but the contents of the reader's life while he is reading it. These are the two, superimposed texts that the book contains. While reading, Marcel is also reading himself into the text: if he is reading the book, the book is also "reading" him into itself. The book bestows its essence on the reader, even as the reader's essence is conferred upon the book—the first of many "seepages and exchanges" between subject and object. While the text is being decoded, the self is being coded into the text—as if the text is really two texts that are co-authored. Mass is never consumed; it is merely converted into other forms: in this case, the mass of the self is converted into the Other (a book) through reading, as it will subsequently be transformed into a book through writing.

In this passage Proust modifies Ruskin's theory of "superimposition" so elegantly stated in *The Stones of Venice*, in which the lightness of the loftier realms of a cathedral are superimposed on the lower, heavier features. Here, Proust superimposes upon the heaviness of the book, the lightness of sunlight and of the ideal self. Later, in the library of the Princess de Guermantes, he superimposes upon the materiality of *François le champi* the immaterial memories associated with this hour in the garden. Proust takes Ruskin's theory of spatial superimposition and adds a temporal quality to it—and he does this throughout *Recherche*, as the material object is superimposed with the spiritual self.

The book has translated the essence of Marcel's self into itself, preserving it between the covers in the invisible ink of associations that are released when the book is once again encountered. It is not necessary to reread the book, but merely to find it again, in order to read the self it sequesters: which is like the first reading of a book, every page of which affords a whiff of immortality. As de Man succinctly avers, "[R]eading is the metaphor of writing" (125). The text not only invites him into its surrogate world, but preserves the essence of his own. As de Man observes, "[T]he text asserts the possibility of recuperating, by an act of reading, all that the inner contemplation had discarded . . . the warmth of the sun, its light, and even the activity that the restful immobility seemed to have definitively eliminated" (119). Reading preserves the "spectacle of Summer" far more completely than would the direct experience of it. Again, de Man's words are instructive: "[T]hese initially static polarities are put in circulation by means of a . . . hidden system of relays which allows the properties to enter into substitutions, exchanges, and crossings that appear to reconcile the incompatibilities of the inner with the outer world" (120).

The book of the Other is merely the objectification of the ideal self. As Finn asserts, "In reading we reach beyond words to make contact with the essence of individuality, and that exercise is really a twin of writing, the silent seeking of our own self beyond our social words" (98–99). Reading is therefore a "pure form of friendship," satisfying in the abstract the spiritual needs of the ideal-hungry personality that Saint Loup satisfies in the flesh, but even more fully.

Reading also re-masculinzes the self inasmuch as the passivity of intellectual pursuits is invested with the virility of active ones: a self put under erasure by the text aggressively superimposes itself upon the text. De Man continues:

> [T]he guilty pleasures of solitude are made legitimate because they allow for a possession of the world at least as virile and complete as that of the hero whose adventures he is reading . . . the passage on reading has to attempt the reconciliation between imagination as action and to resolve the ethical conflict that exists between them. . . . Guilt is always centered on reading and on writing. (120)

The book, like so many other seemingly "static" objects, is invested with an active, kinetic, if not deterministic agency. It is "hot and active," "it relays and 'translates.'" In the final analysis, reading "satisfies the ethical demands of action more effectively than actual deeds" (125).

De Man then raises a critical question: "Is this novel the allegorical narrative of its own deconstruction?" (129). If its unity opens into fragments and discontinuities that resist closure, even this tendency can only be appreciated within the context of the novel's stunning coherence. Its unity is preserved by its discontinuities, further evidencing Proust's tendency toward the "double exposition" of any given binary, including the dyads of unity/discontinuity, whole/fragment. Hence, the novel's discontinuities, far from deconstructing it, call attention to its unities. The narrator's fragmented selves are unified in a way that the novel's fragments are never unified. If the narrator's self resembles a multiple personality fragmented in time whose various selves are in the end therapeutically fused into an ideal core personality, the novel itself resists the assimilation of its free-standing fragments and discontinuities—preserving amidst its overall coherence its fragmentary incoherences. As the moments of Martinville and Hudimesnil evince, *Recherche* is an allegory of reading that paradoxically narrates the possibility and the impossibility of "reading." It is itself a text that refuses to close upon itself, refuses to close around what it discloses. Its multiple disclosures refuse closure.

If the garden tree signifies the tree of knowledge, it also tropes on the trees of Hudimesnil that signify the impossibility of knowledge. Similarly, *Recherche* signifies both the possibility and the impossibility of reading the self—simultaneously discloses and refuses to disclose the self, paradoxically confides in and mystifies the reader. Through the interplay of fact and fiction, of "memory" and figuration, it simultaneously and necessarily constructs and deconstructs itself and its self. It privileges and problematizes interpretation, intentionally obfuscating our very ability to read the self that wrote the work: a self that artfully hides in plain sight amidst its own inventions. The mystifications of Albertine and the trees of Hudimesnil are merely "signs" for a mystifying self that refuses to be "read" in its entirety, in order to keep something to itself. In the end, the self refuses to be "read" even when in the act of being read, even though it figures reading as an avenue to the self. Thus, the "confessions" of the narrating self (Marcel) are qualified by its differentiation from the artistic self (Marcel Proust). An impenetrable mystification inheres in the space between the two, shielding the artistic self from the signs of interpretation, which can approach no nearer the artistic self than its signs upon the page—which is like trying to possess an elusive stag by scrutinizing its tracks in the snow. The author, like his incarnation of the enigmatic feminine sign (Albertine), is himself a sign that refuses to be "read," even in the act of creating his self through a work of art whose ultimate destination is to be read—a self that cannot exist without its "readers," by whom it ironically refuses to be read. The signifying chains that freed the self from its neurotic chains ensure the freedom of that self by standing between it and interpretation. Though bound in a "perpetual alliteration" between the covers of *Recherche*, Marcel and Marcel Proust never merge, refusing to become yet another two-in-one. The self preserves the creative division of itself to preserve its principal dividend: freedom. The artist is always and forever an absent presence, immanent in his or her creations, and nowhere else to be found. All we possess of the self is its creative soul, inscribed in ink upon a page, bound between the covers of a book. As Doubrovsky observes, "[T]he only 'material object' in which the writer is really hidden and potentially presented to himself is words" (140). This artistic self that we would know and possess absolutely is literally a fiction—but one that sings away its captivity in the chains of its own signification.

THE LYCEE OF THE LITERARY SUBLIME: TOWARD AN "EDUCATIVE IDEOLOGY"

Marcel's self-training to be a novelist proceeds from the deep correspondence between self and Other, experienced while reading the book in the garden, to an even deeper alliteration between self and Other, concretized in the style of Bergotte's writing. From his close analysis of Bergotte's style, Marcel's own aesthetic ideology begins to precipitate. As theorized by Rank, this constitutes yet another critical phase in the "apprenticeship" to art. Mimesis of a recognized master keeps a vital breath upon the tenuous flame of the creative impulse. The narrator identifies those elements of Bergotte's style that give him pleasure:

> [A] hidden flow of harmony, a prelude contained and concealed in the work itself would animate and elevate his style . . . he would begin to speak . . . of the "moving effigies which ennoble for all time the charming and venerable fronts of our cathedrals"; that he would express a whole system of philosophy, new to me, by the use of marvelous imagery, to the inspiration of which I would naturally have ascribed that sound of harping which began to chime and echo in my ears, an accompaniment to which that imagery added something ethereal and sublime. One of these passages of Bergotte . . . filled me with a joy . . . which I felt myself to have experienced in some

innermost chamber of my soul, deep, undivided, vast . . . I recognized in this passage the same taste for uncommon phrases, the same bursts of music, the same idealist philosophy . . . by which my own understanding seemed to be enlarged. (SW 71–72)

This passage is significant for a number of reasons. It pays tribute to one of Proust's greatest influences, Ruskin, here quoted without attribution. Further, it defines the elements that are the hallmarks of his own style, the most notable of which is his writing's musicality—here evidenced by the wealth of musical terms deployed to capture the essence of Bergotte's style: "hidden flow of harmony," "prelude," "sound," "chime," "echo," "accompaniment," "bursts of music." He continues: "This is the oral music of Bergotte's prose, what is essential to it and essential in him, a certain arrangement of words which constitutes his originality" (I 788, qtd. in Finn). Proust may just as well have substituted his name for Bergotte's so aptly does this passage describe the elements he incorporates into his own style. If style is the expression of individual genius, then its vocal quality as evidenced in the musicality of its tone and its distinct use of image are its two signature traits. Marcel/Proust's search for an individual genius leads him first and forever to a study of style, whose desired elements he masters and assimilates through mimesis, pastiche, translation—until it is thrown off in the genius of his own style. It is no coincidence that his last work paid homage to the deep alliteration between style and genius: "A propos du style de Flaubert." His valorization of style as the authentic signature of genius is evidenced as well by his love of Ralph Waldo Emerson, "whom Proust had read like a brother, [and who] had said much the same thing: 'A man's style is his mind's voice.'" (Finn 97). Clearly then, if Marcel is ever to liberate the ideal self imprisoned within, concretized in the "genius concept," an original style is not only a prerequisite for that liberation, but the surest evidence of it. Style is the signature genius gives to its work. Style is the symbol-laden effluence of the soul of genius, the visible swell and spray of the deep, far-wandering currents of the creative self—tossing itself off in language, but a language as distinct as one of the seven seas.

Bergotte's style is the surrogate womb for Marcel's ideal self not only by virtue of its musicality and its imagery, but by virtue of the "idealist philosophy" that is "contained and hidden in the work itself," which is akin to Marcel's and whose spirituality the narrator assimilates, producing the telltale pleasure, that metaphysical ecstasy that is the hallmark of the self's recognition of itself in the Other and its assimilation of this Other-as-self into itself. This is the significance of the joy he "experienced in the innermost chamber of his soul, deep, undivided, vast"—an assimilation of the Other by the self which links the "privileged moment" of Bergotte's writing with those of the madeleine tea, the steeples of Martinville, the trees of Hudimesnil, and the paving stones, spoon, and napkin of the Princess de

Guermantes's salon. It is not just a style that Marcel finds, appropriates, and reinvents, but the "idealist philosophy" that comprises the spiritual underpinnings of this style. As the narrator states, "[M]ore than anything else in the world I cherished his philosophy, and had pledged myself to it in lifelong devotion. It made me impatient to . . . attend the class at school called 'Philosophy.' I did not wish to learn or do anything else there, but simply to exist and be guided entirely by the mind of Bergotte" (SW 74). Swann, as always, is his guide to genius, for it is from Swann that "some of the first seeds were scattered for that taste for Bergotte":

> What my mother's friend . . . liked above all in the writings of Bergotte, was just what I liked, the same flow of melody, the same old-fashioned phrases [because time is immured within them] . . . and an invocation, an apostrophe, a lengthy prayer would give a free outlet to that effluence which, in earlier volumes, remained buried beneath the form of his prose, discernible only in a rippling of its surface, and perhaps even more delightful, more harmonious when it was thus veiled from the eye, when the reader could give no precise indication of where the murmur of the current began. These passages in which he delighted were our favorites also. For my own part I knew all of them by heart. (SW 73)

These passages in Bergotte are the aesthetic equivalents of those inspired passages where Proust's narrative unfolds in sustained musical riffs whose prose filaments unfurl with the practiced ease of a fly-fisherman's cast—usually prompted by the fortuitous discovery of the eternal within the ephemeral, and whose signature effect is a style heightened with metaphor, imagery, alliteration, adjectival series, and lateral clauses that expand the central movement as flying buttresses develop an ancient nave. This tension in Bergotte's style between its surface features and its inner musicality not only tropes on Proust's own style, and on all those privileged moments when a lost self is discovered within an object (the madeleine, the steeples, the trees), but on the artistic self latent in the innermost chambers of his own soul, which is roused from its dormancy by contact with something akin to itself: Bergotte's genius in general, and his musical style and idealist philosophy in particular.

In describing the essence of Bergotte's style, Proust is providing what may be the most accurate representation of his own, and of its literary origins (Bergotte/Ruskin). More significantly, his preference for a writing style in which some unnamed essence inheres below the surface, through which it occasionally bursts in long, sustained, recursive lines elevating the spirit in the process, is an aesthetic counterpart to the idealist philosophy that governs his vision of the self-Other dyad, in which some deeper essence inheres in the Other, a quintessence of spirituality, which when liberated from its material body may be assimilated by the self, which then experiences a spontaneous magnification of itself, always manifested as a sense of metaphysical ecstasy.

Proust's own genius is evidenced by his ability to name the unnamed and/or unnamable throughout *Recherche*, and is evidenced here by his analysis of the extent to which style is informed by genius—is indeed the visible locus of genius. Style is the definitive trace of genius.

In addition to its musicality and its idealist philosophy, Bergotte's style is admired for its imagery. As the narrator observes, "[B]y some piece of imagery he would make their beauty explode and drench me with its essence" (SW 72). Along with the aforementioned attributes, metaphor will comprise a signature component of his own aesthetic ideology, even as its ability to effect the two-in-one informs and resolves Marcel's deepest psychological conflict. Metaphor in *Recherche* is not only an expression of genius, but a cure for the pathology of the self—is not only a distinctive element of style, but a profound mechanism for the work's genesis: is both a primary cause and a principal effect of the creative impulse whose result is *Recherche*. The temporal qualities of metaphor not only inform the work's central themes but provide its vast, associative structure as well, not only produce the work's profoundest meanings, but its structural coherence. The cathedral of *Recherche* is deeply informed by metaphor in its entirety and in its most metonymic fragments.

Moreover, Proust's appropriation of music not only as an organizing principle for the plot but as an aesthetic principal of his style is also intimately associated with his original and ubiquitous use of metaphor. Music, as Otto Rank observes, has rhythm which is manifested in temporal repetition: "Music we may therefore regard, analogically, as pure temporal metaphor . . . [it displays] the fundamental essence of metaphor: namely, extension into the infinite" (350):

> For while metaphors of speech only succeed in retaining or recalling some past by association with the present, rhythmic ornament in drawing or music, tends to connect the whole past as such, in abstract form, with the future, since a rhythmic line or a tone-succession can in principle be continued to infinity. (350)

Music, as evidenced by the symphonic structure of the plot, by the architectonics of Vinteuil's "little phrase," by the influence attributed to Wagner's redemptive themes and dialectical treatment of unity and fragment, by the musicality of Proust's style, and by the metaphoric essence of music, deeply informs the essence of *Recherche*.

The structure of Proust's periodic sentences reinforces the musicality of his style insofar as they too gesture toward infinity. Immured within each is an impetus toward the eternal, toward the unending. Metaphors of speech retrieve only metonymic fragments of the past whereas music metaphorically conjoins the entire past and the future in a continuum of time. Again, Rank's theories of metaphor are instructive: as opposed to the "spatial" metaphors of

Homer which seek to eternalize a collective idealized society, "the temporal metaphor of Proust tries to recall a personal past of the individual," and instead of resorting to a collectivized genre to achieve this end, such as the Homeric hexameter, he "creates a mode of expression which is personal to the point of peculiarity" (350). Music is the ultimate metaphor for the extension of the self in time, indeed to infinity. Each periodic sentence masks a desire to extend the self in space and time, across the empty spaces of the page. Each is a fragment of eternity, a "patch of yellow light" in its own right, a "little phrase" of an immortal self.

The extent to which the narrator forms his own creative self in the image of Bergotte is evidenced when he asserts, "I wished that I might have his opinion, some metaphor of his, upon everything in the world . . . upon some of the historic buildings of France, upon certain views of the sea . . ." or similarly have his views "of Notre Dame de Paris, of Athalie, or of *Phedre*" (SW 72)—in short, on all those things that are to comprise the themes of his own work. Genius begins in mimesis of an idealized Other, struggles to free itself through association with an already realized genius. In Bergotte, Marcel discovers not only his style, his idealist philosophy, his most effective figurative devices (imagery and metaphor), but his material. He discovers through Bergotte (Ruskin) those things that are worth writing about, or rather discovers that the things that have always interested him are indeed worthy of great literature inasmuch as they have kindled a similar inspiration in Bergotte. The gap between pupil and master narrows considerably at an early stage of the narrator's creative career. self and Other are brought into deep alliteration not only in reading but in writing: the two sacred pastimes of the ideal self. As Marcel states,

> [I]t happened now and then that a page of Bergotte would express precisely those ideas that I used often at night, when I was unable to sleep, to write to my grandmother and mother, and so concisely and well that his page had the appearance of a collection of mottoes for me to set at the head of my letters. And so too, in later years, when I began to compose a book of my own . . . I would find the equivalent of my sentences in Bergotte's. (SW 73)

This two-in-one alliteration with the Other-as-ideal-self mitigates the sorrows of differentiation so memorably recounted n the "drame coucher." Writing, like reading, remedies, if only temporarily, the pathological wound of the self. The Search is motivated by the desire for a definitive cure, for a permanent solution to the unsolved calculus of neurotic suffering rooted in sexual differentiation. Writing closes the deep wound of differentiation.

The Bergotte passages are noteworthy not only because they demonstrate the influence of a recognized master in the formation of an aspiring artist's aesthetic, but reinforce as well Rank's assertion that the creative impulse for this type of individual is deeply embedded in neurosis, of which art constitutes an objectification, as evidenced by the narrator's assertion that his first literary efforts occurred during that first "black date in the calendar," were a byproduct of the crisis of the good night kiss, were penned on those nights "when I was unable to sleep"—in an effort to symbolically achieve the symbiosis that was in reality denied by his separation from mother and grandmother. Thus, writing becomes the vehicle from the very beginning for externalizing his "scruples and repressions and self-tormentings" (SW 73), and for resurrecting the ideal self profaned in the "drame coucher." Marcel discovers in Bergotte's work a deep correspondence between self and Other, between the texture of his everyday experience and the immortal tissue of lived reality concretized in Bergotte's art:

> And so, when I had found, one day, in a book by Bergotte, some joke about an old family servant, to which his solemn and magnificent style added a great deal of irony, but which was in principal what I had often said to my grandmother about Francoise . . . then it was suddenly revealed to me that my own humble existence and the Realms of Truth were less widely separated than I had supposed, that at certain points they were actually in contact; and in my new-found confidence and joy, I wept upon his printed page, as in the arms of a long lost father. (SW 73)

Bergotte's writing provides the spiritual nipple that gives suck to Marcel's soul in the wake of its separation from the mother. Writing weans his soul from the mother—even if only the writing of an Other, for in reality it is the writing of the self. Bergotte's words are a prophesy of the self—moving beyond its pathological prison, superimposing upon the submerged anchor of the neurotic self, the transcendent spirituality of an immortal self. Bergotte's prose is the great surrogate mother, nurturing and eternal, nourishing Marcel's soul with the mother's milk of identity, eternity, and creativity—and providing for a self that is isolated and alienated from the Other at least one realm where it can savor the "perpetual alliteration" of self and Other.

The father image of Bergotte is also critically important insofar as it reinforces the Rankian assertion that the master-pupil relationship is fundamentally more critical to the artist's development than the father-son dyad. As Rank asserts, "the spiritual relation of pupil-and-master—which Christianity was to set up again as the centre of its doctrine of life—has remained a more important thing to the creative artist than the juridical father-and-son relation which psycho-analysis seeks to regard as fundamental, whereas it is spiritually of a secondary order" (53–54). In *Recherche*, the true fathers of Marcel's development are those spiritual and aesthetic law givers: Bergotte, Vinteuil, and Elstir, as evidenced by the dominant role assigned to each relative to the biological father, with whom he is "generally shown failing to communicate" (Collier 15).

The narrator concludes the "privileged moment" of Bergotte's style by confessing his desire to meet the author himself, inaugurating a pattern that repeats throughout the novel, that indeed drives his entire search, which is an idealistic search for the original, material counterparts of his idealized and spiritualized imagination—which is a search to concretize the genius of the Other in order to objectify his own. It is not enough to encounter genius in the abstract world of art; Marcel must meet it in the flesh and blood, as an inspiration to his own most ardent desire, which is to make the ideal real. His disappointment with the man Bergotte reprises the "drama of disappointment" with Berma and the Balbec church. Instead of "the sweet Singer with the snowy locks," instead of the Homeric, muse-like figure of his imagination, something altogether different and bitterly disappointing greets his senses:

> a common little thick-set peering person, with a red nose curled like a snail shell and a black tuft on his chin. I was cruelly disappointed . . . in the squat figure, packed tight with blood vessels, bones, muscles, sinews, of the little man with the snub nose and black beard who stood before me. All the Bergotte whom I had slowly and deliciously elaborated for myself, drop by drop, like a stalactite, out of the transparent beauty of his books, ceased . . . to be of any use, the moment I was obliged to include in him the snail-shell nose and to utilise the little black beard. (WBG 417)

This passage (and others akin to it) is Proust's response to Sainte-Beuve, his refutation of the Sainte-Beuvian theory that an artist's work is deeply informed by the details of his daily existence: a theory predicated on the false assumption that the artist's art imitates his life. Proust, like Rank, asserts the precise opposite: that the artist's life is a product of his or her art, serves the creation for which (and through which) he lives. Proust's view is endorsed by Rank: "[T]he mistake in all modern psychological biography lies in its attempt to 'explain' the artist's work by his experience. . . . The real artist regards his work as more important than the whole of life and experience, which are not a means to production—almost, indeed, a byproduct of it . . . sometimes, indeed, production may be simply a means to life" (50–51). The art work does not therefore "express" the artist's personality, so much as it justifies the personality it helps to create in order to stimulate further production. Hence, the disconnect between the art and artist, who offers no visible evidence of his genius—of his objectified ideal, which exists in ink and on paper, and literally nowhere else: certainly not in the flesh and blood caricature of genius that is the artist.

Writing occurs in the contested space between self and Other, material and spiritual, ideal and real, individual and collective: is the byproduct of a nexus of conflicts. We thus we find Proust organizing his life entirely around his art: from the cork-lined bedroom in which he lives and writes to the sorties mounted into society, whose principal aim is to gather material for his work. Even those invited to his bedroom served artistic needs insofar as they unwittingly posed for their portraits in *Recherche*. As Albaret notes, "[W]hat interested [Proust] in people, at least during the time I knew him, was the material they might provide for his book. . . . [H]e never went out, except with his book in mind. When he set out it wasn't at random but always with a definite objective—for he was a hunter of details, a pilgrim in quest of his characters" (239). This theme is reiterated throughout Albaret's memoirs: "To finish his book—that was all that mattered. And from the autumn 1914 onward, his whole life was organized around that compulsion more than ever before" (45); "The miracle with M. Proust was his will power. And his will power was all directed toward his work" (65). What leaves the strongest impression upon Albaret is "his devotion to the work to which he completely sacrificed his health" (80)—living out an ideology of sacrifice that ultimately requires the artist to surrender his own life to art after first necessitating the sacrifice of others to it. As Proust observes to Albaret, "I have to have peace and quiet. I am married to my work. All that matters is my writing" (173). This tendency to subordinate life to art is evidenced as well in the career of the fictional writer, Bergotte, whose behavior is also "the result of subordinating his life to his work,"

> [who] arranges his life for the sake of his writing, having affairs with little girls to whom he pays large sums because he knows that the emotional effect they have on him is a source of inspiration. . . . [A]nd if love brings suffering, then that too, he knows, will help his artistic production by setting his soul in movement. (Bucknall 115)

This observation prefigures the narrator's conscription of Gilberte as a procuress of young girls ostensibly for the same purpose, and which culminates in Marcel's "arrangement" with Gilberte's daughter, Mlle de Saint Loup: the final incarnation of the muse-as-mistress, of the youth he has lost, and of the two-in-one, inasmuch as she personifies the "perpetual alliteration" of the Méséglise and Guermantes ways. The biographer would be better advised to try and understand the artist's lifestyle in terms of his art, including his desire for young girls, instead of the reverse. As Rank asserts, "[T]he biographical presentation, even when it can be done with certainty, seems to us inessential. . . . Thus the factual and concrete biography of Michelangelo and Shakspere [sic] does not enable us to understand their work the better" (57). The artist's lifestyle is more an effect of his art than a cause of it, and therefore it is folly to look toward the artist's outward experience for the keys to his or her genius. As Albaret observes, "[T]o think M. Proust's books are a factual account of his life is to give little credit to his imagination" (86). As tempting as it may be, one must resist this tendency to draw too close a correspondence between the artist's work and his life, between Marcel and Marcel Proust.

Despite Marcel's disappointments with Bergotte the man, his close identification with Bergotte's art signifies a critical stage in his "apprenticeship to signs"—and particularly to the signs of style. As Rank theorizes, this process "begins by identification with a master and is then 'artistically' developed and perfected on the pupil's own lines" (Rank 54). The dynamics of this apprenticeship, and particularly the tendency toward aesthetic independence, is not only evidenced in the master-pupil relationship of Bergotte and Marcel, but in the influence of Ruskin upon Proust (which I will revisit shortly). The Bergotte-Marcel dyad reinscribes the "educative ideology of the artistic Greek nation, even as it comprises a variation on the Greek concept of the muse, first embodied in Homer" (54). The Bergotte-Marcel, the Elstir-Marcel, and later the Vinteuil-Marcel dyads reinscribe the Greek ideal of the master-pupil relationship insofar as they embody a "high spiritual relation which had as its basis and object a 'pedagogic' training for the boy," but which like the Greek paradigm also assimilated sexual-erotic desires, though in Marcel's case these are always displaced onto a member of the opposite sex (Gilberte, Odette, Albertine), who is nevertheless intimately associated with the genius. As Rank affirms, "[I]n the dynamism which leads him to create, the artist suffers from a struggle between his higher and his lower self" (61). Further, this conflict is "perhaps the profoundest source of the artistic impulse to create" insofar as it evidences

> the struggle of the individual against an inherent striving for totality, which forces him equally in the direction of a complete surrender to life and a complete giving of himself in production. He has to save himself from this totality by fleeing, now from the Scylla of life, now from the Charybdis of creativity, and his escape is naturally accomplished only at the cost of continual conflict ... [and] intensified in him to a point which drives him with dynamic compulsion from creative work to life, and from life back to new and other creativity. According to the artist's personal structure and spiritual ideology, this conflict will take the form of a struggle between good and evil, beauty and truth, or, in the more neurotic way, between the higher and lower self. (60, 62)

In Marcel, this struggle plays itself out between the polarities of profane and sacred desires, between incestuous, matricidal, and homoerotic impulses on the one hand and creative impulses on the other. Further, the Gilberte-Bergotte, Albertine-Vinteuil, Odette-Elstir liaisons evidence the intimate alliteration between the carnal and the artistic impulses, dramatize the peculiar intimacy of the narrator's higher and lower selves. In *Recherche*, the fundamental conflict between life and art is crystallized in the conflict between profane desire and the desire to write. The ubiquity of this conflict comprises as well a resourceful variation on Ruskin's theory of superimposition in which the spirituality of the creative impulse is superimposed on the sensuality of fleshly desire.

Proust's narrator similarly depicts this conflict between life and art in the terms of a struggle between good and evil, between his higher and lower selves: as evidenced not only by the sinner's damnation to sorrow, but by his redemption to art. The work everywhere dramatizes the superimposition of art on life. Whereas life arouses the appetites of a baser self, stimulates matricidal and homosexual, sadistic and hedonistic urges, impels him to consort with prostitutes and lesbians, homosexuals, bisexuals, and sadists, art by contrast signifies the transcendence of the spiritual over the material. *Recherche*, for all its depictions of the profane, is an extremely moral allegory. Its ultimate wisdom is not existential but Catholic: its final order expounds a Catholicism of genius.

THE PUPIL AS MASTER: IDOLATRY AND INSURRECTION

The pupil's imitation of a master triggers a struggle to free the creative self from the master's influence. Mimesis gives way to rebellion in the quest to authenticate genius. We find less evidence of this liberatory struggle in the Bergotte-Marcel dyad than we do in the actual Ruskin-Proust alliteration. As Collier observes, it is from Ruskin that he derives his idealist philosophy: "Proust's model of romantic idealism and actual disappointment is already the moral fabric of Ruskin's writing" (43). The idealization and disappointment of Venice for Ruskin furnish the example that will characterize the entire career of Proust's narrator Marcel, whose "Ruskinian yearnings" follow the same pattern of idealization and disappointment. Both writers subscribe to a religion of genius, as Collier observes: "Ruskin and Proust both treat art so reverently in their works that it tends to take on the role of an ethic or even a religion" (15). The impressionism of *Recherche* is also indebted to Ruskin: "Ruskin it was whom Proust quoted describing Turner's art as being based on painting what he saw, not what he knew, and Ruskin's Turner is commonly acknowledged to be one of the major figures behind Proust's Elstir," with his metaphorical "transposition of land and water" (Collier 46). Proust's repeated deployment of the "reciprocal metaphor" is also Ruskinian in origin. Collier continues, "Proust has followed Ruskin in seeing the bright ground as a composite of liquefied stone and petrified sunlight" (46).

Proust visits the same Venetian artworks as Ruskin, with Ruskin in hand, reading Ruskin's original descriptions of the Baptistery in St. Mark's, before representing these same works in his own hand in a deliberate attempt to prove himself the worthy successor to Ruskin. The entire Venice section of *Recherche* is a monument to the master, Ruskin, in which Proust attempts to out-Ruskin Ruskin. As Collier states,

> [I]n *La Fugitive*, Ruskin's depictions of blue shadows in terms of water, and of yellow stone as petrified sunlight, are modulated by Proust; the fields of Combray are rewritten in the marine terms of Venice, and the church of

Combray . . . becomes the great marine vessel of St. Mark's. . . . In all of these examples, Ruskin's original text is lovingly recomposed, reformulated and transformed in the Proustian mosaic. (5)

Albaret's memoirs confirm the decisive influence of Ruskin and Venice upon *Recherche:* "It was in 1901 or 1902, during the two or three years when, he told me, he'd made three of his most important discoveries: the English writer Ruskin; the cathedrals, especially Amiens and its angel; and Venice and Venetian painting" (229). The assertions of Collier and Albaret evidence the shift from imitation of a master to an original application, if not an outright transformation, of a master's aesthetic ideology. A process that commences with close identification with Ruskin ends by being "'artistically' perfected on the pupil's own lines." From this point in his career, Proust's craft evolves beyond pastiche, translation, criticism, and mimesis into original fiction, into which these former modes of writing are assimilated.

It should be noted that Proust first visits Venice five months after Ruskin's death, "as if the living presence of Ruskin prevented Proust from visiting the city which he imagined so powerfully from Ruskin's writings" (Collier 12)—a visit that he perhaps undertakes in a final effort to "struggle free of the father-figure Ruskin" (15), literally writing his way out of the master's shadow by writing about those very water-shadows of which Ruskin composed so imaginatively in *The Stones of Venice*. Proust differentiates himself from Ruskin in another key respect. As Collier states, "Proust heightens the painterly aspect of the young Marcel's version of Ruskin, and he heightens the young man's romanticism . . . the young Marcel is more romantic (and less religious) than Ruskin" (42–43).

It is art's relation to religion, in fact, that first prompts the pupil's revolt against the master. For Ruskin, "'idolatry' occurs when we idolise an artistic object independently of its spiritual support. He is very close to the traditional Biblical attack on 'graven images.' . . . But in his preface to *La Bible d'Amiens*, Proust, moves away from Ruskin's critique of those who idolize art at the expense of a religious truth to which it should be subservient" (Collier 15). Proust detects a hypocritical contradiction between Ruskin's theme and his form, for while admitting "the piety of Ruskin's overt argument, [he] discovers idolatry in the artistry of his arguments and his prose style: 'At the very moment he was preaching sincerity, he was himself lacking in it, not by what he said, but by the way in which he said it.'" (qtd. in Collier 15). The evolution of Proust's relationship to Ruskin (fictionalized in Marcel's relationships to Bergotte, Swann, and Elstir) illustrates Rank's theories on the importance of the master-pupil relationship to artistic production:

The first stage in the growth of an artist is that which we have described as his "nomination" and which marks the subordination of the individual to one of the prevailing art-ideologies, this usually showing itself in the choice of some recognized master as the ideal pattern . . . at first, his individuality vanishes, until, later, at the height of achievement, he strives once more to liberate his personality, now a mature personality, from the bond of an ideology which he has himself accepted and helped to form. This whole process of liberation from a personal or ideal identification is particularly intense and therefore difficult for the artist. . . . In this creative conflict it is not only the positive tendency to individual self-liberation from ideologies once accepted and now being overcome that plays a great part. There is also the creative guilt-feeling, and this opposes their abandonment and seeks to tie down the individual in loyalty to his past. This loyalty is again opposed by a demand for loyalty to his own self-development. (371–72)

The educative dynamics of the Ruskin-Proust correspondence are reprised in the Freud-Rank relationship, which illustrates Rank's theories on the master-pupil relationship. Proust's translation, imitation, and ultimate interrogation of Ruskin frees him to move beyond Ruskin into the uncharted fictional territory of his own genius, even as *Trauma of Birth* (1924) heralds Rank's emergence from Freudian theory as an original theorist in his own right. Collier observes the critical connection between the completion of Proust's apprenticeship to the master and the commencement of his own masterpiece: "[W]ith his own work on Ruskin finished, Proust was able to give free rein to his own hero's complex quest for artistic truth, and to focus it on Venice. It is generally agreed that Proust started work on A la Recherche du temps perdu in about 1908, two years after his translation of Ruskin ended . . ." (19).

The final stages of the master-pupil dyad enact an allegory of death and resurrection, of fratricide and rebirth, which informs the fictional landscapes of Venice and the Guermantes salons. Indeed, the tomb of the artist Dandolo in the Baptistery of St. Mark's overwatched by John the Baptist not only informs the Ruskin-Proust relationship, but the Marcel-mother dyad and the artist-art dynamic. Collier writes:

John the Baptist watches over the immortalised Andrea Dandolo: but the same scene would very well describe the genius of Ruskin presiding over the hero at this stage of his quest—burying one self, resuscitating another, and preparing to live on forever in the mosaic of the work of art cystallising the mosaic of his life. . . . [T]he whole topos of the motionless sleeper watching at the heart of his petrified creation is of course prepared right at the start of the Recherche, with its creator caught in his dream thought of falling asleep, and becoming a church. (119)

The image of the "sleeper watching at the heart of his petrified creation" also tropes on the dead mother (grandmother) whose spirit is eternally entombed in the masterpiece of *Recherche*, even as it tropes on the soul of Proust that sleeps eternally within it. As Collier states, "*La Prisonnière* and *La Fugitive* are constantly shimmering with the reflected promise of resurrection through the forms of the phoenix, the peacock, the Fortuny dress and the Carpaccio painting" (128). If Proust's interrogation of Ruskin's idolatry signifies the birth of his own genius he nevertheless immortalizes the dynamic of the master-pupil relationship by situating his rebirth to art in the sediment of redemptive images that immortalize Ruskin's influence: St. Mark's, the Baptistery, the mosaics, *The Stones of Venice:* a fitting tribute to the influence of a genius who immortalized the mosaics of St. Mark's by a genius about to create a literary mosaic of the self.

THE TOMB AT THE CENTER OF THE CREATION: TOWARD AN IDEOLOGY OF SACRIFICE

> Others die, so that I may rise from my death.
> —Doubrovsky

The creative impulse, as theorized by Rank, is not only informed by an "educative ideology," but by an ideology of sacrifice. The image of the sleeper entombed in his own creation is a powerful one that merits and rewards further scrutiny insofar as it symbolizes the mother (grandmother) as well as the novelist himself entombed and eternalized in *Recherche*. To what extent was the mother's life sacrificed to the son's art? And to what extent are the narrator's matricidal impulses informed by the need for a living sacrifice to his work? Further, to what extent does this oedipal variation exemplify the parasitic tendencies not only of a pathological self, but of the creative impulse immured within it? Ironic, to think that the definitive work of high modernism could be deeply informed by a pagan ideology of sacrifice that ritualizes the self's negotiations with the beyond. For clearly, the life of the mother that is offered to art purchases the immortal life of the artist-son. This raises yet another critical question: To what extent is the mother's eternal absence a further stimulus to creativity, if for no other reason than to convert it into an eternal presence? To what degree is the creative impulse informed by this "tendency to reproduce something absent" (Rank xlviii). Is Marcel/Proust's willingness to suffer morbidly for his art a form of penance for the sin of matricide? Does the mother's sacrifice to art make his martyrdom to it not only easier but inevitable? And is writing *Recherche* therefore not just an act of creation, but of expiation: Proust writes:

> [I]t is the cruel law of art that human beings should die and that we ourselves must die after exhausting the gamut of suffering so that the grass, not of oblivion but of eternal life, may grow, the thick grass of fecund works of art, on which future generations will come and gaily have their picnic lunch, without a thought of those who sleep beneath. (PR 1116)

Art is a deeply ambivalent "sign": signifying at once the morbidity of the artist and the immortality of his art. Rank notes the extent to which the creative urge is informed by an ideology of sacrifice: "[The artist] needs, as it were for each work that he builds, a sacrifice which is buried alive to ensure a permanent existence to the structure, but also to save the artist from having to give [sacrifice] himself"(49). Instead, s/he kills himself in work, martyrs herself to her muse. As Proust confides to Albaret, "Dear Celeste, I am exhausted, I can't go on, and yet I must. If I don't finish I shall have given my whole life, sacrificed everything, for nothing" (334). Proust's experience is not atypical, as Rank avers:

> [T]he frequent occasions when a great work of art has been created in the reaction following upon the death of a close relation seem to me to realize those favorable cases for this type of artist in which he can dispense with the killing of the building's victim because that victim has died a natural death, and has subsequently, to all appearances, had a monument piously erected to him. (49)

This alliteration of matricidal and creative impulses is also noted by Doubrovsky: "If the artist, in effect, installs himself in death, he does so the better . . . to deny death by inventing an afterlife. The unconscious literally kills, so that the written word may literally resuscitate" (44). He concludes, "[T]o have pleasure/ to write, is, then, ideally to masturbate upon a tomb. . . . [T]o write is to save the one you love from oblivion" (43):

> [T]o assure "an immortal and compensatory glory" for the alter ego who is adored/profaned, loved/hated in the hell of ambivalence means literally to compensate for the real evil you have done—that is, for the unconscious, imaginary death you have desired—by conferring symbolic immortality. (Doubrovsky 44)

Proust commenced work on *Recherche* in the years immediately following his mother's death (1905), and was perhaps prevented from setting to work on it as long as she was alive by his emotional dependence upon her. *Recherche* is the St. Mark's "piously erected" to eternalize the soul of the sacrificial victim entombed within it: the mother, and after his own death, the artist. Mother and son are finally conjoined in an eternal embrace within the literary cathedral of *Recherche:* a symbiosis of spirits in death that belies the separation of their bodies at birth and throughout life, a separation that was the source of the novelist's greatest anguish, the root cause of his self-pathology, and hence the most significant source of his art. In the final analysis, the sleeper Dandolo entombed in his own creation, over-watched by John the Baptist tropes on the "sleeping" mother over-watched by Marcel, on the "sleeping" Marcel over-watched by his mother, and on the "sleeping" pupil (Proust) over-watched by the master (Ruskin) who helped mother his own work.

The novel's end is deeply alliterative with its beginning insofar as it fulfills the profane wish of the "drame coucher" for the two-in-one, now sanctified in art. As Doubrovsky observes, it is "the dead mother who is at the (buried, repressed) center of the work" (143). He continues: "The work of art is a work of death. It remains completely locked in the neurotic structure of a 'death wish' for the one you love best. In the case of Proust . . . the complete unconscious formula would be: 'to write . . . is to kill the mother' (39). Proust's own words would seem to reinforce Doubrovsky's assertion: "A book is a great cemetery in which one can no longer decipher the half-effaced names on most of the graves" (PR 1018–19).

Yet, I would argue that the book (and by implication, the writer) does not remain "completely locked in the neurotic structure of a 'death wish.'" Marcel's "death wish" for the mother is in reality a wish to free his ideal self from the bind of "separation anxiety": is in truth a wish for immortality. His "death wish" is really an effect of the creative impulse, and is exculpated by it. However, if the creative impulse liberates Marcel from the "obsessional cage" of neurotic dependency on the mother, the self is wounded anew by the "neurotic structure" of guilt, which becomes yet a further impetus to create, in what becomes a self-sustaining feedback loop of profanation and productivity. The self is not "completely locked in a neurotic structure," but completely locked in a neurotic-creative dynamic. Doubrovsky's analysis merits further attention:

> [H]e took advantage of those he loved . . . by feeding upon them. In a much less innocent way, he has not simply "used" them once they are dead; he has devoured them alive. The "materials" of the literary work are first a living "material" that has been parasitically absorbed . . . the vampirism of his book only takes to its extreme the vampirism of his life. (40–41)

Here the profane and sacred selves converge. The pathological self and the creative self are alike parasitic. The profane parasitism of the self in love is absorbed into the spiritual parasitism of the self that creates. It is even possible that the parasitism of the creative self has been honed by the parasitism of the pathological self, whose pathology is not only a cause of the creative urge, but is to a significant degree cured by it. Like the burrowing wasp, the creative ego parasitically absorbs the deep tissue of the Other, who provides the "material" for its own liberatory development. The Other is food for the pathological and creative selves—for the spiritual epicure that is the creative self, who works its epic cure on the profane self. The ideal self has more than a touch of the hymenoptera.

Loss stimulates the creative impulse—and does so ubiquitously. Rank cites, for example, the careers of Shakespeare and Mozart, whose "*Hamlet* and . . . *Don Juan* are familiar examples of the reaction after a father's death, while Wagner's *Lohengrin* followed on the death of the composer's mother.

These works are supreme examples of artists negotiating with the problem of the Beyond" (49n). If the examples of Shakespeare, Mozart, and Wagner are not enough to redeem the sacrifices necessitated by art, then Rank offers a fourth example of this ideology of sacrifice, Christianity:

> Christianity is the prime drama of all European art, at least in its significance as a new ideology of sacrifice, corresponding to the death and rebirth cycle. . . . But this represents only a supreme spiritualization of the primitive myth in which the individual sacrifices himself so as to produce the world from his body: an ideology which we have seen to be the prototype for all artistic production. (293)

Proust's appropriation of so many other aspects of this "prime drama" (the quest to eternalize the soul, redemption through suffering, atonement of guilt through confession, the cathedral not only as a reliquary of art, but as an organizing principle for his novel, the didactic allegories of the Garden of Eden, Sodom and Gomorrah, Paradise Lost, and Mary Magdalene) would seem to warrant his appropriation of its ideology of sacrifice as well, foregrounding martyrdom (his mother's and his own) in the quest for spiritual immortality. As Rank affirms, "[T]he fundamental idea is that for all created things there is a need not only for a creator, but a piece of life" (293). In the end, it is life that must be sacrificed to art: first his mother's and then his own. "The modern artist has," as Rank avers, "actually to sacrifice life to make his work live, and this sacrifice involves both his own life and that of others" (72). This creative ideology of sacrifice reinscribes pagan creation myths in which "the construction of the world also, apparently, demands a living sacrifice. . . . [T]hese myths therefore show us not only the first, but the most gigantesque type of artist, who creates the world not so much in his own image as from out of himself" (210).

As the climactic passages of *Recherche* evince, it is from within himself that the narrator realizes he must extract his creation. In modern art, as in pagan creation myths, the need for a living sacrifice is displaced from the self onto the Other, though remnants of it are found in the artist, in the masochistic impulse to punish the self as a form of self-sacrifice. The impulse toward self-sacrifice coexists with the tendency to sacrifice the Other, as evidenced in the narrator's masochistic and matricidal impulses, even as both tendencies are yoked to the higher spiritual ideal of eternal salvation through art. As Rank attests, "Naturally men try to divert this self-sacrifice onto others or to represent it as punishment," in the process renouncing "sexual generation in favour of the belief in metamorphosis [which] thus makes of death only a change of form" (211).

The personal quest for immortality, to eternalize the individual soul, is one of the most important sources of the creative impulse in *Recherche*—one that, moreover, deeply informs the narrator's matricidal and sadistic impulses.

Hence, the creative impulse is not only parasitic, but pagan inasmuch as it privileges the following quid pro quo: it confers immortality on the life sacrificed to it. Therefore, it "has always the character of a building-sacrifice" (293). Rank continues: "[T]he creator must give a part of life—in fact, his own life—in order to make it eternal in his work of art. The sacrifice of another life is only a sham sacrifice which does not save him from self-sacrifice, though it may be the immediate instinct of self-preservation to find a substitute" which is "somehow withdrawn from its proper destiny of death and fixed in an intransient existence" (293). Though initially displaced onto the Other, in the end it is the creator's own life that must be sacrificed to art, to complete the achievement which alone ensures the immortality of his or her soul. The tomb that lies at the center of his creation will in the end contain not only a chosen Other but the idealized self. As the poet Schiller observes, "What would live in song immortally/ Must in life first perish" (qtd. in Rank 35).

NEGOTIATING WITH THE BEYOND: TOWARD AN IDEOLOGY OF IMMORTALITY

The impulse toward immortality, toward eternalization of the individual soul, is one of the deepest sources of the creative urge—as abundantly evidenced in the narrator's career and the work's title. *Recherche* narrates a search for a self that is not only continuous in time but which by virtue of its temporal invincibility transcends time. As Rank affirms, the origins of the artist's ideology of sacrifice are bound up in the problem of the beyond, and whether the sacrifices are made by a chosen Other or by the self, they are an essential precondition for (and an inevitable byproduct of) the impulse to create.

To the extent that art eternalizes the soul of the artist, it supplants religion in his or her life. A second means of immortalizing the soul becomes as superfluous as having a second heart. Consequently, the collective immortality of religion is replaced by the individualized immortality of a religion of genius. As Rank asserts, "[T]he idea of the collective soul was gradually transformed into the idea of the individual god, whose heir the artist later became. . . . The individual artist . . . no longer uses the collective ideology of religion to perpetuate himself, but the personal religion of genius, which is the pre-condition of any productions by the individual artist-type" (45). The artist therefore rejects the "dominant immortality-ideology of his age—whether religious, social, or other . . . because it is collective, whereas what he aspires to is an individual immortality" (72). Barbara Bucknall endorses Rank's assertion: "In the religion of art, the hope of immortality which traditional religions offer as a gift of God is held out by the art work itself" (85). This casts a useful light on the "final order" of *Recherche*, in which society's catastrophic decline into decadence and destruction is offset by the narrator's redemption through art. As in Sodom and Gomorrah, the unfaithful many die so that the One may live—or rather, the One martyrs himself to art to eternalize the one and the many who are sacrificed to it.

The scene in the Baptistery of St. Mark's represents a creative fusion of the oppositional ideas of collective and individual immortality insofar as Marcel's personal resurrection through art is prefigured while standing within the ultimate symbol of collective immortality: the cathedral. The trope of the cathedral, which until this point in his career has functioned exclusively as a monument to art, is now wedded to its traditional function as a symbol of humanity's collective redemption. The fusion of art and religion under the "sign" of redemption in the novel's climax embodies yet another manifestation of the two-in-one. The conflict between the individual artist and the collective ideology of his or her age is thus resolved by the individual's creation of a religion of genius. As Rank observes,

> Finally, in art, which has developed out of the collective consolation-ideology of religion . . . the individuality-conflict is solved in that the ego, seeking at once isolation and union, creates, as it were, a private religion for itself, which not only expresses the collective ideology of the epoch, but produces a new ideology—the artistic—which for the bulk of them takes the place of religion . . . there is a deification of the genius-concept and an adoration of works of art which is comparable only to the worship of statues of gods. (86)

Marcel's idolatry of the genius concept as evidenced by his obsessive "adoration of works of art" and by the repeated pilgrimages to art that he undertakes is comparable to the pagan and Christian "worship of statues of gods." Further, Marcel also "seeks at once isolation and union." Indeed, his greatest most insistent conflict is born of the contradictory needs for differentiation and association, for independence from and dependence upon the Other. Further, Bergotte, Berma, Vinteuil, and Elstir evince a fictional "deification of the genius concept" which reflects a "personal craving for immortality of the ego" (87). Marcel's spiritual ecstasy is also informed by the religious experience, as Rank observes: "[I]t is on the identity of the spiritual . . . that the pleasurable effect of the work of art ultimately depends, and the effect is, in this sense, one of deliverance" (as it was with the three steeples), of finding "himself again in his accomplished work," and is characterized "by a feeling of oneness with the soul living in the work of art" (110). The joy of the artistic "sign," as with the religious "sign," is produced by the visible objectification of the soul: which is bound up with its deliverance from the temporal into the eternal. Rank continues:

> Thus the will-to-form of the artist gives objective expression, in his work, to the soul's tendency to self-eternalization, while the aesthetic pleasure of the enjoyer is enabled, by his oneness with it, to participate in this objectification of immortality. But both of them [artist and individual] . . . enjoy, as

high pleasure, the personal enrichment of that individuality through this feeling of oneness. They have yielded up their mortal ego for a moment . . . to receive it back in the next. (110)

The mortal self is at last contiguous with the objectification of its immortal self, externalized first in time, then in a timeless work of art. The sorrows of sexual differentiation are absorbed into the ecstasies of artistic association, which bring the isolated self into "perpetual alliteration" with the world and itself, across time and space.

The individual artist's liberation from the collective ideology of religion into a personal religion of genius is replicated in the struggle the artist wages to free himself from prevailing aesthetic ideologies—including most particularly those of a recognized master, with whom the artist originally and preconditionally identifies. Again, Rank's observations are instructive:

> [I]n this ceaseless struggle for liberation of the self from the moral, social, and aesthetic ideologies and the people who represent them, the individual goes through a disjunctive process of which I have regarded the process of birth as the prototype. . . . [I]t is, broadly, the attempt of the individual to gain a freedom from dependence of any sort upon a state from which it has grown . . . the basic conflict is always the same: the overcoming of previous supporting egos and ideologies from which the individual has to free himself according to the measure and speed of his growth, a separation which is so hard, not only because it involves persons and ideas that one reveres, but because the victory is always . . . won over a part of one's own ego. . . . [E]very production of a significant artist . . . always reflects, more or less clearly this process of self-liberation and reveals the battle of the artist against the art which expresses a now surmounted phase of the development of his ego. *In some artists the representation of a process of personal development seems to be the chief aim of their work.* (374, my emphasis)

Rank's observations not only inform his own liberatory struggle against the orthodoxy of Freudian theory, as well as Stephen Dedalus's neurotic struggle with orthodox Catholicism, but Proust's struggle for aesthetic independence from Ruskin: a "process of personal development" that he similarly objectifies in his work. The primal need of the creative impulse to assert itself not only brings the artist into sometimes morbid conflict with collective and collectivizing ideologies, but also often necessitates the sacrifice of life to art: not only the life of the Other, but ultimately the life of the artist.

ART AND THE FLIGHT FROM ART: RENUNCIATION, DIVERSIFICATION, AND ANALYSIS

This brings us to yet another species of conflict that influences the creative impulse, and to yet another critical phase in Marcel's "apprenticeship to signs": one that is incisively ficted in *Recherche* and that deeply informs the liberatory struggle of the creative self. Having struggled to free the creative self from the influence of collective ideologies, having struggled to liberate it from the self, the self now struggles in turn to free itself from the creative self, which threatens to totalize it under the "sign" of art. A self that was liberated by the creative impulse becomes oppressed by it, struggles to free (or differentiate) itself from the creative urge.

Those metafictive and ubiquitous passages in *Recherche* where the artist writes about art evidence a liberatory impulse: to free the self from domination by the creative impulse. The psychology of differentiation deeply informs the relationship between creativity and criticism. In Proust, the two impulses are always playing off one another: the impulse to write and to write about writing, the seemingly contrary impulses toward fiction and literary criticism. If *Recherche* reveals anything, it is that the two are bound in a peculiar intimacy that deeply informs the psychology of invention. Rank theorizes this phase of a creative career as an epic struggle waged between the artist and his or her art.

The liberatory impulse exerts a governing determinism in the career of the artist. Whereas in the early stages this impulse prompts the individual's rebellion against collectivizing ideologies, as embodied in religion, politics, work, and marriage, as well as a liberatory struggle against neurosis, so at the height of artistic achievement this liberatory instinct prompts, if not a flight from art, then at least an attempt to mitigate its dominating effects. Rank's assessment merits attention:

> [T]he artist type, with his tendency to totality of experience, has an instinct to flee from life into art, since there to a certain extent he can be sure of matters remaining under his own control; but this totality tendency itself, which is characteristic of the really productive type, in the end takes hold of his creation also, and this totality of creation then threatens to master the creative artist as effectually as the totality of experience [and this] makes all productivity, whether in itself or in a particular work, as much a danger for the creative ego as was the totality of experience from which he took refuge in his art. Here the conflict of the artist versus art becomes a struggle of the artist against his own creation . . . which forces him to complete self-surrender in his work. How the artist escapes this new danger is one of the obscurest and most interesting problems of the psychology of creative artists. There will of course be special modes of escape for each artist. (385)

Bucknall reinforces the centrality of Rank's assertions, noting that "the artist . . . must lose all awareness of himself as an individual as he is swallowed up in the contemplation of the object he is to depict" (15). We gain a sense of the terrible demands placed upon the artist by his art, and in particular upon Proust by his work, from Albaret: "When I think now of the desert all around him, and I hear again the echo of those nights, I think 'What loneliness! And what strength of mind to have chosen it, and having chosen it, to have endured it'" (172) How the artist negotiates with the demands of art is, as Rank asserts, one of the most interesting, yet least understood areas of creativity.

In the final, as in the initial, stages of his career, the artist's actions are determined by an impulse toward self-liberation. This is the essence of the determinism that shapes his or her career—as it shapes Marcel's—and which is symbolically embodied in the series of privileged moments where some sublime essence awaits liberation from its imprisoning object (the madeleine, the steeples, the three trees et al.): all are metonymic projections of the creative impulse's struggle to liberate itself from within the narrating self. *Recherche* is deeply informed by this dialectic of imprisonment-liberation, from its opening to its closing passages. The privileged moments leverage the liberation of the creative self from within the self, which lacks the will to effect this liberation on its own. They function as midwives to the birth of the creative impulse. This is not only the primary function of the privileged moments, but of love, whose sorrows enervate the creative self. It is finally the purpose of those masterpieces of art that affix Marcel's gaze throughout The Search because they bring his creative urge into direct contact with the abstractions of that impulse, in the process enervating it anew. The signs of memory, love, and art are midwives to Marcel's creative self, insofar as they facilitate the materialization of that self in art. The search for essences in the material world is in reality a search for the sublime within: a search that is fugitive until it discovers the means to become what it has always desired: a creative self—a self that literally creates itself.

Once liberated however, the creative impulse grows so powerful it oppresses the self, literally absorbing all matter of the self (and all that matters to it) into itself. The art that had been a means to freedom becomes in the end a source of imprisonment, necessitating the psychic liberation of the artist, which it achieves through three "special modes of escape": renunciation, diversification, or analysis of the creative impulse. All three strategies of differentiation are evidenced either in Proust's career or in the career of his narrator, Marcel. Before addressing the strategies of diversification and renunciation, I want to focus on the psychological implications of the tendency to complement, and in some instances supplant, creativity with analysis of creativity.

In fiction this tendency assumes the form of metafiction (or writing about writing). This metafictive impulse is an effect of the self's negotiation with the creative impulse's tendency to totalize the self. It arises, ironically, from the same need that originally informed the creative impulse: the need for freedom, or self-differentiation. Now, however, it is the creative impulse itself, and its tendency toward totalization of the self, that prompts this liberatory urge. The metafictive word detaches the creative ego of the artist from a state of undifferentiated identification with his art, thus reinscribing the role of the word in general, indeed of all language, whose goal, we may recall, "is to dominate the world around," which it does by detaching the self from the world through language. Language, thus, achieves for the self what birth does for the body—a birth to individuation, to creative differentiation. The birth of language is also the birth of the individual self. Thus, language and identity are inseparable. Language makes possible the detachment of the self from the world, enabling it to define itself as different from all Others. The pivotal, redemptive role that language plays in *Recherche* foregrounds the useful interpretation of it from postmodern perspectives, as a rich body of recent scholarship evinces, and as the readings of Deleuze, Doubrovsky, Kasell, de Man, Kristeva, and Gray in particular evidence.

At the height of the creative process, the differentiation of the self from the creative self vanishes, necessitating a re-differentiation whose primary vehicle is a metafictive impulse, in which art is accompanied by the analysis of art, in which creation is wedded to criticism, invention to interpretation, in which the reflections of the creative self give rise to a creative self-reflexivity. As the self was once absorbed in life, or in neurosis, so it becomes absorbed in art—sacrificed once again, as it was in the beginning, by the devotion of the creative self to its art. This necessitates the rebirth of an individuated self, which it achieves metafictively by writing about writing—or as in Shakespeare's case, meta-dramatically, through the layering of a play-within-the-play. This metafictive layering of meaning enables the self to go on dwelling within its work as a self-differentiating entity: one who not only creates but observes itself in the act of creating—thereby preventing its entire self from being absorbed by the creative process.

In Proust's career we find the creative impulse arising from his literary criticism (*Contra Sainte-Beuve*) and in the end returning to it (*Du style de Flaubert*). Consequently, the critical impulse is both a cause and an effect of the creative impulse. The ego, threatened with total domination by creativity, sets up between itself and art an extra layer of differentiation—by writing about writing. This metafictive strategy of self-possession is ubiquitous in Proust.

The creative ego preserves a measure of freedom from the creative impulse by transforming the writer into a scientist, by fleeing from creation into analysis of creation, from invention into interpretation, and from metaphors into maxims. Proust anticipates his posthumous interpreters—by interpreting his own invention. He becomes not only his own writer, but his own critic. The artist consciously reflects upon his art in order to avoid complete absorption by it, to leave a portion of the self to itself, to detach a portion of the self from the creative ego, which it does creatively. To avoid totalization by creation, the ego confronts the artist with a scientist: a self that scientifically analyzes its own creation. The creator confronts creativity with an analysis of creativity to protect the ego from being subsumed by creativity—and then, moreover, displaces this analysis onto the creative plane. As Rank asserts, "[T]his is the diversion of creation into knowledge, of shaping art into science and above all into psychology":

> Spiritual self-representation in the work is always one essential element in artistic creativity and in art, but it is only in modern artists that it becomes a conscious, introspective, psychological, self-analysis . . . [a type who] passes suddenly from the formative artist into the scientist, who wishes . . . to establish, psychological laws of creation or aesthetic effect. This diversion of artistic creation from a formative into a cognitive process seems to me to be another of the artist's protections against his complete exhaustion in the creative process. (387)

Rank's observations are significant because they prompt a critical reassessment of the Proustian maxim, which has come under attack by postmodern criticism as evidence of a tendency to essentialize experience or to "absent" the self in universal maxims. These maxims, by contrast, deeply inform the self's liberatory struggle to free itself from art through analysis of art. Those passages in which the narrator comments on his craft, defines his aesthetic ideology, or depicts the complex process of invention are the fictional counterparts to those meta-dramatic moments in Shakespeare when he comments on the craft of acting, of which the "Mouse Trap" scene in *Hamlet* is perhaps the most striking, though by no means the only, example. In Proust, this metafictive impulse asserts itself in those passages where he analyzes the style of Bergotte, dramatizes the disjunction between the artist and his art, confides his doubts about his talents, describes his despair of ever setting to work, or analyzes the essence and implications of Berma's theatrical genius, of Vinteuil's musical genius, or Elstir's genius for impressionism. By metafictively commenting on his art, the artist avoids being subsumed by it, retains a measure of differentiation from it. Creativity not only helps differentiate the self from the world but from creativity. As Rank observes, "[C]onscious reflection about creativity and its conditions and about all the aesthetic laws of artistic effect [ensures] the survival of the ego amidst the all absorbing domination of creation" (385).

Analysis of art is but one means, however, by which the creative ego escapes from its own creation. We also find evidence of the self's attempt to keep itself from being entirely absorbed by art in the artist's vacillation between genres or between entire art mediums. The self avoids totalization by the creative impulse by dividing that impulse amongst several works, by diversifying it across various genres. This is evident in Shakespeare's vacillation between poetry and drama early in his career, and between the sonnets and dramas of his later career. It is evident as well in Rodin's fluctuation between painting and sculpture; in Michaelangelo's vacillation between the same two media, in Da Vinci's fluctuation not only between art forms (painting and sketching) but between disciplines (art, science, engineering, medicine, etc.), in Goethe's vacillation between poetry and drama, the novel and the epigram; and finally in Proust's own vacillation between novels, essays, translations, pastiches, letters, and journalism. As Finn observes, "Proust was a social chronicler and journalist, a productive essayist and critic, an inexhaustible (if perpetually exhausted) correspondent, a translator, and a master of pastiche . . ." (102). Experimentation in various genres spares the artist from complete absorption in any one genre; the demands made upon the creative ego by one work often necessitate the creation of a second in order to preserve the autonomy of the creative ego. Rank writes,

> [O]ne means of salvation from total absorption in creation . . . is the division of attention among two or more simultaneous activities; and it is interesting to note that work on the second activity is begun during work on the first, just at the moment when the latter was threatening to become all absorbing. (285)

Proust, thus, commences work on the Ruskin translations hard on the heels of *Jean Santeuil*'s failure, even as *Recherche* begins emerging from the final chapters of *Contra Sainte-Beuve*. What the creative ego needs to sustain it, to protect it against complete emotional identification with one unrecognized work, or a work recognized as a failure, is a second work, which serves to liberate it from the first. The creative ego protects itself from domination by a single creation through multiple creations, which also protect it against the failure of any one creation.

This fluctuation between genres manifests yet another Rankian theory insofar as "the second work is often the antithesis in style and character to the first, though it may be a continuation at another level" (285). If the first half of this assertion is born out by the antithetical natures of *Jean Santeuil* and the translations of Ruskin, then the second half of it is similarly evidenced by the similarity between the final chapters of *Contra Sainte-Beuve* and *Recherche*, which indeed is a "continuation of it at another level." Proust found his true creative voice at the end of *Contra*, in which we already find the Guermantes appearing—at which point he could no longer delay the creative impetus of the reformulated work within him kicking for deliverance. As Jephcott observes, "Proust now became increasingly absorbed in the writing of *Against Sainte-Beuve* until a point about the middle of 1909 when the process of creation became strong enough to shake off the theoretical ballast of that work, and Proust began to write the opening sections of a new version of his novel" (210). In *Contra*, he makes the critical discoveries that lead to the transformation of *Jean Santeuil* into *Recherche*. The privileged moments of involuntary memory are no longer merely significant in themselves, but become the driving force of the plot insofar as they are linked to the "protagonist's progression towards the revelation of his artistic vocation and of the true nature of reality. At one stroke, Proust has discovered both the form and the meaning of his novel" (211). As Proust states in *Contra*, "[T]he artist's task . . . is that of recreating a 'self' which is 'deep within us'" (qtd. in Jephcott 208).

Sainte-Beuve prefigures *Recherche* in other important ways. As Jephcott notes, "[I]n the last sections of *Against Sainte-Beuve* . . . Proust's fictional characters drawn from society proliferated until they outgrew the conception of the book and began to people a new world—that of *In Search of Lost Time*" (204). The fluctuation between literature and literary criticism, between *Jean Santeuil* and the Ruskin translations, between *Contra Sainte-Beuve* and *Recherche* dramatizes the unstable, yet essential coexistence within Proust's creative ego of two muses: the artist and the art critic. This division of the creative ego between two competing, yet antithetical discourses comprises yet another successful survival strategy of the creative ego, which avoids complete absorption by either muse by swearing absolute allegiance to neither. In the end, both discourses are incorporated into *Recherche* (in yet another example of a conflict that is harmonized in art) where the art critic assumes the guise of Swann and the artist the identity of Marcel (and his surrogates: Berma, Bergotte, Elstir, and Vinteuil)—in a work whose many syntheses include the synthesis of literature and literary criticism. This is only possible of course "with artists who have various interests and capacities; thus Goethe indulged his scientific, and Schiller his philosophical, studies at periods apparently of weakness in poetic activity, but really . . . to find respite from that creativity" (Rank 386). Similarly, the Ruskin translations rescue Proust's creative ego in the wake of his failure and perhaps fatigue with the novel, *Jean Santeuil*, even as *Recherche* rescues him from the theoretical and critical fatigue of *Contra Sainte-Beuve*. The great cycle of apostasy from art and rebirth to it (as evidenced by the *Jean Santeuil-Ruskin-Contra Sainte-Beuve-Recherche* progression) mirrors the plot of *Recherche*, for which it provides the prototype, and into which it is absorbed. As Bucknall affirms, the narrator's "eventual realization of his vocation as a writer will take on the aspect of a reconversion after years of straying from the true path" (28). This development of a "second sphere of interest—which is frequently a second form of artistic achievement" is a critical and effective survival strategy of the creative ego, is an effective defense against those "periods of disappointment, depression, and even illness [which] are likely to occur, which are then not so much a consequence of exhaustion as a flight from it" (Rank 386).

Whereas analysis and diversification of the creative impulse comprise two means by which the creative ego mitigates the aggressions of that urge, there is yet a third: abandonment, in which the work is "simply set aside for the time being"(386). This adjustment informs the narrator's repeated postponement of his work, as if he instinctively senses and fears its totalizing tendencies with respect to the self—as if sensing the long solitary devotion and the Herculean labor it will require of him. As Rank observes,

> [T]he creative process . . . always contains in any case a time conflict, which expresses itself in the difficulty the artist finds both in beginning and in finishing his work. Just as he can escape from threatened domination in the midst of his creation, so he can hold back instinctively as long as possible from the beginning of it. (386)

Rank's observations inform Marcel's long delay to writing, which is a byproduct of the "ego's necessary protections against being swallowed by creativity" (386).

The narrator's delay masks a deeper fear, however: the fear of death. Rank continues: "[T]he particular creative process, if it involves an exhaustive output, is by the same token a symbol of death"—even as the completed work is a symbol of eternity. This ambivalence toward the creative impulse stems from the contradictory needs of a self that wants to live and a self that wants to live eternally. For the self that wants to live, the creative process comprises a form of death, figurative and literal, to the extent it will deprive it of living and to the extent it drains off the life forces in creativity. As Rank states, "[T]he artist is both driven on by the impulse to eternalization and checked by the fear of death" (386). Bucknall agrees: "At the heart of the Proustian religion of art, as of the Christian religion, lies a mystery of death and resurrection" (120). As it does with Hamlet, the narrator's delay, his "continual postponement of the act of writing" produces his "deepest sense of guilt" (Bucknall 119). Yet, the guilt inspired by his delay, like that inspired by matricidal and homosexual tendencies, is beneficial to his art, for "by a fruitful paradox, the narrator . . . has accumulated a capital of guilt and suffering on which he can draw for artistic inspiration. By the same token, the act of writing will help to annul that guilt and suffering" (120). Thus, his art is both the cause and the cure of his guilt. The demands that art makes on the creative ego require an almost complete surrender of that ego to creation, even as it rewards this self-surrender with a spirituality that is apostolic not only after life, but during it. Bucknall writes,

> To feel that one should be kind, sympathetic and hard-working, willing to dedicate one's life and even to die in the service of an ideal; to feel an intense emotional allegiance to anything which is presented as both spiritual and a duty; to attend spiritual seances while doubting the reality of an afterlife; to visit churches for their artistic rather than their religious associations; to feel bitter disappointment at the failure of physical union to lead to the inter-penetration of souls; and finally to remain in doubt as to whether this set of values corresponds to anything real: all this is both true

of Proust's narrator and typically modern. The reader of *A la Recherche du Temps perdu*, seeing in the narrator a pilgrim as bewildered and doubting as himself, is all the more inclined to accept as valid those messages which the narrator hesitantly imparts. (164–65)

As Rank's interpretation of the psychology of the artist shows, the dominant need of the artist throughout his or her career is for self-liberation: first from the collectivizing ideologies of religion and society; subsequently from the self-destructive forces unleashed by neurotic fear and from the collectivizing influence of art as embodied in a master; and finally from the demands made on the creative ego by creation itself. A career that commences with a retreat from life into art ironically concludes with a flight of self-preservation from art into life, from art into an analysis of art, or from one work of art into another. This ability to detach the self from whatever threatens to absorb it must be asserted throughout the artist's career. Against each in its turn, the artist struggles "in order to arrive at that state of detachment which is so essential to the creative artist" (Bucknall 42). Differentiation is both a cause and effect of the creative impulse. If the self's differentiation from the Other produces the sorrows of *Recherche* that incite the creative impulse, then by contrast the tyranny of the creative impulse prompts the self to differentiate itself from the creative self. The self differentiates itself through art, and differentiates itself from art through analysis of art.

The ironic pleasure of reading Proust derives from reading a self which, like the Sapphic sublime or the trees of Hudimesnil, refuses to be read. The self we read in *Recherche* is not Proust's, nor perhaps even Marcel's, but our own. *Recherche* is an allegory of the self that refuses to close around its own disclosures—whose signs do not form a circle that ends where it begins, but a spiral that turns, without closing, upon its self.

If, like the steeples of Martinville, *Recherche* selectively surrenders its essence to the interpretive gaze, then similarly like the trees of Hudimesnil it partially mystifies the possessive gaze of criticism. The "sign" floats continuously between the mystifications of the text and the demystifications of interpretation. In our desire to possess its meaning, we are left in possession of meaning's immortal fragments. We may bring to light the meaning of a "little phrase," of a "patch of sunlight," or of a crumb of madeliene, but as for the work itself, it resists the chains of signification with which we would make it our captive. Among its inscrutable signs, we discover the traces of a self's apprenticeship to art. As Germaine Brée succinctly observes, "[N]o other novelist has so intimately linked within a single book the story of the origination of a work and its realization; no other novelist has so specifically delineated the spiritual genesis of a vocation" (217). Yet, like the madeleine, the steeples, the trees, and the Sapphic sublime, *Recherche* is itself a sign that simultaneously discloses and mystifies itself, that refuses closure in the act of disclosing itself. Though ficted from the tension between criticism and creativity, in the end *Recherche* eludes containment under either sign—exists beyond the essentializing reach of interpretation. In this, it alliterates with the three figures so perceptively theorized by Otto Rank: the hero, the neurotic, and the artist. As he states in the "Preface" of *Beyond Psychology*,

> My own life work is completed, the subjects of my former interest, the hero, the artist, the neurotic appear once more upon the stage, not only as participants in the eternal drama of life, but after the curtain has gone down, unmasked, undressed, unpretentious, not as punctured illusions, but as human beings who require no interpreter. (qtd. in Taft 296)

conclusion

The Art of Madness

Happiness is beneficial to the body but it is grief that develops the powers of the mind.

—PR

THE WOUND AND THE WORD

The origins of the creative impulse are complex. Aside from Joyce's *Portrait*, few works in the modernist canon dramatize those origins as insightfully as *A la Recherche du temps perdu*. Similarly, few theorists demystify the origins and effects of the creative impulse as coherently and usefully as Otto Rank, as evidenced in the work that comprises his most mature articulation of those theories, *Art and Artist: Creative Urge and Personality Development*. Rank's theoretical elucidation was the result of a life-long interest in the depth psychology of the hero, the artist, and the neurotic, and advances our understanding of the complex origins and effects of the creative impulse beyond Freudian theory's preoccupation with sublimated sexual impulses. Rank theorizes the origins of the creative impulse from diverse psychological perspectives, developing the influence of an "educative ideology" and an "ideology of sacrifice," of the will to eternalize the soul and the "will to form." Yet Rank's greatest contribution to the psychology of the artist is revealing to what degree the creative impulse, particularly as evidenced in the career of the modern artiste manqué, is informed by "morbid crises of a neurotic nature," whether these arise from the individual's conflict with the collective ideologies of church, state, and society, or are embedded in conflicts of a more personal nature. Rank's legacy is the pioneering work that revealed the deep alliteration between neurosis and creativity, that theorized creativity as the objectification of neurotic conflict. It is from this psycho-critical perspective that *Recherche*, as a case study in the career of the artiste manqué, can be usefully informed by Rankian theory.

As evidenced from the first "black date in the calendar" and the "drame coucher," the pathology of the narrating self is deeply rooted in the sorrows of differentiation, in "separation anxieties" associated with the mother. The desire to mitigate, if not eliminate those sorrows is what prompts The Search and arouses the creative impulse. Ensuing sorrows related to the pathology of differentiation and the desire to transcend it sustain, unify, and fulfill The Search.

The drama of the good night kiss is the black hole at the center of the Proustian universe, the dark center of gravity around which all matters revolve, and from which only the light of creativity escapes. All else in the novel collapses into this dark gravitational field of damnation and oblivion, save the soul of the narrator. As Walter Benjamin observes in "The Image of Proust,"

> [S]ince the spiritual exercises of Loyola there has hardly been a more radical attempt at self-absorption. Proust's, too, has as its center a loneliness which pulls the world down into its vortex with the force of a maelstrom. And the overloud and inconceivably hollow chatter which comes roaring out of Proust's novels is the sound of society plunging down into the abyss of this loneliness. (qtd. in Bloom 46)

In the climactic passages of *Recherche*, all die so that the individual might live eternally: the salvation of orthodox religion yielding to the redemption of an unorthodox religion of genius. The son's original and mortal sins (profanation and matricide) are midwife to the writer's salvation in eternity. If Combray is a paradise, it is a paradise lost to original sin. Hence, this first "black date in the calendar" signifies the birthdate of twin selves: a pathological and a creative self. The Search primarily narrates the epic struggle waged between these conflicting selves, motivated respectively by profane and sacred desires, which are respectively oriented toward life and art.

Good and Evil cohabiting in the Garden of Original Desire.

Despite Proust's refutation of Ruskin, and despite its own celebration of the profane, the "final order" of *Recherche* is deeply moral, inscribing a Catholicism of genius in which the narrator's soul is redeemed by art for the original and mortal sins it commits: against the mother, the Other, and the self. Combray is an Edenic topos of original sin, nonetheless fatal for its pastoral beauty. Rene Gerard, in "The Worlds of Proust," underscores the dark determinism of the "drame coucher":

> [T]he decisive choice has already been made. The seed of Cities of the Plain can already be found in Combray. All that is necessary to move from one universe to the other is to give in to the incline of the slope, to that move-

ment which increases steadily and takes us ever further from the mystic center. This movement . . . becomes more rapid in the child who gazes at the gods of Combray and prepares to succumb to every kind of eroticism. (qtd. in Bloom 79)

Of all moments from time past with which Proust could have commenced his epic narrative, he chooses to begin with this first "black date in the calendar"—and for good reason. This moment signifies the true "birth date" of his immortal soul, insofar as it dramatizes the violent birth of the creative self—or if not its birth, then at least its profane conception in the seamed sheets of an incestuous desire. His life will be a labor (prolonged for decades, arrested by dependency on the mother, enacted in secrecy), to beget the strange offspring he carries within: a bastard conceived from the unholy matrimony of desire and guilt, suffering and imagination, whelped in the sacrificial blood of matricidal and suicidal impulses. Combray casts a shadow over the entire landscape of *Recherche*. The deep wound that opens between mother and son at birth is closed with the winding shroud of words, is stitched in ink upon a page.

This is the originary darkness that is Combray, sealed in the vaults of time, to which the narrator returns: as if to the scene of an original sin, of a bloody oedipal crime, and of his real birth, of his psychic and spiritual rebirth, of his birth to art—a rebirth all the more spiritual after the living death of indifference, concretized in the spiritual sterility of the sanitarium. The Search of the narrator reenacts one of the primal desires of humanity: to regain an Eden lost to sin. The Search not only reinscribes Christian myth but Arthurian romance, insofar as it depicts a heroic quest to liberate from the tower of time, the beauty of truth imprisoned within, is at once an allegory of the Crusades and the quest for the Holy Grail. The narrator's external pilgrimages to art objectify the self's inward pilgrimage to creativity. And the idolatrous relics it seeks in reality, from Balbec to Venice, merely embody the immortal artifact it carries within: The Book.

Marcel's epic labor is to liberate from within himself a quintessential, creative self: a struggle projected onto privileged objects in the material world, dispersed throughout The Search, imprisoning within themselves a fugitive fragment of his self, whose liberation heralds the revolutionizing liberation of the creative force immured within. The "privileged moments" of *Recherche* objectify the central drama of the novel, which is the epic struggle waged by the profane self to liberate its ideal self. Doubrovsky underscores the paralyzing morbidity of Marcel's bind, "from which you can neither free yourself nor separate yourself: insoluble conflict, producing contradictory behavior (adoration and profanation in sacrilegious gestures . . .) and leading into a progressive inertia (bedroom-bed-paralysis)" (77). Doubrovsky continues:

> Because the obsession with the two-in-one, with the 1 + 1 = 1, which the Narrator projects in all his relationship with others . . . is already nostalgia for an original fusion, for a lost age, where all difference is abolished . . . and *where Proust's deepest desire to write originates* . . . the serenity of visceral enclosure is affirmed, the joy of the primitive circuit. (78, my emphasis)

The urge to create is deeply informed by neurotic conflict ("where Proust's deepest desire to write originates"). Proust's own assertions reinforce Rank's theories concerning the neurotic origins of the creative impulse: "[I]t is only while we are suffering that our thoughts, as though stirred by perpetual changing movements, bring up within our range of vision, as in a storm, all that boundless world . . . of which we had no view from our ill-placed window, for the calm of happiness leaves it all too smooth and below our range of vision." Proust continues:

> Perhaps only in a few great geniuses does this upsurging constantly go on without their having need to be stirred by suffering; and yet, perhaps, when we study the abundant and regular development of their joyous work, we are too much inclined to infer that their lives were joyful also, whereas, on the contrary, they may have been continually filled with sorrow. (PR 1014)

Love, to the extent it makes the artist suffer, is likewise a boon to the creative impulse. As Proust asserts, "[E]very person who makes us suffer we can associate with a divinity"—inasmuch as they kindle the divine spark of creation within the artist (PR 1015).

The "madness" that is experienced may even be willed. The creative self instinctively senses that the cosmic light it needs may only be found on the far side of a darkness that is entirely inward. The pilgrimages along the Méséglise and Guermantes ways provide a foretaste of the pilgrimages to love, society, and art that organize The Search, whose external "ways" objectify the search for an inward path to salvation, often obscured amidst the labyrinthine corridors of a pathological self. These external pilgrimages (the "two ways," Balbec, Venice) are allegories of the self's holy crusade to locate and liberate the creative self within.

In freeing the artist from neurosis, creativity frees him or her to create about neurosis, to transform a cause of art into an effect of it. As Proust observes, "[T]he suffering caused him by others, his attempts to forestall it, the conflicts provoked by his suffering and the other cruel person—all that, interpreted by his intelligence, might furnish the material for a book" (PR 1016). Creativity does not, however, enable the artist to escape neurosis, but merely provides a means of coping with it, of mitigating its most destructive elements. The artist is never entirely "cured" of neurosis, nor is such an absolute cure desirable—inasmuch as the conflict associated with it enervates the creative impulse. As Doubrovsky observes, "To write is not, as the theory would lead you to hastily conclude, 'to emerge' from neurosis in the least; it is to adhere to it. . . . In fact, the narrator lodges his enterprise of liberation in the very location of his most intimate servitude" (121).

The "location of [Marcel's] most intimate servitude" is the bedroom of his boyhood, the scene of the "drame coucher," which reprises the scene of the original wound: the birthing bed that violently severs the living connection between mother and self. Marcel's bed is the site of the recurring wound that reopens every night during the "good night kiss" trauma-drama. This bed of original sorrows also prefigures the bed of deliverance from sorrows; the boyhood bed of profane desire heralds the bed of writing which liberates the self from those sorrows, which is also a bed of martyrdom and immortality. The bed is an ambivalent trope of profane and sacred desires, of death and resurrection, to which the self is bound like Prometheus to his rock, and where it converts its sleepless sorrows into the wakeful dreams of art. Like Prometheus, the self risks its soul to steal light from the gods: a divine spark it gives to humanity. If the artist sings, it is because of his chains—like a caged bird. The bars that imprison the body cannot constrain the musical bars that liberate the soul, inscribed in "the necessary rings of a beautiful style," even as the iron shackles of neurosis cannot clip the angel wings of creativity.

Marcel's name is incomplete because he lacks the identity for which he is searching: an artist. He is half of a metaphor in search of its mate. Half of a self in search of its ideal self. Only when that search for identity is complete, when the book is written, will the two halves of the metaphor that are narrator and author be conjoined in a single name: only then does Marcel become Marcel Proust. However, as this occurs beyond the bounds of the narrative, it can only be signified on the book's binding or title page: the only place that binds Marcel Proust to Marcel.

Marcel escapes the closed sign of neurosis through invention: through an idealizing imagination, whose unfettered virtual reality is a remedy to the enclosures of the neurotic bind. The claustrophobic walls of Marcel's Combray bedroom are an objectified topos for the neurosis that closely circumscribes the self, even as the figurations of the magic lantern trope on the remedial effects of creativity in dissolving the walls of neurotic fear. The constricted chest cavity of an asthmatic seizure also reiterates the closure of neurosis on a figurative and literal level, as the effect par excellence of neurotic enclosure: a choking off of that which is essential to life. As the walls of Marcel's bedroom are absorbed into the illusory projections of the magic lantern, so too will neurosis be absorbed into the figurations of *Recherche,* even as the claustrophobic walls of a Combray bedroom give way to the cork-lined walls of Boulevard Haussmann.

Art breaches the neurotic enclosure, realizing the liberatory struggle of the creative impulse, even as a galloping Golo dematerializes the prison walls of the narrator's bedroom. The writer's "signs" are a prisoner's graffiti: symbols that not only dematerialize the walls of his or her neurotic enclosure, but which would be impossible without the suffocating presence of those walls. If neurotic fear collapses the walls of the lungs in suffocating asthma attacks, then the creative urge is the medication that dilates the self.

The art of *Recherche* is deeply associated with the neurotic sorrows of desire. As Proust affirms, "[T]he women he has loved most deeply . . . were only posing for the writer at the very moment when, against his will, they were causing him the most suffering" (PR 1016):

> I realised clearly that she did not love me and I was forced to reconcile myself to merely learning from her what it is to experience suffering, love, and, at first, even happiness. And when we endeavour to extract the general qualities from our sorrow and to write about it, we are somewhat consoled, perhaps for a still different reason . . . writing comprise[s] for the writer a healthful and indispensable function, the fulfilling of which brings happiness. (PR 1018)

Writing heals the pathology of the self: recuperates the Platonic "pharmakon." The wound, however, is never entirely closed, for this would close it off as a source of creativity. Proust writes:

> [W]hen we say that his loves and his sorrows have been helpful to the poet and have aided him to construct his work, that unknown women have . . . brought each her stone for the building of the monument they will never see, we do not sufficiently take into consideration that the life of the writer does not end with his work. . . . Viewed as an omen of misfortune, the work should be regarded solely as an unhappy love which is the certain forerunner of others and will result in the poet's life resembling his work. (PR 1019)

How to comprehend this statement, whose deflationary characterization of the art work as "an omen of misfortune" seems so out of place in a work that is nothing if not a monument to the cult of genius. Writing is not only a cure to present sorrows, but the guarantee of future misfortunes: some of which it creates, some of which it seeks in order to create. The very sacrifice of life to art creates sorrows, which the artist then uses to make further art. The very primacy of art in the artist's life creates sorrows in love—which the artist similarly converts into art. If sorrow begets creativity, then creativity begets further sorrow, is indeed an "omen of misfortune."

In contradistinction to Doubrovsky's assertion, neurosis is not a closed structure, an "obsessional cage" for the artiste manqué. The closed pattern of neurosis is breached by the red thread of creativity which bleeds beyond its closely circumscribed margins—as in a Navajo blanket. As Proust observes, "[I]t is true, we are obliged to go through our own individual suffering again, with the courage of the doctor who repeats on himself the dangerous inoculation":

But at the same time, we have to represent it to ourselves in a general form and this enables us to a certain extent to escape its strangling grip ... and is not without even a certain joy ... one can win release form suffering, even if only by drawing from it the lessons it has to teach. The intelligence does not recognise in life any closed situations without an outlet. (PR 1020)

Hence, "the dull ache of our heart can raise, as it were, a banner for each fresh sorrow, the permanent symbol of an inner image." Proust continues:

[L]et us accept the physical injury it inflicts because of the spiritual wisdom that it brings; let us allow our body to disintegrate, since each fresh particle that breaks off, now luminous and decipherable, comes and adds itself to our work to complete it at the cost of suffering [and thus] make it more and more substantial as emotions gradually chip away our life. (PR 10021)

If we would understand the personality of the modern artist, we must also understand the personality of the neurotic, his spiritual progenitor. This is why Rank approaches the creative personality through an analysis of the "productive neurotic type," or "artiste manqué" (25). Marcel's "apprenticeship to signs" exemplifies this "interdependence of production and suffering" in which production is conceived as a "forcible liberation from inward pressures," as a "creative development of a neurosis in an objective form "(52, 43). Like Goethe, Proust was "able to balance the destructive elements in him creatively, by absorbing them into his [work]" (81). The illusory thus plays an "absolutely vital character" in the artist's liberation from neurotic fear (100). Rank regards the "neurotic as a failed artist." Unlike the artist, the neurotic "fails to overcome his mortal fear because he has nothing to compensate it" (101). For the modern (and postmodern) artist, art is all the compensation needed to cope with neurotic fears. The pleasure he or she thus derives from the creative act is not only "nourished from positive sources but may even be just a condition characterized by the absence of fear" (107).

To escape the neurotic shore, the poet invents the sea—and a raft of words to voyage across it. Yet, s/he returns to feed upon the wound, in what is tantamount to a perpetual ingestion of the nutrient-rich, neurotic afterbirth. Art is, consequently, the byproduct of a tendency to ideologize a personal conflict, to "create for himself some ideology for the objectification of his psychic tensions" (Rank 370). This tendency is, moreover, bound up with the problem and the process of "identification." According to Rank, "[O]ne can say of the artist that he does not practice his calling, but is it ... the artist needs his calling for his spiritual existence"(371). This conclusion bears significantly upon the career of Proust's narrator insofar as the quest for art is inseparably yoked to his search for spirituality, as evidenced by Proust's appropriation of the greatest symbol of religious spirituality: the cathedral. The question of creativity thus resolves itself into a question of identity, as evidenced by *Recherche*, which is nothing if not a search by the self for a deeper correspondence with itself, for a self with which it more completely, if not absolutely identifies: for a self that is more inclusive, that is deeply informed by the spiritual—a self that is revealed by, and which is immanent in, art.

This concern with depth identity explains the inherent and unavoidably "confessional" nature of modern and postmodern art. As Rank observes, the aim of the modern artist "is not to express himself in his work, but to get to know himself by it . . . he cannot express himself without confessing, and therefore knowing, himself" (390). This tendency toward confessional truth in art, however, reprises the original conflict that created the need for the consolation of illusion in order to cope with suffering. The less illusory his art, the more it prolongs his suffering—a problem the artist solves by building into his or her work levels of "truth": corresponding to the degrees of self-identification with those truths. Hence the need for a fictional Marcel who, while confessing some "truths" (incestuous desires, matricidal impulses, sado-masochistic tendencies), provides Proust a means of distancing himself from others (homosexuality). This narrative construct enables him to negotiate the conflicting demands art and life, fiction and reality, illusion and experience, self and society. Proust creates a narrative apparatus that permits various levels of sincerity, which permits him to confess many "truths" while keeping others to himself. The degree of fact or fiction at any given point in the narrative is a function of the ego's distance from the narrating voice, which is forever violating its own gag order, in what constitutes a struggle between antithetical tendencies: to mystify and demystify the self—a struggle between a volitional desire to disclose much and an unconscious desire to disclose all.

The pages of *Recherche* are a contested ground that marks the site of repression and the return of the repressed. Incestuous, oedipal, matricidal, homoerotic, sadistic, masochistic, voyeuristic, and exhibitionistic impulses struggle against the ego's self-censorship. This eruptive force of the repressed unconscious prompts a contrary impulse toward mystification of the self through strategies normally associated with dreams: displacement, condensation, transposition. These are now absorbed into the narrative in an effort to negotiate the conflicting demands of the unconscious and conscious mind for expression and preservation respectively. The "caged obsessions" are continuously slipping the shackles of silence, flooding the page in signifying chains, like the uniformed inmates of a sanitarium after a breakout. The result is the poetic bedlam of the Proustian unconscious, loosed upon the page in incestuous and matricidal impulses, in sadistic and masochistic tendencies, in homoerotic and creative urges, in dreams and involuntary memories, and in the ubiquitous practice of vices across race, class, and gender. *Recherche* is one vast negotiation between the conscious and unconscious mind, in which the instincts of the former are as repressive as the impulses of the latter are eruptive. The result of this psychological dialectic is a conscious prose deeply informed by the material of the unconscious mind—is the singular harmonization of the volitional and the involuntary that is Proustian narrative.

As Rank theorizes, the modern artist produces in "response to pressure from the most diverse influences" (77). Whereas an educative ideology, an ideology of sacrifice, the desire to replace what is lost, and the will to form all inform the creative impulse, "the most decisive part of creative dynamism originates in this conflict of opposing tendencies and their settlement in the harmony of the work" (409). Proust offers an even more nuanced interpretation of the dialectic between suffering and creativity: "It is our moments of suffering that outline our books and the intervals of respite that write them." I would add a further qualification: it is the writing of our sorrows that brings respite from them. Sorrows that impregnate the self are objectified in art. Art materializes the darkness of the self—and by so doing immortalizes it. Regarding the wound that gives rise to the word, I yield the last word to Proust: "[O]ne might almost say that works of art, like artesian wells, mount higher in proportion as the suffering has more deeply pierced the heart" (PR 1022).

THE ARCHITECTURE OF DESIRE: NEGOTIATING THE OTHER

The profane desire that is thwarted by the mother is displaced onto the feminine Other, through whom the self desires to fulfill its wish for the two-in-one (Gilberte, Albertine, and platonically Odette and the Duchess de Guermantes). Cruelly, the sorrows of differentiation return to wound the self anew, as it discovers the ineffaceable breach between itself and the Sapphic Other. It copes with these sorrows by seeking not an Other, but a same: an idealized objectification of the self, personified in Saint Loup, but thinly veiling the self's deeply homoerotic desires.

Woman is the elusive signified that forever escapes ontology, the slippery sign that by its very flux cannot be signified, much less possessed. The Sapphic Other is doubly fugitive, twice mystifying. Woman is the shadow of the great mother who sleeps at the heart of *Recherche*. Woman inherits the mother's ability to inspire possessive desire, as well as her capacity to wound by virtue of her separation from the loving son. If the mother inflicts the wound that inspires sadistic, matricidal, masochistic, and ultimately creative impulses, then woman compounds this original wound by reinforcing the sorrows of sexual differentiation, further enervating the creative urge, by intensifying the need to objectify suffering in order to mitigate the destructive force of it.

Hence, the mutual hymenoptera of self and Other.

The "perpetual alliteration" between mother and feminine Other is just one of the work's ubiquitous juxtapositions, which fosters the heartbreak and facilitates the continuity of the self across space and time. As Bersani observes, "[M]etaphorical connections among apparently dissimilar incidents provide a literary documentation of the unity of personality" (122). The architectonics of *Recherche* are deeply informed by Proust's temporal metaphor, and by the metaphor of the cathedral in particular. The book, like a cathedral, signifies the eternity of the soul. The book, like a cathedral or any ancient architecture, bears the "stain of time," exists not only in the three dimensions of space but in the fourth dimension of time, which is for Proust, as it was for Ruskin, critical:

> The greatest glory of a building is not in its stones nor in its gold. Its glory is in its Age. . . . It is in that golden stain of time that we are to look for the real light and colour and preciousness of architecture; and it is not until a building has assumed this character . . . and its pillars rise out of the shadows of death, that its existence, more lasting as it is than that of the natural objects of the world around it, can be gifted with even so much as these possess, of language and of life. (*Seven Lamps* 233–34)

Was it because the little patch of sunlight in Vermeer's "View of Delft" evoked Ruskin's "golden stain of time," that Proust loved this painting above all others? Inspired by Ruskin's temporal view of the great cathedrals, Proust composes *Recherche* so that its "pillars rise out of the shadows" of Aunt Leonie's impending death, out of the shadows of a mother's oblivion, first tasted on the eve of the kiss good night, out of the gloom of his separation from the maternal sublime, which tropes on the first violent separation of self and Other. The cathedral, like the book, is a free-standing work, lonely in its grandeur, isolated from its immediate surroundings, a trope of the self differentiated from all Other, and redolent of the three spires of Martinville, isolated on a darkling plain. If the cathedral is an objectification of the spiritualized and differentiated self, then similarly the immortal self is a monument to the ethos of the cathedral, a topos of redemption and eternity, "embody[ing] in ourselves the teachings and the truths which it represents" (Johnson 147).

Finally, the architectural organization of the great Romanesque cathedral not only tropes on the novel structure of *Recherche*, but on the nature of the self-Other dyad which comprises its very foundation. As Johnson observes, the narthex-sacristan-nave progression beautifully captures the *Combray-Swann in Love-Within a Budding Grove* progression, in which the "depth of the narthex . . . gives so much by its extent the illusion of being the real church that we are completely dazzled when the sacristan opens up the far end, which is only the second portal, the real one of the nave, and the nave opens up to us in its immensity" (157). More importantly, however, this architectonic principal also governs the nature of the self-Other relationship insofar as the Other is figured as a cathedral which similarly contains an inner essence, deep and hidden, which can only be apprehended by crossing the "threshold which leads to the kingdom of the spirit and [by penetrating] more deeply at the same time into the work and ourselves" (Johnson 157).

Metaphor is a means by which the self asserts itself across space and time, by which it also transforms the Other into a projection of the self. Metaphor is not only instrumental in stabilizing and transcending the discontinuities of the self, but is the principal medium for the redemption of the self through art. As Bersani asserts, "[I]t is the discovery of metaphor that confirms Marcel's sense of his literary vocation in A la Recherche . . ." (225). Metaphor is what enables him to "re-create the people and situations from his past as aspects of his own individuality" (236); they provide "at every moment the instruments of combat that transform a discouragingly alien world into the substance of self-affirmation . . . and allegorical representations of the self" (245, 247). Jephcott concurs: "[T]he principle of these laws, as applied to literature, was that of metaphor, which alone, for Proust, is capable of showing the true unity of experience"—the immanence of the eternal in the temporal (282). This law is given its most succinct formulation by Proust: "[T]ruth will only begin when the writer takes two different objects, poses their connection . . . and encloses them in the necessary rings of a beautiful style" (PR 1008).

Language itself is metaphorical, comprised of signs which are not the things themselves, but merely stand-ins for them. Rank theorizes language as "one vast metaphorical comprehension of the world [and thus] no word has any but a metaphorical meaning" (236–37). *Recherche* is one vast "perpetual alliteration" of its metonymic fragments. The words themselves are immersed in the associations they awaken and reawaken: signifying chains that float in a solution of associations. Each sign simultaneously signifies something and transcends itself in associations, alliterating with other self-transcending signs in a vast associative web that signifies the "communal life led by our ideas." The meaning of *Recherche* inheres partially in its signs, but more essentially in the associations they awaken, in the vast system of temporal dialectics: between the material and the immaterial, object and subject, present and past, space and time. And the vehicles for realizing this associative "wisdom" are metaphors that dematerialize the object and spiritualize the subject, that are sheathed alike in object and subject, so that both are set in motion in space and time. As Proust concludes, "[W]ithout that relationship there is nothing" (PR 1009): only the sterility of a subjectless objectivity, of a despiritualized materiality, of an impoverished (and therefore false) realism—a hollow, fatuous, pseudo realism in which the material is evacuated of the immaterial, the object divorced from the subject, a realism that is only half alive because it is "satisfied merely to 'describe things,' to furnish a miserable listing of their lines and surfaces, [and which] is, notwithstanding its pretensions to realism, the farthest removed from reality, the one that most impoverishes and saddens us" (PR 1009).

In collapsing the subject-object binary, in "restoring the tangled participation of each within the other" (Gray 9), Proust models the very postmodern perspective that will come to characterize the criticism of his own text, collapsing the distinction between critic and author, between criticism and creativity, "for in the widened cultural context of postmodernism, criticism becomes creative activity—criticism's claim to objectivity now debunked, and the myth of theory's separateness collapsed. A postmodern perspective restores the tangled participation of each within the other, abolishing the imposed boundaries that have segregated the two" (9). The subject usurps the object as the critic authors the text.

Metaphor is the vehicle of a metaphysical synthesis that redeems and eternalizes the soul of the narrator: a synthesis born in the anguish of a son's separation from his mother, which becomes the womb of the ambivalent disjunction between self and Other; a self tragically divided by the contrary yearnings for symbiosis and independence; a conflict which is not resolved until the narrator's liberation to art, in which the tension between self and Other, the ideal and the real, is resolved through their symbiosis on the plane of illusion. Metaphor fulfills the wish for the two-in-one.

Desire for the Other is a function of the Other's ability to not only occupy space, but to move in time as well, to metaphorically transcend its own three-dimensional materiality and expand into a four-dimensional spirituality. As Bersani asserts, "[M]etaphorical expression is . . . a means of assimilating the outer world to the accumulated past that makes up Marcel's inner world . . ." (148–49). This is what Proust opposes to mere "realism," to a reductive, mimetic, "faithful" transcription of the material world. The three-dimensional Other holds not the least interest for Proust unless and until it acquires a fourth dimension through its association with another place, another time, or to a work of art. Thus, the Duc de Guermantes "is no longer the rich, vain coureur Marcel is disappointed to meet, but part of a harmonious set of associations among the names of different regions in France and among different periods in time" (Bersani 150). Any given person, place, or thing in the novel justifies its presence by virtue of its being part of a web of associations, as evidenced by the Guermantes who are but "the present links in a historical chain which is otherwise wholly spiritual" (Bersani 154).

This is the essence of the selective vision that either grants or denies access to the privileged salon that is Proustian aesthetics—and whose exclusivity is an analog for the Jockey Club of Swann and Saint Loup, for the exclusive salons of the Duchess de Guermantes and Mme Verdurin, and for the select races of Sodom and Gomorrah. Membership in the exclusive club of Proust's "privileged moments" is highly selective, privileging either some form of the genius concept or deep correspondence with the self. The highly codified and select aesthetic that governs inclusion in the narrative produces signifying practices that are individualized in the extreme. It is a process of artificial selection that favors things that are part of a temporal pattern. As Joseph Wood Krutch observes,

> [E]very moment implies the past and the future because its true significance lies in its being part of a pattern extending from the past into the future. Living experience cannot be fully significant because it is isolated and transitory; it becomes significant only when it is contemplated in connection with those parts of the pattern that time separates but which really belong together. (Intro x)

Proust composes *Recherche* by re-composing the immortal fragments that time has decomposed. The existence of any and every metonymic fragment is due to its being part of a pattern in time, to its participation in the "perpetual alliteration" of past, present, and future. This is the source of that "freshness of vision which makes his novel unlike any other,"

> whether narrating a series of events, describing a scene, or cataloguing the contents of the mind of a character at any moment, he is certain to select incidents, to set down particulars, and to list details which most would have omitted in favor of certain others now in their turn passed over by Proust. The result is the creation of a strange new world. (Krutch xiii)

The result is the peculiar salon that is Marcel's narrative, the marvelous masked ball that is Proustian sensibility. The people, places, and things that populate *Recherche* are like the members of the select or secret societies whose codes he decodes. All trope on the exclusivity of the Proustian universe, whose metaphoric selectivity privileges the sameness of difference, the spirituality of matter, the temporalization of space, and the spatialization of time. Every metaphoric fusion of objects disjoined in time or space represents a displacement of the original subject-object disjunction, of the primal separation of Marcel and mother. Doubrovsky's assessment is instructive: "[W]ith the same stroke, metaphor comes into being; the 'two' terms or 'objects' are now 'one' (50).

THE LAST JUDGMENT:
FIGURING THE "FINAL ORDER" OF *RECHERCHE*

Deleuze asserts, with respect to the final judgment of *Recherche*, that "the third order, dominated by the idea of death, seems absolutely catastrophic and unproductive" (140):

> [T]here remains the third Proustian order, that of universal alteration and death. . . . Whereas the first two orders raised no promise of reconciliation . . . there is now, on the contrary, a reconciliation to be found, a contradiction to be surmounted. (139)

I would like to revisit Deleuze's problematic assessment. Unlike the first two orders, which are dominated by the idea of death (the death of the ideal in the real), the third order is dominated not only by death, but by resurrection and remystification. If this final order is, on the one hand, dominated by the death of society, whose decline is initiated by malice, accelerated by vice, and brought to catastrophic closure by the Great War (almost as biblical retribution for its sins of decadence and vice as embodied in Sodom and Gomorrah), then it is also, by contrast, dominated by the redemption of the individual-as-artist, whose deterministic plot of decline is suddenly transformed into a plot of incline prompted by his spiritual rebirth to art and personal transcendence of Death through art.

It is also dominated by the remystification or spiritualization of the real by involuntary memory. The dramatic, chiaroscuro tone of this final order is due to the juxtaposition of the ideas of death and transfiguration. If Proust is writing the obituary of society, he is concomitantly immortalizing the artist in general and eternalizing his own soul in particular. If in his penultimate portrait of Charlus's decline, he presents us with a rogue's gallery of pimps, prostitutes, perverts, and proprietors, with coke fiends, gigolos, and pedophiles, with the likes of Big Jule, Algeria Jenny, and Pamela the Charmer, then by contrast in the ensuing retrospective on Venice images of resurrection proliferate: of the Virgin Mary, Dandolo's tomb, the phoenix, the mosaics, and the Baptistery of St. Mark's.

Unquestionably, the brothel scene reinscribes the biblical doom of Sodom and Gomorrah, as evidenced not only by the sudden bombardment that accompanies Marcel's exit from this house of vice, in which the "siren shrieked forth, followed at once by a violent barrage of fire," but by the biblical imagery of fire and brimstone raining down upon the heads of the hedonists, whose "repugnant" appearance was "probably due to indulgence in degrading forms of enjoyment" (PR 967).

Several of these Pompeiians, on whom the fire of heaven was already raining down, "descended into the passageways of the underground railroad, which were as black as catacombs. . . . Engulfed in this strange element, Jupien's habitués felt as if they had traveled far and come to witness some natural phenomenon, such as a tidal wave or an eclipse . . . they celebrated secret rites in the darkness of the catacombs, as in some Pompeiian palace of ill repute, to the accompaniment of the volcanic thunder of bombs" (PR 970). Celeste Albaret notes the significance of this Last Judgment:

> [T]here was a whole world, a whole society and a way of living that he'd once known and that was crumbling gradually, in the midst of a new world

coming into being. He had realized this; I'm sure he foresaw it right from the beginning. As a moralist, he tried to describe all this in its human aspects, with all its beauties and also all its follies. He was terrible in his judgments, and he foretold the fall—anyone who doesn't see that in his work hasn't understood it. (242)

I believe the "final order" of *Recherche* is more redemptive than the Old Testament morality of the judgment seemingly rendered on society in these passages. The catastrophic closure of society contrasts with the redemption of the narrator, which nevertheless sustains and deepens the moral tone of the denouement. Further, this redemptive denouement is prefigured by the images of renewal with which Proust seeds the landscape of damnation. Even amidst the proliferating images of the apocalypse, amidst the fire and brimstone of an "absolute catastrophe" conjuring the fate of the denizens of Pompeii, Sodom and Gomorrah and the catacombs, Proust ushers in a Rembrandtian ray of resurrection, embodying the regenerative effects of war: "Already anticipating the end of the war, new styles of dancing were being developed everywhere and were being madly indulged . . . along with this, certain artistic opinions, less anti-Germanic than during the early years of the war, were becoming current and bringing a breath of air to stifled minds" (PR 970)—heralding the youthful renewal of a postwar Europe, but more significantly prefiguring Marcel's own rebirth to and through art. Even vice is invested with an invincible persistence, refusing to perish amidst the carnage and chaos: a rank weed that grows corrupt, but grows imperishably—itself an alternative and prophetic emblem of eternity.

The modern concern for a unity that definitively closes off meaning opens into a postmodern narrative that unwrites itself. *Recherche* stops short of the catastrophic closure toward which it dramatically gestures in this "final order" whose finality it unwrites. Its final gesture is to figure a catastrophic closure that opens upon itself. The last laugh is left, not to a judgmental self, but to the imperishable fragments of time, whether they proliferate under the signs of vice or virtue, society or art, damnation or redemption. *Recherche* lapses into a self-reflexive paradox in which the harsh judgments that rain down like aerial bombs on vice are softened by the immutability of vice. The last word, like the first, is left to time, in a final order that embraces the immortality of vice as well as virtue: in a world where the only virtue is a vice-redeeming art, and whose narrative arms after hurling thunderbolts at vice, open into a conciliatory embrace of the imperishable—even if it is the immortal fragments of vice that survive amongst the apocalyptic ruins.

In the last analysis, *Recherche* transcends its own penultimate judgments of a vice-ridden society and self, unwriting itself in a farewell gesture toward the renascent, the recuperative, and the redemptive, in which even the judgments against vice are absorbed into a final awareness of its immutability.

Proust's last judgment situates vice in the fictional mosaic of immortal fragments that inform The Search. This final judgment enacts its own peculiar wisdom inasmuch as it is grounded in "the point of view from which we come at last to regard the world"—and particularly the world of vice.

Whereas society is seemingly consigned to oblivion for its sins against human nature (and against humanity in general), the individual who confesses his sins in art thereby atones for them, and is redeemed by and through his art. Yet, Proust's "final order" evinces hope for the collective as well as for the individual, for the seeming destruction of a decadent society by war is contradicted by the hopeful images of its own inevitable renascence: even if only the renascence of vice and the renewal of the pursuit of pleasure, of dancing, and of the creative impulse. These are the blades of society's grass whose emergence from the volcanic, Pompeiian wasteland of postwar Europe he already foresees.

Roger Shattuck problematizes the work's redemptive ending as its singular flaw: "Here, I have my principal criticism to make of the book as Proust left it":

> This total reorientation of the action, embodied in the transformation of Marcel's life in the final pages, demands some corresponding elevation in style to lift us out of the level established by twenty-six hundred pages of prose. . . . He has unlimbered so much of his arsenal that one feels he has no reserve left to throw into his final passage. . . . And the fact is . . . that Proust has . . . anticipated this final revelation so many times, that much of the dramatic effect of the end is vitiated. (127)

I would argue that, on the contrary, Proust's effect at the end is deliberately and appropriately understated. After the figurative pyrotechnices, the prosaic sturm and drang of the preceding passages, in which the decline into decadence of society is metonymically replicated by the collective fall of its most elite members (the Guermantes), Proust applies a deft Wagnerian touch: drawing the music of his epic work to a close that is suffused with the spiritual light of a lasting repose.

Proust's vision, as embodied in this final order, is neither moral nor immoral, but amoral. If it indeed signified the "absolute catastrophe" of which Deleuze writes, it would signal a moral order as well: one connoting the absolute destruction of an immoral society a la Sodom and Gomorrah and the redemption through art of a penitent individual. Proust rejects such an unambiguous moral denouement in which evil and good are absolutely divided, in favor of a more modern (even postmodern) morally ambiguous final order in which vice and virtue are invested with a similar immutability.

Ironically, Proust ends by reinscribing the Ruskinian marriage of art and religion by investing art with the redemptive power of religion. Having liberated art from the service of religion (its rightful place, according to Ruskin), Proust elevates it to the level of religion, as a vehicle (and perhaps in modern society the sole remaining vehicle) of spirituality. After its long eclipse by Darwinian theory, metaphysical doubt, and the industrial age, spirituality is reborn in *Recherche*—but even more significantly, it is reborn not in the great collective institution of orthodox religion, but through an individualized religion of art. Further, spirituality is recuperated by Proust not merely for the artist, but for the individual insofar as it is mortal experience that is invested with the spirit of the immortal sublime. Moments we experience between the womb and the tomb twinkle with stardust. And these moments are enough to give to experience a smile of the eternal, to imprint upon its mortal rubble a "little patch of yellow light."

Yet, the truly heroic achievement of *Recherche* is that Proust manages to reconcile these two seemingly antithetical realms, to unite the romantic and the existential (the Chateaubriand and the Sartrean halves of his soul) in a romantic existentialism, to synthesize them in a spiritualized materiality. His journey is not merely a bildungsroman of the artist, but an "apprenticeship" toward the sign (Deleuze 14), an evolution toward a kind of "wisdom," toward a philosophical reintegration of the ideal and the real, of the spiritual and the material. This is perhaps the greatest of all morals to be gleaned from *Recherche*: the search of Proust's narrator is in reality the search of all humanity for a spirituality that has been under assault since Carlyle's *Sartor Resartis*—and which is increasingly lost amid the rampant materiality and dehumanizing conditions of the modern and postmodern age. As William Henry Hudson observes in his introduction to *Sartor Resartis*, "[S]pirit is the only reality. Visible things are but the manifestations, emblems or clothing of spirit" (x). What Hudson observes of Carlyle applies with equal veracity to Proust who, like Carlyle, utilizes "his own experiences for the human setting of his philosophy . . . these experiences possessed far more than a merely personal interest and meaning" (viii). Hudson continues: "[T]he moral significance of Carlyle's 'symbolic myth'" derives from it purpose, which is "nothing less than spiritual rebirth" (ix). Whereas Carlyle, like Ruskin, utilizes the "symbolic myth" as the vehicle of spiritual rebirth to and through religion, Proust deploys it as the vehicle of spiritual rebirth to and through a religion of art. His great gift to humanity is the discovery, the awareness, that life itself is yet enough to meet our spiritual needs: as long as we let it get through to us, as long as we are truly alive. When we open *Recherche*, it is experience (respiritualized) that comes flooding back into our souls. Life is the logical, inevitable, and revelatory destination of *Recherche*. The ultimate intertextuality is that between *Recherche* and the pages of our own experience, which it helps us to "read" and to live anew. As his narrator asserts in the novel's penultimate passage, "[T]hey would not be my readers, but readers of themselves" (PR 1113).

There is amongst the catastrophic ruination of the end a spiritual revelation. "We must," as Delueze reminds us, "consider these signs from the viewpoint of the final revelation. This revelation is identified with art, the highest kind of signs. But in the work of art, all the other signs are included, find a place with relation to the effectiveness they had in the course of the apprenticeship" (83–84). Deleuze continues: "[T]he time regained of art encompasses and comprehends all the others, for it is only within time regained that each line of time [wasted, lost, or rediscovered] finds its truth, its place, and its result form the viewpoint of truth" (87)—which is conferred ulteriorly. The wisdom of this third moment of desire is associative. As Joseph Wood Krutch observes, Proust's "theory was that the quality of direct experience always eluded one and that only in recollection could we grasp its real flavor . . . because its true significance lies in its being part of a pattern extending from the past into the future"(x).

The temporal wisdom of this retrospective view recuperates a narrative mastery problematized by the signs of Sapphic desire, and into which the discontinuities, contradictions, and uncertainties of the self are absorbed. The spiritual nausea produced by the existential sign of desire's second moment is superseded by a spirituality that arises from the real—and which is, in the final analysis, life-affirming. Perhaps devoid of meaning before the womb and after the tomb, experience is reinvested with a "spiritual glamour" that satisfies the soul's dual needs for spirituality during life and for immortality after it. The "wisdom" that is *Recherche* privileges the perspective that human experience is not dependent for its spirituality or meaning on what transpires beyond the grave. The truly revolutionary and redemptive "wisdom" of *Recherche* is that life's experiences are "charming enough in themselves" (SW 325). Art in general, and *Recherche* in particular, restores to modern experience a spirituality in decline since the advent of the industrial age. The wisdom of *Recherche* is its faith that the real can fulfill the desires of the ideal: that the two are indeed one. It is, in the last analysis, a wisdom that privileges the alliteration between the idealism of the imagination, the immediacy of the senses, and the soul's hunger for immortality.

This is not to suggest that the novel's meaning can be essentialized from any theoretical perspective, much less from a Rankian psycho-critical framework. Theorizing *Recherche* from a Rankian perspective can serve criticism through a selective "reading" of those passages that metafictively inform the creative process. As Doubrovsky reminds us, "[I]n criticism there is something for everyone—as long as you see that whatever metalanguage is used, there is no ultimate decoding of the metaphorical language of the work into a rigorously metonymic language that would lay out its meaning" (115). In the final analysis, because we make meaning of fragments, the meaning we make is fragmentary: a "little patch of yellow light" projected onto the canvas of the work it interprets.

Marcel is forever negotiating between the conflicting needs of desire and art, and the landscape of this conflict is the feminine, whose mystification nevertheless resists possession either as an object of desire or as a "sign" that can be definitively captured in art. Desire for the metaphor of the feminine ends with the possession of feminine metonyms: a mole, a neck, a bent knee. The desire to totalize possession of the feminine collapses in a thousand partial possessions. The epic structure of desire Marcel raises in his imagination collapses into a rubble of fragments in reality—and *Recherche* is largely the saga of this catastrophic implosion of the architecture of desire, from whose rubble, however, the dove of art arises. The roar emanating from *Recherche* is the thundering downfall of desire—offset when the dust settles by the immortal flutter of figuration.

References

Aciman, Andre. "Letter From Illiers-Combray: In Search of Proust." *The New Yorker* Dec. 1998: 81–85.

Albaret, Celeste. *Monsieur Proust.* Ed. Georges Belmont. Trans. Barbara Bray. New York: McGraw-Hill, 1973.

Appignanesi, Lisa. *Femininity and Creativity: A Study of Henry James, Robert Musil, and Marcel Proust.* New York: Harper & Row, 1973.

Bataille, Georges. "Proust and Evil." *Modern Critical Interpretations: Marcel Proust and Remembrance of Things Past.* Ed. Harold Bloom. New York: Chelsea House, 1987. 51–62.

Beckett, Samuel. "Memory, Habit, Time." *Modern Critical Interpretations: Marcel Proust and Remembrance of Things Past.* Ed. Harold Bloom. New York: Chelsea House, 1987. 19–36.

Bell, William Stewart. *Proust's Nocturnal Muse.* New York: Columbia UP, 1962.

Benjamin, Walter. "The Image of Proust." *Modern Critical Interpretations: Marcel Proust and Remembrance of Things Past.* Ed. Harold Bloom. New York: Chelsea House, 1987. 37–50.

Bersani, Leo. *Marcel Proust: The Fictions of Life and Art.* New York: Oxford UP, 1965.

Bloom, Harold. "Introduction." *Modern Critical Interpretations: Marcel Proust and Remembrance of Things Past.* Ed. Harold Bloom. New York: Chelsea House, 1987. 1–18.

———. "Marcel Proust." *The Books and School of the Ages.* New York: Harcourt Brace, 1994.

Brady, Patrick. *Marcel Proust.* Boston: G.K. Hall, 1977.

Brée, Germaine. *Marcel Proust and Deliverance From Time.* Trans. C. J. Richards and A. D. Truitt. New Brunswick, N.J.: Rutgers UP, 1955.

Bucknall, Barbara J. *The Religion of Art in Proust.* Chicago: U of Illinois P, 1969.

———. *Critical Essays on Marcel Proust.* Boston: G.K. Hall, 1987.

Campbell, Joseph. *The Hero With A Thousand Faces.* Princeton: Princeton UP, 1949.

Carlyle, Thomas. *Sartor Resartus: On Heroes and Hero Worship*. Intro. by W. H. Hudson. New York: E. P. Dutton, 1956.

Cattaui, Georges. *Marcel Proust*. Trans. Ruth Hall. New York: Funk and Wagnalls, 1967.

Collier, Peter. *Proust and Venice*. Cambridge: Cambridge UP, 1989.

Deleuze, Gilles. *Proust and Signs*. Trans. Richard Howard. New York: George Braziller, 1972.

De Man, Paul. "Reading (Proust)." *Allegories of Reading*. New Haven and London: Yale UP, 1978. Qtd. in *Modern Critical Interpretations: Marcel Proust and Remembrance of Things Past*. Ed. Harold Bloom. New York: Chelsea House, 1987. 117–34.

Derrida, Jacques. "The End of the Book and the Beginning of Writing." *Of Grammatology*. Trans. Gayatri Chakravorty Spivak. Baltimore: Johns Hopkins UP, 1976. 16.

De Souze, Sybil. "Why Vinteuil's Septet?" *The Religion of Art in Proust*. Chicago: U of Illinois P, 1969. 109–17.

Dezon-Jones, Elyane. "Death of My Grandmother/ Birth of a Text." *The Religion of Art in Proust*. Chicago: U of Illinois P, 1969. 192–204.

Doubrovsky, Serge. *Writing and Fantasy in Proust: La Place de la madeleine*. Lincoln: U of Nebraska P, 1986.

Ellison, David R. "The Self in/as Writing." *Modern Critical Interpretations: Marcel Proust and Remembrance of Things Past*. Ed. Harold Bloom. New York: Chelsea House, 1987. 147–56.

———. *The Reading of Proust*. Baltimore: Johns Hopkins UP, 1984.

Finn, Michael R. *Proust, the Body, and Literary Form*. New York: Cambridge UP, 1999.

Flugel, J. C. *The Psycho-Analytic Study of the Family*. London: Hogarth, 1931.

Girard, Rene. "The Worlds of Proust." *Modern Critical Interpretations: Marcel Proust and Remembrance of Things Past*. Ed. Harold Bloom. New York: Chelsea House, 1987. 63–87.

Graham, Victor E. "Proust's Alchemy." *The Religion of Art in Proust*. Chicago: U of Illinois P, 1969. 58–69.

Gray, Margaret E. *Postmodern Proust*. Philadelphia: U of Pennsylvania P, 1992.

Hodson, Leighton. *Marcel Proust: The Critical Heritage*. New York: Routledge, 1989.

Hudson, W. H. *Sartor Resartus: On Heroes and Hero Worship*. Intro. by W. H. Hudson. New York: E. P. Dutton, 1956.

Humphries, Jefferson. *The Otherness Within: Gnostic Readings in Marcel Proust, Flannery O'Connor, and Francois Villon*. Baton Rouge: Louisiana State UP, 1983.

Jephcott, E. F. N. *Proust and Rilke: The Literature of Expanded Consciousness*. New York: Harper and Row, 1972.

Johnson, J. Theodore Jr. "Marcel Proust and Architecture: Some Thoughts on the Cathedral-Novel." *The Religion of Art in Proust*. Chicago: U of Illinois P, 1969. 133–61.

Johnson-Roullier, Cyrainia E. *Reading on the Edge: Exiles, Modernities, and Cultural Transformation in Proust, Joyce, and Baldwin.* New York: State U of New York P, 2000.

Kasell, Walter. *Marcel Proust and the Strategy of Reading.* Amsterdam: John Benjamins B.V., 1980.

Klein, Dennis B. *Jewish Origins of the Psychoanalytic Movement.* New York: Praeger, 1981.

Kohut, Heinz. *The Restoration of the Self.* New York: International Universities P, 1977.

——. *The Search for the Self: Selected Writing of Heinz Kohut (1950–1978) Vol. 1.* Ed./Intro. by Paul H. Ornstein. Madison, Conn.: International Universities P, 1978.

——. *The Search for the Self: Selected Writings of Heinz Kohut (1978–1981) Vol. 3.* Ed. Paul H. Ornstein. Madison, Conn.: International Universities P, 1990.

Kolb, Philip. "Proust's Protagonist as a 'Beacon.'" *The Religion of Art in Proust.* Chicago: U of Illinois P, 1969. 50–57.

——. *Marcel Proust: Selected Letters Vol. 4 1918–1922.* Trans. by Joanna Kilmartin. London: HarperCollins, 2000.

Kristeva, Julia. *Time and Sense: Proust and the Experience of Literature.* Trans. Ross Guberman. New York: Columbia UP, 1996.

——. *Proust and the Sense of Time.* Intro./Trans. by Stephen Bann. New York, Columbia UP, 1993.

Krutch, Joseph Wood. "Introduction." *A la Recherche du temps perdu.* Trans. C. K. Scott Moncrieff. and, for *Le Temps retrouvé*, Frederick A. Blossom, 2 vols. New York, Random House, 1934.

Lacan, Jacques. *Structuralism.* Ed. Jacques Ehrman. New York: Anchor Books, 1960. 101.

——. "Fetishism: The Symbolic, The Imaginary, and the Real." *Perversion: Psychodynamics. . . .* Ed. Sando Lovand. New York: Random House, 1956.

Lamos, Colleen. *Deviant Modernism: Sexual and Textual Errancy in Eliot, Joyce, and Proust.* Cambridge: Cambridge UP, 1999.

Landow, George P. *The Aesthetic and Critical Theories of John Ruskin.* Princeton, NJ: Princeton UP, 1971.

Macksey, Richard. "The Architecture of Time: Dialectics and Structure." *Modern Critical Interpretations: Marcel Proust and Remembrance of Things Past.* Ed. Harold Bloom. New York: Chelsea House, 1987. 89–98.

Maxwell, Donald. *The Abacus and the Rainbow: Bergson, Proust, and the Digital-Analogic Opposition.* New York: Peter Lang, 1999.

Miller, Milton L. *Nostalgia: A Psychoanalytic Study of Proust.* Boston: Houghton Mifflin, 1956.

Moss, Howard. *The Magic Lantern of Marcel Proust*. New York: MacMillan, 1962.

Nin, Anais. *The Diary of Anais Nin: Volume One (1931–1934)*. Ed. Gunther Stuhlman. New York: Harcourt Brace, 1966.

O'Brien, Justin. "Albertine the Ambiguous: Notes on Proust's Transposition of the Sexes." *PMLA* 64.5 (Dec. 1949): 933–52.

Painter, G. D. *Marcel Proust: A Biography*. Boston: Little Brown, 1959–1965.

Poulet, Georges. "Proustian Space." *Modern Critical Interpretations: Marcel Proust and Remembrance of Things Past*. Ed. Harold Bloom. New York: Chelsea House, 1987. 99–116.

Proust, Marcel. *A la Recherche du temps perdu*. Trans. C. K. Scott Moncrieff. and, for *Le Temps retrouvé*, Frederick A. Blossom, 2 vols. New York, Random House, 1934.

———. *Jean Santeuil*. Paris: Gallimard, 1952.

———. *Contre Sainte-Beuve*. Paris: Gallimard, 1954.

———. *Le Bible d'Amiens de John Ruskin*. Paris: Mercure de France, 1926.

———. *Sesame et les lys: des tresors des rois; des jardin des reines de John Ruskin*. Paris: Mercure de France, 1935.

Rank, Otto. *Art and Artist: Creative Urge and Personality Development*. Foreword by Anais Nin. Trans. Charles Francis Atkinson. New York: W.W. Norton, 1932.

———. *Beyond Psychology*. New Jersey: Hadden Craftsmen, 1958.

Richard, Jean-Pierre. *Proust et le monde sensible*. Paris: Seuil, 1974.

Rivers, J. E. "Proust and the Aesthetic of Suffering." *The Religion of Art in Proust*. Chicago: U of Illinois P, 1969. 118–32.

Seiden, Melvin. "Proust's Marcel and Saint-Loup: Inversion Reconsidered." *The Religion of Art in Proust*. Chicago: U of Illinois P, 1969. 92–108.

Shattuck, Roger. *Proust's Binoculars: A Study of Memory, Time, and Recognition in A la Recherche du temps perdu*. New York: Random House, 1963.

Splitter, Randolph. *Proust's Recherche: A Psychoanalytic Interpretation*. Boston: Routledge and Kegan Paul, 1981.

Stambolian, George. *Marcel Proust and the Creative Encounter*. Chicago: U of Chicago P, 1972.

Taft, Jessie. *Otto Rank: A Biographic Study Based on Notebooks, Letters, Collected Writings, Therapeutic Achievements and Personal Associations*. New York: The Julien P, 1958.

Terdiman, Richard. "The Depreciation of the Event." *Modern Critical Interpretations: Marcel Proust and Remembrance of Things Past*. Ed. Harold Bloom. New York: Chelsea House, 1987. 125–46.

Updike, John. "The Man in Bed." *The New Yorker* April 2000: 89–92.

Wilson, Edmund. *Axel's Castle: A Study in the Imaginative Literature of 1870–1930*. New York: Charles Scribner's Sons, 1931.

Index

Albaret, Celeste, 173–174, 176–177, 194–195, 198, 201, 207, 230
Alden, D. H., 71
Appignanesi, Lisa, 7, 59, 60, 74
artiste manqué, 14, 176, 217, 223

Baker, Russell, 16
Balzac, Honore, 171, 183
Bataille, Georges, 44, 76
Beckett, Samuel, 7, 55
Bell, William Stewart, 7, 8
Benjamin, Walter, 218
Bersani, Leo, 8, 53, 71, 89, 130, 167–169, 226–228
Bloom, Harold, 40, 44, 49, 81, 219
Blossom, Frederick A., 6
Bové, Carol Mastrangelo, 173
Bové, Paul, 6, 8, 9
Brady, Patrick, 7, 99–101, 167
Brée, Germaine, 7, 17, 214
Bucknall, Barbara J., 118, 195, 204, 207, 212–213

Campbell, Joseph, 47–49
Carlysle, Thomas, 233
Cattui, Georges, 7
Chateaubriand, Rene, 233
Christianity, 203, 219
Collier, Peter, 148–149 152–153, 155, 162–164, 179, 197–199

Darwinian theory, 233
Da Vinci, Leonardo, 211
Deats, Sara, 5

Dedalus, Stephen, 206
Deleuze, Gilles, 7, 8, 15, 23, 33, 35, 40–41, 68, 97, 100, 102, 104, 106, 111, 117, 120–121, 123, 137, 160–161, 168–169, 170–171, 173, 209, 229, 232–234
de Man, Paul, 7, 44, 146, 173, 185–187, 209
Derrida, Jacques, 7, 8, 15, 97
Doubrovsky, Serge, 7, 8, 12, 15, 25, 37, 38, 98–99, 121, 130–131, 134, 167, 173, 175, 176, 184, 188, 200–202, 209, 219 220, 222, 229

educative ideology, 217
Eitingon, Max, 13
Emerson, Ralph Waldo, 189

Finn, Michael R., 182, 183, 186, 189, 211
Flaubert, Gustav, 183
Flugel, J. C., 48
Freud, Sigmund, 8–10, 12–15, 33, 40, 58–60, 78, 127, 176, 199, 206, 217

Gerard, Rene, 218
Gide, Andre, 126
Goethe, 211–212, 223
grammatology, 8
Gray, Margaret, 7, 8, 16, 69–74, 88, 89, 97, 111–116, 137–141, 165–167, 175, 209, 228
Gregh, Fernand, 172

Hamlet, 213
hermaphroditic, 41
Hodson, Leighton, 71, 172
Holy Grail, 219
Homer, 192, 194, 196
Hudson, W. H., 233
Humphries, Jefferson, 7
Huxley, Aldous, 2
hymenoptera, 95, 103, 131, 202, 226

ideal hunger, 19, 25, 37, 42, 94, 146, 147, 156, 182
ideology of immortality, 204
ideology of sacrifice, 42, 200, 217

Jephcott, E. F. N., 107–110, 116–117, 122–123, 129–130, 168, 211, 212, 227
Johnson, J. Theodore, 129, 226, 227
Joyce, James, 5, 217
Jung, Carl G., 13

Kant, Immanuel, 115
Kassell, Walter, 7, 86–87, 143–145, 151, 155–156, 175, 209
kitschification, 16
Klein, Dennis, 9, 11, 12
Kohut, Heinz, 10, 25, 37, 146
Kristeva, Julia, 7, 8, 15, 26, 27, 28, 29, 34, 39, 41, 42, 43, 76–79, 82, 88, 97, 147, 153, 174, 209
Krutch, Joseph Wood, 146, 229, 234

Lacan, Jacques, 7, 8, 9, 15, 88, 144
Landow, George P., 18
Last Judgment, 230
"Leda and the Swan," 132, 138, 140

Mallarmé, 43, 96
Marxist, 9
maxims, 210
merger hunger, 10, 22, 25, 37, 68, 83, 94, 121, 156, 183
meta-dramatic, 51
Michaelangelo, 211
Miller, Henry, 13
Miller, Milton, 8

Milton, 47
mirror hunger, 19, 25, 37, 42, 94
Moncrieff, C. K., Scott 1, 2, 6
Moss, Howard, 24, 25, 26, 27, 34, 41, 138
Mozart, Wolfang Amadeus, 202, 203

New Criticism, 7
Nietzsche, Fredrick, 11, 14
Nin, Anais, 4

objective correlative, 147
O'Brien, Justin, 74
Oedipus complex, 14, 15, 48, 219

Paradise Lost, 47, 203
pastiche, 182
Plato, 161
Pompeiian, 232
profanation, 77–78, 94, 184
Prometheus, 221

queer studies, 9

Rank, Otto, 4–5, 9–12, 14, 15, 36, 42, 51, 55, 58, 60–63, 72, 84, 93, 97–98, 126, 151, 176, 177, 178, 180, 183, 188, 190, 192–196, 199–209, 212–215, 220, 223–225, 227, 234
Rawlings, Marjorie Kinnan, 3
Richard, Jean-Pierre, 178
Rilke, Rainer Maria, 107–109
Rodin, 107, 210
Rogers, J. P. W., 5
Ruskin, John, 1, 17–19, 24, 116–117, 129, 149, 161–162, 164–165, 183, 189–190, 192, 197–201, 206, 211–212, 217–218, 226, 232

Sainte-Beauve, 194
Saint Simon, 177
Sand, George, 148
Sartre, Jean Paul, 233
Schiller, 204, 212
Schopenhauer, 14
Schwob, Marcel, 126

self-nomination, 180
self-training, 181, 188
separation anxiety, 10–12, 14, 22, 29, 36, 37, 40, 45, 202, 218
Sévigné, Mme de, 148, 177–178
Shakespeare, William, 202–203, 210
Shattuck, Roger, 7, 8, 29, 39, 112, 174, 232
Sipiora, Philip, 5
Sodom and Gomorrah, 203, 231
Stambolian, George, 7
Sturman, Douwe, 1, 2
sublimation, 13, 15
sublime, 17–19, 116
superimposition, 197

Taft, Jessie, 13, 126, 142, 215
Terdiman, Richard, 49
Titian, 177
Trilling, Lionel, 8
Turner, Frederick, 177, 197

Updike, John, 1

Vermeer, 64, 66, 113, 170, 226

Wagner, Richard, 12, 113, 171–172, 191, 203
Wyeth, N. C., 3

Zola, Emile, 65